# COUNTERFEITING

## IN COLONIAL AMERICA

# COUNTERFEITING

# IN COLONIAL AMERICA

*by Kenneth Scott*

WITH A FOREWORD BY U. E. BAUGHMAN, CHIEF, U. S. SECRET SERVICE

NEW YORK

OXFORD UNIVERSITY PRESS

1957

TO MY FRIEND

ERIC P. NEWMAN

# CONTENTS

# FOREWORD

THIS fascinating account of the doings of counterfeiters of another era supports a belief of the United States Secret Service that so long as there is a medium of exchange there will always be attempts to imitate it. Stringent punishments have had some deterrent effect. As the book points out, counterfeiters have been dragged to the gallows and hanged by the neck. Some have had their ears cropped or their hands cut off. Some have been branded with hot irons, and others have been sentenced to spend their lives in prison. Despite the severe penalties, however, the crime of counterfeiting has never been wholly and completely suppressed, and probably it never will be, because some men are always seeking nefarious ways to get rich.

In the pages that follow, you will find this statement: 'Counterfeiting in the colonial period both by individuals and increasingly by organized and co-operating gangs posed a constant threat to the credit and commerce of the provinces.' Counterfeiting in our own times is no less a threat to the credit and commerce of the United States. An unstemmed flood of counterfeit money today could wreck the economy of our country. It is the responsibility of the Secret Service to prevent any such disaster, but counterfeiting is a crime against all the people, and the co-operation of the public therefore becomes an essential element in the successful suppression of this crime.

This unusual book might have been a dull and pedantic recital of counterfeiting activity in Colonial America. Instead, it is a lively combination of true detective and adventure stories told in terms of real people of the past, people with quaint names like Barnaby Budd and Thankful Baker and Abigail Conwell, people whose methods for fleecing the innocent were little different from many such methods in use today. The citizen can learn a great deal from these historic case histories and will find them enjoyable reading as well.

The research which was necessary before this book could be written was obviously tremendous and careful. It seems to me that the results were well worth while.

U. E. BAUGHMAN
Chief, U. S. Secret Service
Treasury Department

*Washington, D.C.*
*February 1957*

## ACKNOWLEDGMENTS

THE writing of this book has been made possible through the help of the staffs of the Connecticut State Library, the Hall of Records in Annapolis, Maryland, the Hall of Records in Dover, Delaware, the New Hampshire Historical Society, the Historical Society of Pennsylvania, the New-York Historical Society, the American Antiquarian Society, the American Numismatic Society, the Chester County Historical Society, the Reserve Room of the New York Public Library, the Library of the New York Bar Association, the Manuscript Division of the Library of Congress, the Adriance Memorial Library in Poughkeepsie, the Manuscripts Division of the New York State Library, the Law Library of the Court of General Sessions of the County of New York, the Newport Historical Society, the Rare Book Department of the Boston Public Library, the Public Library of Morristown, New Jersey, the Columbia University Library, the Wagner College Library, the Office of the Prothonotary of the Supreme Court in Philadelphia, the offices of the clerks of court of Albany, Dutchess, New York, Orange, Queens, Suffolk, and Ulster counties in New York, of Bucks, Chester, Cumberland, Lancaster, Philadelphia, and York counties in Pennsylvania, of Newport, Providence, and Washington counties in Rhode Island,

and the office of the Clerk of the Supreme Court of New Jersey.

The author wishes to express his gratitude for help and encouragement to Mr. Eric P. Newman of St. Louis, Missouri, Mr. Charles E. Baker, Editor of *The New-York Historical Society Quarterly,* Mr. Carstairs Bracey, of Bracey, Virginia, Mr. James Brewster, State Librarian of Connecticut, Mrs. Kathryn C. Buhler, Assistant Curator of the Department of Decorative Arts of Europe and America of the Boston Museum of Fine Arts, Mr. Clarkson A. Collins, 3rd, Librarian of the Rhode Island Historical Society, Mr. Stephen G. C. Ensko of New York City, Mr. Harley L. Freeman of Ormond Beach, Florida, Miss Edna Jacobsen, Chief of the Manuscripts Division of the New York State Library, Mr. James A. Murphy, Law Librarian of the Court of General Sessions of the County of New York, Mr. William M. E. Rachal, Editor of the *Virginia Magazine of History and Biography,* Mr. Donald A. Sinclair, Curator of Special Collections of the Library of Rutgers University, Mr. Donald T. Smith, Librarian of Wagner Lutheran College, and Mr. R. N. Williams, 2nd, Director of the Historical Society of Pennsylvania. And I wish to give special thanks to my wife, Aurelia G. Scott, for her unstinting assistance.

K.S.

# COUNTERFEITING

## IN COLONIAL AMERICA

# Chapter 1

## INTRODUCTION

COUNTERFEITING in all countries is as old as money it-self, and the English colonists in North America were familiar with the crime and the punishments inflicted in the mother country upon offenders. Forging the coin of the realm in England was high treason and the penalty was that the offender be drawn to the gallows and not be carried or allowed to walk, although as a rule a sledge or hurdle might be used to preserve the criminal from the extreme torment of being dragged on the ground or pave-ment; that he be hanged by the neck and then cut down alive; that his entrails be taken out and burned while he was yet alive; that his head be cut off and his body divided into four parts, and that his head and quarters be at the king's disposal.

In 1553, in the first year of the reign of Mary, it was made treasonable to forge such pieces of foreign coin as were current in the kingdom, and later, in 1572, in the reign of Elizabeth, the counterfeiting of such foreign coin was made misprision of treason by act of Parliament, and the punishment of a convicted offender was loss of profits of lands during life, forfeiture of goods, and imprison-ment for life.

Despite the harsh penalties, counterfeiting flourished in

England, where, indeed, so many offenses were punishable
by death that people grew callous. In many instances the
authorities were lax and often hesitant to carry out sentences, so that persons were frequently discharged by proclamation. Neither coiners nor the general population considered coining and clipping as serious wrongdoing. On
28 April 1770, a coiner, James Oldfield, was executed at Ty-
burn and on the occasion the Reverend James Booth said of
counterfeiting: 'It is amazing to think that so many are
endeavouring to extenuate this crime, and speak of it as
if it were of a trifling nature, and commit it in so daring a
manner.'

Often it was not 'healthy' for officials to be zealous in
prosecuting counterfeiters. Thus a Mr. Deighton, a super-
visor of the excise, who had brought about the arrest of
numerous coiners in Yorkshire in 1769, was shot down
within one hundred yards of his home, and his dead body
was stamped on and abused. About three years later John
Munro, a justice of the peace of Albany County in New
York, who had busied himself with the arrest and examination of suspected counterfeiters, wrote to Governor
Tryon to ask to be excused from further service as a
magistrate. 'What can a Justice do,' wrote Munro, 'when
the whole Country combinds against him . . . my property is destroyed night and day & durst not say ill done.'

Counterfeiting of copper money reached scandalous
proportions in England, where that type of coin was introduced in the reign of Charles II. Counterfeiting of it was
not punishable until 1742, when this offense was made a
misdemeanor and it was enacted that forgers of halfpence
and farthings should suffer two years' imprisonment and
find securities for their good behavior for two years more.
Legislation did little to check the evil, and in 1753 it was

reckoned that two fifths to one-half of the copper money circulating in England was counterfeit. Immense quantities of blank flans were manufactured in Birmingham — and the manufacturing was not a crime — and then sold through middlemen to coiners. An act of Parliament of 1771, to be sure, made forging, buying, selling, receiving, or paying of counterfeit copper money a felony, but the mischief continued unabated.

The flans were coined in London particularly and also in the slums of Birmingham with dies so contrived that the pieces already looked worn when struck. Often, too, new coins were fried for a time after supper in a pan to darken them. One writer in 1800 comments of an earlier period: 'Scarcely a wagon or coach departs from the metropolis which does not carry bags and parcels of base coin to the camps, seaports, and manufacturing towns.' On 31 March 1774, Sir John Fielding dispatched five armed men to a house on Fish Street Hill, where they discovered eight coiners making coppers. The magistrate had learned of their activities when the night before the counterfeiters had sent a child for some beer with new halfpence to pay for it. When the landlord happened to observe to the little girl that the coppers were warm, she innocently replied that her daddy had just made them.

Many of the counterfeiters who were veritable pests in the British colonies in North America were American-born, but others were old hands at the business when they set foot in the New World. One such was Joshua Dean, a London convict, described as a very sly and artful fellow, a jack of all trades, and a great artist at coining, who, when convicted of counterfeiting the paper stamps in England, was transported to the plantations for life and was purchased as a servant by Alexander Spotswood of Germanna,

Virginia, Postmaster General of America. Dean, who had often slipped his neck out of the halter by breaking jail in England when imprisoned for coining, escaped from Germanna in June 1737 and apparently was never retaken.

At the beginning of December 1770, the ship *Trotman*, commanded by Captain Blickenden, arrived in Maryland with a number of coiners who were transported for having presented the British public with too many specimens of their ingenuity. A few days after they were landed notice was given the inhabitants of Annapolis in the *Maryland Gazette* that counterfeit dollars and shillings manufactured by the convicts had already appeared and that great caution was to be observed in receiving and paying away coin.

Many circumstances conspired to make the way of the counterfeiter in the New World an easy one. When paper bills of credit were emitted, nothing was easier than to take or send some samples to England, to Amsterdam, to Germany, and especially to Ireland, and have plates made for imitating them or actual counterfeits struck off. Thus Peter Long of Philadelphia in 1739, through his cousin, Robert Jenkins, sent directions, with samples, to an English printer for counterfeiting the bills of New Jersey and of New Castle. Long admonished that the paper, ink, type, flourishes, and every spot and tittle must be minded or the false bills would be of no value. A great advantage in having bills or plates made in Europe was that the act was apparently not punishable there and the chances of detection were remote in any event.

As the court records of the eighteenth century show, many counterfeiters were induced to take up that nefarious business because of extreme poverty and large families for which provision had to be made. Others, such as Ebenezer Seamore and Samuel Ford, succumbed to temptation because of temporary financial difficulties. Some, like the silversmith Gilbert Belcher, deliberately adopted a career of crime. 'No gain,' said Belcher in his dying speech, 'afforded me so much pleasure as that which I acquired by illicit means.' The counterfeiters came from all social classes: farmers, sailors, weavers, carpenters, cordwainers, perukemakers, boatmen, tailors, victuallers, bakers, schoolmasters, millwrights; well-to-do merchants, doctors, deacons, justices of the peace, members of the legislatures became involved, and because of the technical skill required for making coin or plates, many printers, blacksmiths, and silversmiths (including some noted ones such as Samuel and Gideon Casey, Abel Buell, and Garret Onclebag).

A large number of the colonists rarely handled coin, gold pieces especially, and were therefore not familiar enough with the genuine readily to detect the false. A large percentage was unable to read or write and would accept bills, particularly unfamiliar ones of neighboring or distant colonies, which contained glaring errors of all kinds. Frequently the money makers even made mistakes in spelling, and this was above all true of bills forged in Germany, where English was not known by the printer. Thus on bills made in Hammelbach JUSTICE was spelled INSTICE; again, DROIT was made DPOIT and COUNTERFEIT was turned into COUUTERFEIT; TWO CROWNS was converted into TWO CROWES; THOMPSON was written as THONNON; the second D was omitted from the word WOODBRIDGE; Raper (a signer's name) was copied as Reper; Parker was spelled with an H; the E was left out of the last syllable of DECEMBER and the B out of PUBLICK; the M in the word QUARTAM was upside down.

Poor, simple people were taken in by such crude counterfeits and turned out to be the losers, for the merchants and wealthy persons would detect the false money and refuse to accept it. Governor Gabriel Johnston in a speech to the Council and House of Burgesses of North Carolina in 1735 complained of 'the great Number of Counterfeits, which are gone abroad into all the parts of the Province, by the villanous Arts of wicked and ill disposed persons, and to the utter undoing of many poor industrious Families.' Persons who did not discover manifest errors in spelling could scarcely be expected to observe differences in paper that was too thick, too thin, too white, or too bluish, letters which were too large or too small, irregular and misshapen, ink that had turned yellow or was too red, too black, or too pale, words which were run together, demi-lions that looked like owls and crowns that resembled apple dumplings or caps, a sun too large or a rainbow too small, and spots or dots which were left out. When a really gifted artist, such as Samuel Ford, went to work, the provincial treasurers themselves could not tell a false bill from a genuine one. The counterfeiting of the bills of Virginia in 1773 was so clever that the business of that colony practically came to a standstill. James Hill, George Washington's steward on the Custis plantations, wrote Washington that he dared not take money for corn he had sold but required the purchaser to give a note of hand. When two important horse races took place at 'Leedes Town on the Potomack,' a New York newspaper reported that not half the money that would normally have been wagered was bet, since the Marylanders would not stake their property against the Virginia currency which had been counterfeited in a manner so unparalleled.

False coins, usually Spanish and Portuguese gold and silver, were those most generally imitated. Often the work was careless, as when milled pieces of eight, dated 1754,

were struck with the name PHILIP instead of FERDINAND
on them, or when the pieces were too light or rang false
or showed quicksilver oozing out of them or would shatter
when thrown on the ground or showed the marks of filing
to remove the nob left where the metal had been poured
into the mold. On the other hand, the public was defense-
less against such masterpieces as the doubloons which were
circulating in and about Philadelphia in 1748 and 1749.
A merchant took one of them to a goldsmith and asked if
it was good, to which he received an affirmative reply. The
merchant, who still had doubts, sent it to a second goldsmith, who also reported that the piece was genuine. At
this the merchant sent the doubloon to a third goldsmith,
who tested the interior of the coin and found it was only
one-half gold. Small wonder that Christopher Sauer, publisher of the *Pennsylvanische Berichte,* asked editorially:
'If, then, goldsmiths cannot differentiate the coins by their
appearance, how is the farmer, who has, indeed, had little
gold in his hands, to recognize them?'

The laws of the colonies varied so greatly that counterfeiting in one province might be punishable by death
but in another merely by a fine, while in Connecticut one
who skipped bail was normally left unmolested, since the
authorities were well satisfied to collect the bond for the
treasury of the colony. On many occasions the authorities
of one government refused to co-operate with those of
another, as when a sheriff from New York seized a gang of
counterfeiters near Sheffield in territory claimed by both
Massachusetts and New York. The jails of the day were
extremely weak and poorly guarded, so that a counterfeiter
who was caught knew that he had a better than fifty-fifty
chance to slip out of the prison at night. The money maker
was well aware of the fact that it was almost impossible

for the king's attorney to get a conviction unless two or more of a gang would turn crown's evidence against their associates. Further, if a money maker was convicted and sentenced to death, there was frequently pressure brought to bear on the governor to grant a pardon, as in the cases of Berry and Mark in New York and of Haines, Cooper, and Budd in New Jersey. Good behavior in Connecticut jails could usually persuade the General Assembly to have a counterfeiter serving a life sentence released within a few months or a year. The legislators did not need to be told that a prisoner did not pay for his keep in jail and that the burden of supporting his wife, children, or aged parents then fell upon the community in which he had resided.

The land was covered with thick forests and deep, almost impenetrable swamps, which were favorite haunts of counterfeiters. Sometimes an enterprising artist like Owen Sullivan would have a well-furnished workshop inside a hill and friendly neighbors who had secret passages, trap doors, and hidden rooms beneath their fireplaces. Backwoods districts were far away from the officers of the law, and often whole communities were engaged in the counterfeiting business or sympathetic to those who were so occupied. Such, for example, was a section of the Oblong in Dutchess County, 'where,' wrote a New York newspaper in 1756, ' 'tis said a large Gang of Villains have harboured for a considerable Time past, few of which but have a Crop or a Brand-Mark upon them, as it is a Sort of Disgrace for one reputed honest to be seen among them.' Such gangs grew up and flourished everywhere, so that a New York paper in 1768 observed: 'It is said that there is a Clan of these Gentry of at least 500, who correspond thro' all the colonies, as far as North Carolina.'

The trouble and confusion created by counterfeiters was enormous. Issue upon issue of bills had to be recalled and replaced, only to have the new emissions promptly forged. The amount of bogus paper and coin put off was great in proportion to the total amount of money in circulation. Peter Long passed nearly £6,000 without being detected; John Davis had £3,500 in false bills on him when arrested; Owen Sullivan made some £24,000 of Rhode Island and New Hampshire currency alone, not to mention great sums in New York bills; Samuel Ford was so successful and prolific that his associates called him 'the treasurer of the three provinces.' One can understand the exasperation which led Colonel Schuyler to propose in the New York Assembly in 1773 that the plate for making thin sheets of paper, which were to be pasted on New York bills, represent 'an eye in a cloud, a cart and coffins, three felons on a gallows, a weeping father and mother, with several small children, a burning pit, human figures being forced into it by fiends, a label with the words "Let the name of a Money Maker rot," and such other additions as the commissioners might think proper.'

Lieutenant Governor Patrick Gordon of Pennsylvania, in a speech to the Assembly on 30 March 1727, warned of the perils of counterfeiting, saying: 'It may not unjustly be compared to the Poisoning the Waters of a Country; the blackest, and most detestable Practice that is known, and which the Laws of Nations, and those of War condemn even in declared Enemies, for as that destroys the Lives of the innocent in taking their Natural Food, this would effectually overthrow all Credit, Commerce and Traffick, and the mutual Confidence that must subsist in Society, to enable the Members of it to procure to themselves and Families their necessary Bread.' Gordon might have been surprised at the zeal with which his own country, England, poisoned the financial wells of the patriots during the American Revolution by counterfeiting their paper money and by forging on a wholesale scale at a later date the French *assignats,* even as during World War II the Germans, at times, printed five, ten, and twenty pound notes of the Bank of England at the rate of 1,800 an hour.

# Chapter 2

## WAMPUM, BOSTON MONEY, AND FOREIGN COIN

THE early settlers in the British colonies in North America made use of various media of exchange, one of which was the wampum which served the Indians as money. It consisted of cylindrical pieces of shell drilled through the center, polished on stones, and strung on threads like beads. There were two kinds, that made from the blue eye of the quahog shell and that fashioned from the white periwinkle shell. The dark variety was priced at twice the white and the value of the shell money was governed by the price of beaver skins in the London market.

The Indians often counterfeited their wampum, dying the white beads a bluish black and thereby doubling their value if they could be put off on the unwary. In addition Roger Williams charged that the Indians counterfeited the dark beads with 'stone and other materials.' On 30 May 1650, the director and council of the Dutch Colony of New Netherland prefaced an ordinance for the better regulation of the currency with this complaint: 'We have by experience and for a long time seen the decline and daily depreciation of the loose Wampum, among which are circulating many without holes and half finished, also some of Stone, Bone, Glass, Muscle shells, yea even of Wood and Broken Beads.' The General Court of Electors of Rhode Island in May 1647 ordered that false strings of wampum offered by the Indians in exchange or barter should be confiscated to the public treasury, and by 1662 the General Court of Commissioners of the same colony declared that since the wampum had sunk to so low a rate that it could be considered only as a commodity, it was unreasonable that it should be forced in payment on any man. After this date, indeed, it ceased to be current as a medium of exchange in Massachusetts.

Other articles were, to be sure, used for payment in the early days. For example, on 18 October 1631 it was ruled in the Massachusetts Bay Colony that corn should pass for the payment of all debts at the usual rate at which it was sold, unless money or beaver skins had been expressly named in the contract. In Virginia, tobacco was the common medium of exchange until November 1645, when a law was enacted that the inhabitants should cease trading for that commodity and use a metallic currency, but the law was not implemented and tobacco continued to be used as currency.

The advantage of coin as money was obvious and the colonists employed silver and gold pieces, chiefly those of Spain and Portugal. In their act of 1645 the Virginians provided that the coin to pass current should be Spanish silver, with pieces of eight reals valued at six shillings and all other Spanish silver coins valued proportionately. In addition it was ordered that 10,000 pounds of copper be bought at the rate of eighteen pence per pound and coined into twopenny, threepenny, sixpenny, and ninepenny pieces, while the law decreed that capital punishment should be inflicted upon counterfeiters and passers of false money.

Sixty-five years later, in 1710, a law was passed in Virginia which established the foreign silver coins that should be current and the rates at which they should pass. Any person or persons who should coin, counterfeit, falsify, or debase these pieces or should aid, consent, or counsel in so doing should, upon conviction, be adjudged as offenders in treason and suffer the pains, penalties, and forfeitures mentioned in the act of Parliament of the eighteenth year of the reign of Queen Elizabeth. Not long thereafter, in November 1714, all unmilled British gold coin, all Spanish and French coined gold, all sequins and Arabian pieces of gold, all moidores of Portugal, and all lesser pieces of that species were made current in Virginia, and the counterfeiting of them was proclaimed high treason and subject to the same penalties as in England. An act of February 1729 also made the counterfeiting of the current copper coinage a treasonable offense. In 1698 a certain Edward Brotherton was found guilty of 'possessing counterfeit money' by the justices of Accomack County, but what penalty was imposed, if any, is not recorded.

In Massachusetts foreign coins circulated freely, and in 1652 the government of that colony set up a mint and began the emission of silver coins, shillings, sixpence, and threepence. The coinage of these was soon discontinued because lawless individuals began to clip pieces off the edges. One such offender was a Frenchman named Peter Lorphelin, who on 8 August 1679 was accused of having made rash and insulting speeches at Boston at the time of the recent great conflagration in that town. His words gave rise to the suspicion that he had had a hand in the matter, so he was taken up and jailed. The authorities ordered that his chest and writings be examined by the constables in the presence of some gentlemen appointed to see it done.

To their surprise a search of his chest disclosed two or three crucibles, a melting pan, a strong pair of shears for clipping money, several clippings of the Massachusetts coins, and various suspicious instruments. When questioned about these discoveries, Lorphelin called God to witness that he had never clipped money but had taken the instruments out of a privateer's chest in Boston harbor when he had been sent by the authorities to search the chests of some privateers.

The justices rightly took his story for a bold and impudent falsehood and had him recommitted to the prison, from which, within a day or two, he sent a letter owning that his words had been a lie and asserting that four or five years before his arrest a woman, whose name he did not know, had brought him the instruments and clippings from a privateer who had lodged with her. The court of assistants meeting in Boston on 2 September 1679 decided that this account also was a fabrication, and that the crime of clipping was proved against Lorphelin, and sentenced him to stand upon the pillory two hours, to have both his ears cut off by the executioner, to pay all costs and fees, and to provide a bond of £500, with two sureties satisfactory to the governor and council for his good behavior in the future.

The second coinage of Massachusetts was that known generally as the 'Oak Tree' and consisted of shillings, sixpence, threepence, and twopence, all of which were provided with two raised concentric rings, the outer near the edge of the coin in order to prevent clipping. Over a period of some thirty-four years the 'Oak Tree' and later 'Pine Tree' pieces were coined. They, along with the Spanish silver in circulation, were counterfeited. A Suffolk County Court in 1674 found John du Plisse guilty of dispersing pewter counterfeit money and ordered that he furnish a bond of £40 for his good behavior and for his appearance before any authority within the county to answer for his crime if called when within the colony. It would seem that the justices were giving du Plisse a chance to quit the colony and avoid punishment for his crime.

Further cases of coining in Massachusetts in the seventeenth century are recorded, and doubtless there were numerous other counterfeiters at work there who were not apprehended. Joseph Blandchard, the son of George Blandchard, and George Grimes, at a court of assistants in Boston on 1 September 1674, were charged with coining base money and passing the same, and the justices bound them over in bail of £20 each to appear at the next county court to be held in Cambridge. Their fate is not known, but such is not true of Martin Williams, a bricklayer, described as a stranger, late resident in Salem, who, at a court of assistants held on 16 October 1691, was indicted for having at Salem in April of that year counterfeited five pieces of eight and for having, at about nine o'clock the same evening he made them, passed off one of his products. He pleaded not guilty but the jury decided otherwise, and Captain Richard Crisp, its foreman, informed the court that he was found guilty of passing base money. The sentence pronounced was that he stand in the pillory in Boston on three separate lecture days, one hour each time after the lecture, with a paper signifying his crime, and that he pay all charges and fees.

In 1674 George Grimes had been charged with coining, and in March 1690 another Grimes, this one named William and a resident of Billerica, was accused of having made two New England shillings out of pewter or lead and of having tried to pay them away. Fortunately for him, at a court of assize held at Charlestown in January 1697, the grand jury brought in his indictment ignoramus. About a year later in Boston the authorities became concerned about the activities of one John Wedgewood and had him brought before the court of general sessions in that town on the charge that he had set up a furnace for making counterfeit coin in his lodgings at the house of a widow named Ruhanna Eldridge in the north end of town. It is not recorded whether he was convicted and punished or was as fortunate as William Grimes in escaping through the inability of the grand jury to find a true bill. Further, even though a counterfeiter was presented by a grand jury, it was usually very difficult to secure a conviction, unless one or two accomplices could be induced to give evidence for the crown.

The Province of New York was constantly plagued by the importation of bogus Massachusetts and Spanish coin and the striking of such money in New York. In 1680 John Archer, sheriff of New York, presented two rascals from New Jersey, John Burrell and William Shore, whom he arrested in New York City for bringing into that town and passing there various false Boston coins. Burrell confessed his guilt, so got off by making restitution to those who had suffered loss through the cheat and by paying a fine. Shore was so ill-advised as to try to brazen out the affair, was tried, convicted by the mayor's court, and given thirty lashes well laid on.

Fines and lashings were not deterrent to the lawless element that was inclined to make money the easy way. Toward the end of December 1683 the governor and council of New York issued a warrant for the apprehension of passers of false coin and pointed out that several counterfeit Boston, Spanish, and other kinds of money were circulating in the city. Early the next year the governor received information of bad coin from Boston and base Spanish silver, all apparently made in neighboring colonies, and he issued his proclamation to check its circulation in New York. At best, however, the action of governor and council can have had but a temporary effect, for in April 1685, Captain Jonathan Selleck complained to his excellency and the council of the great amount of clipped Spanish coin in New York, and Selleck declared that he had received from one individual, Benjamin Blagge, £16 of clipped money to the value of 290 pieces of eight.

Even prominent and wealthy individuals sometimes would take a chance when it came to passing false coin. Such a case is that of Gabriel Ludlow, who was born in 1663 at Castle Cary, Somerset, England, and arrived in New York in November 1694, where he built and owned vessels in the coasting trade and set up a place of business in Queen Street. Three years after his arrival he married Sarah Hanmer, daughter of the Reverend Joseph Hanmer, chaplain of the king's forces in the Province of New York, and in 1697 he became a vestryman of Trinity Church. In 1698 this prosperous and well-connected merchant found, as he claimed, seventy-three bad dollars, allegedly received in trade. He was brought before the authorities and charged with having arranged with a Mr. Montagne, an apprentice to a Mr. Wenham, to pay away the false money in return for a small commission for each one thus passed. Merchant Ludlow was tried by a special sessions held in the same Trinity Church of which he was a vestryman, and he got off upon conviction with a light sentence which required him to pay all costs, to make good all damages, to give security for his future good behavior, and to pay a fine of £3 for the use of Trinity Church. His

conviction was no block to his advancement, for the following year he was made clerk of the New York Assembly
and the year after that clerk of the vestry of Trinity
Church.

The Earl of Bellomont, the royal governor, on 15 May
1699 wrote to the Lords of Trade in disgust with reference
to Ludlow: 'I am sorry to say it but 'tis an undoubted
truth, the English here are soe profligate that I can not find
a man fitt to be trusted, that's capable of businesse. . . .
I was obliged to employ one Ludlow a merchant to be
Clerk of the Assembly this Session, one that was lately
convict of cliping and coining in this towne. I think proper
to acquaint your Lordships of this circumstance, that you
may see how impossible a thing it is to make a right choice
of men in this place, and what sort of men I have to doe
with. Those that are honest of the Dutch, being formerly
kept out of imployment and businesse are very ignorant,
and can neither speak nor write proper English.'

In 1703 another person of some standing in the community, Garret Onclebag, a silversmith of talent but of
bad character, pleaded guilty to a charge of coining and
passing false money and, like Ludlow, suffered nothing
worse than paying fees and a fine of £20 and providing a
bond of £100 for his good conduct in the future. Three
years later, however, two coiners of false dollars, Bartholomew Vank and Thomas Roberts, were convicted and
received much less tender treatment than the more prominent Ludlow and Onclebag. They were publicly whipped
at the cart's tail in the Broadway in sight of the Town
Hall, at the well in Broadway, at the end of Beaver Street,
at the end of Pearl Street, at the cage, at the most public
part of the market place at Burghers Path, at the corner of
Wall Street, and at the City Hall — three lashes at each

place. One week later they had to sit for one hour in the
pillory, with an inscription in capital letters setting forth
the nature of their crime affixed over their heads.

As early as 1638 the Maryland Assembly passed an act
making it treason to counterfeit the king's coin and when,
in 1661, the legislative body provided for the setting up
of a mint to strike silver money, it was voted that every
offense of clipping, scaling, counterfeiting, washing, or in
any way diminishing such coin was to be punishable with
death and forfeiture of all lands and goods to the Lord
Proprietor, an act which in 1676 was confirmed among the
perpetual laws. Then in 1707, since 'divers evil disposed
persons' had recently forged several foreign coins, encouraged thereto by the fact that there had been no con-
dign punishment provided by law for such offenders, the
legislators passed a law which provided that those convicted of counterfeiting foreign gold or silver money
should for the first offense be pilloried, whipped, and have
both ears cropped, while for the second each such offender
was to be branded on the cheek and banished.

The 'evil disposed persons' were Richard Clarke and his
prodigal companions, one of whom was Benjamin Celie.
Complaint was made early in 1705 that Celie and Clarke
were riding armed, threatening the death of several of her
majesty's good subjects, putting the inhabitants in terror
of their lives, and robbing their houses. A plan was concerted by the authorities whereby the rangers, under the
command of Lieutenant Charles Beale, were to capture
the rogues, but Beale failed to do his duty with any sort
of discipline or sense, and the miscreants escaped. By
March, however, Celie was taken up and imprisoned in
the jail of Ann Arundel County, from which he broke out,

on Sunday, 25 March, in the company of an Indian and a felon. Soon, however, he was recaptured and, together with Humphry Hernaman, who had aided him in breaking jail, was transported to Barbados.

Clarke himself managed for a long time to elude the officers of the law, thanks to the help of his numerous friends and associates. In Ann Arundel County he had so many near relations that the government could not discover his haunts. By many he was considered a stout fellow and, since he was born in the country, other natives of Maryland, large numbers of whom were public officials, had a feeling of sympathy for him and were therefore backward or altogether unwilling to bring him in. Edward Mariarty admitted he had let Clarke have horse and boat, and others, in an attempt to repair their shattered fortunes, assisted Clarke in counterfeiting large quantities of Spanish pieces of eight and lion dollars of the Low Countries, which they made of pewter, glass, and other mixed metals.

Another accomplice in coining and general misbehavior was Captain Silvester Welch, who, it was discovered, often harbored and abetted Clarke and his companions and entertained them at his home. It reached the ears of Governor Seymour and his council that on St. Stephen's day, 1707, Clarke and a certain Harrison had been reveling and firing pistols at Welch's house. The captain, arrested and strictly examined, told how, at about ten o'clock on a Sunday night in July, in John Jacobs's pasture, he met with Clarke, who was mounted on a gray horse and had a pistol stuffed in his jacket on his left side, a naked rapier hanging on his wrist, and a good lusty stick in his hand.

Joseph Hill, another crony of Clarke's, was a member of the House of Delegates and was expelled from that body 'for adhering to, assisting & corresponding with the said

Clarke.' Richard Snowden told of harboring, entertaining, and concealing Clarke, for all of which he professed to be 'very sorry.' He told the officers how Thomas Winter had put Clarke's sails in his (Snowden's) house and how several women visited the fugitive there. Finally, he related, Clarke's wife arrived, told him that his sloop was seized, whereat he at once rushed out, bade God bless them all, and went away. William Chew of Baltimore County warned that there were 300 men in that county who 'would stand by Clarke.' It is no wonder that the government was greatly perturbed.

On 30 January 1707, to be sure, Clarke had made a gesture, probably none too sincere, of yielding himself, for he wrote a letter to Governor Seymour which he then dropped at David Bell's mill. In it he expressed 'a deep sensce of the Horrour and detestation of his Crimes and that he lyes under the Denomination of a Traytor to her Majesty and Offers to Submitt himself to his Excy$^s$ Mercy.'

His deeds, however, ill suited his words, for it was presently discovered that with his gang of runaway rogues he had concerted to seize the government magazine, burn the town and port of Annapolis, steal a ship and hoist the Jolly Roger. The efforts of government were redoubled and in March 1708 Clarke was taken and brought before the governor and council. His confession justified no further consideration nor was it such as to induce the council to seek a royal pardon for him, so it was ordered in April that Clarke, 'attainted of high Treason and Fellony,' be executed on 'Friday next.'

Even as early as the seventeenth century it appears, particularly from what is known of the career of Robert Fenton, that counterfeiters were forming in gangs and maintaining relations with coiners in the same colony and other colonies. Fenton is first heard of in Philadelphia in 1683, when he, Charles Pickering, and Samuel Buckley were arrested and charged with coining New England shillings and Spanish silver pieces made of silver alloyed with copper. It was brought out in a statement by Pickering that one John Rush had said he spent half his time in coining bits. Pickering, on conviction, had to make good all losses incurred by those who had received his bad money and was required to pay a fine of £40 toward building a courthouse, while Buckley was fined £10 for the same purpose. Fenton, since he had frankly confessed his guilt and was only Pickering's servant, was sentenced to sit in the stocks for one hour.

John Rush, whose name had been mentioned during the examination of the coiners, was not picked up promptly and thus had several days which he put to good use in destroying evidence before he was arrested. At his examination he apparently talked himself out of the unpleasant situation. In 1691, however, his luck ran out when he was on board a vessel bound for Jamaica. The master, Cornelius Jacobs, somehow discovered that his passenger was a coiner, and, although Rush managed to heave one parcel overboard, Jacobs seized on him a bag containing £9.15s. in counterfeit coin. Rush was imprisoned in Jamaica, taken back to New York, and then dispatched under guard, with his bag of coin as evidence, to Philadelphia, where it was presumed that his crime had been committed. In the light of the general insecurity of the jails of the day and the fact that he had to be transferred from constable to constable throughout the Jerseys en route to Pennsylvania, it is not improbable that he took to his heels at some point, for there is no record of his being examined or tried in Philadelphia.

Fenton, apparently none the worse for his hour in the stocks, transferred his activities to Connecticut, where he had a shop, presumably a smithy. There on 13 January 1699, he was apprehended and examined by William Pitkin, assistant, who asked him if he had any false money. To this Fenton replied in the negative, but a search of his pockets led to the discovery of five pieces of eight, three half joes, and one eightpence, all of which were judged to be false. At this he broke down and decided to tell the truth, or at least some of it. He confessed that in the summer of 1698 he had been employed by John Potterfield, with whom he had made false bits and pieces of eight. Another counterfeiter, John Tedman of Long Island, had induced him to make stamps and tools for coining pieces of eight, half pieces, and bits, and together they had struck off such coins made half of silver and half of alloy. Fenton admitted that he had also fashioned other such stamps and tools for Thomas Messenger, a joiner with a shop at the south corner of School Lane in Boston. Further, he implicated in coining a Mr. Hornbuckle of Northampton, who had struck pieces of eight that were made of a mixture of half copper and half block tin.

At this time Connecticut appears to have had no law to deal with coiners of foreign money, so Fenton was lucky enough to escape punishment. It is not likely that in that day of no newspapers the authorities in Connecticut knew of his conviction in Philadelphia for coining or of his forging in 1691 imitations of the first paper bills of credit in America and passing the same in Boston. The evidence which has survived of his activities in Connecticut, Massachusetts, and Pennsylvania shows that he had extensive connections with the counterfeiters in three colonies and points to a general understanding or perhaps confederation among the coiners and passers of the seventeenth century.

In the Jerseys both Spanish and New England coin circulated freely, and in 1683 there were complaints that counterfeits of this currency were being made or at least widely disseminated within the province, to the injury of its inhabitants and those of neighboring colonies. As a result a law was passed in West Jersey requiring the authorities to search for and arrest the offenders. It was provided that a grand inquest be impaneled for investigating the matter and that those convicted should receive such punishment as the court might impose.

There is no record of arrest or convictions at the time, but early in August 1698 Emmanuel Smith was brought before the grand jury in Burlington on the charge of clipping the current coin. The jurors did not find a bill for want of evidence, so Smith was bound over to the next court which was to be held on 3 November. This time the crown produced witnesses, John Buntin and Richard French, but again the grand jury returned the indictment ignoramus on the ground that no clippings had been found in Smith's chest.

It is quite possible that Smith was actually guilty of clipping, but it was extremely difficult to prove the crime, as his case shows. Suspicion again fell upon him, for at a session of the court held in Burlington in August 1701, Thomas South testified before the grand jury that in November 1700, Elizabeth Hill, who was making the bed in a chamber upstairs, called to him to come up to her. He did so and, on looking in her father's closet, among other assorted items found a coffee dish containing clippings of coin to the value of ten or twelve shillings. South picked up the dish, examined the clippings, and was told by

Elizabeth that she knew nothing about them unless her father had received them from Emmanuel Smith. At this Elizabeth was sworn and she stated that South had never been in her chamber or her father's closet and that she had never seen any clippings in her father's house. Obviously someone was lying, and the king's attorney apparently thought it was the girl, for he attempted to have Seth Hill indicted. The grand jury, however, returned the indictment ignoramus, and Hill was bound over to the May 1702 sessions, at which he was acquitted by proclamation.

In the fall of 1702, William Dickinson was committed to the jail of Burlington County for making false coin but managed to break out and escape, leaving behind him a black mare, which was sold to pay prison fees. Again, in May 1707, Benjamin Dunham was arrested on the charge of having clipped Spanish 'Ryals and half Ryals' and passed them. He was tried at Perth Amboy in November and, despite the testimony of five witnesses against him, was found not guilty, so that the court ordered his tools and money to be returned to him, a detail which suggests that some legal technicality or the downright disinclination of the jury to convict under any circumstances led to his acquittal.

It was indeed not until 1731 that a coiner was convicted in New Jersey, and then because he pleaded guilty. In December 1730, Duncan Campbell of New Brunswick, a laborer, passed a counterfeit pistole to Matthew Risley. Later Campbell was arrested and indicted at the supreme court in May 1731 for having made and passed pistoles. For his offense he stood two hours in the pillory in Amboy, two days later was given thirty-nine lashes on the bare back at the cart's tail, and two days after his flogging was given thirty-one more stripes. His ordeal, however, was not completed, for he was charged with a similar wrong-doing in Monmouth County and was ordered sent there for a trial, the result of which is not recorded.

The first paper money emitted in New England consisted of bills of credit issued in 1690 by the Massachusetts Bay Colony to pay its troops who had made the expedition against Canada in the French and Indian War. It is interesting to note that Robert Fenton, who had had years of experience as a coiner, was one of the first if not the first to try his hand at altering the paper currency. By 1691 Fenton and Benjamin Pierce of Woburn in Middlesex County had raised thirty-seven bills of 2/6 each, some to 10s. and others to 20s., with which they purchased goods from the wife of Nathaniel Jewell of Boston, so that the merchant sustained a loss of £22.10s. Jewell, upon the direction of some magistrates, prosecuted the offenders at several county courts both at Cambridge and Charlestown, and the rogues were found guilty. Fenton, however, avoided the sentence and judgment by appealing to the court of assize, and no sentence was pronounced against Pierce. In this way Jewell obtained no recompense for his loss and the great expense of prosecuting the criminals, so he appealed to the General Court in Boston to satisfy his claim for damages.

Actual counterfeiting, as distinct from the altering done by Fenton and Pierce, came somewhat later, and the first *cause célèbre* was one involving a good-sized gang. Under the date of 22 July 1704, Judge Samuel Sewell of Massachusetts wrote in his diary: 'It begins to be known that the twenty shilling bills of credit are counterfeited.' Two days later a proclamation concerning the matter was issued by Joesph Dudley, Captain General and Governor of the

Massachusetts Bay Colony, and printed in America's only newspaper of the time, the *Boston Weekly News-Letter*. The governor warned that some evil-minded persons, designing to 'cheat and cousen' her majesty's good subjects, had counterfeited the twenty shilling bills, and therefore he ordered all holders of any notes of that denomination to bring their bills, before 1 August, to the council chamber in Boston either on Tuesdays or Saturdays from eleven to one o'clock or on Thursdays from three to five. There one or more of the commissioners who had signed the money would determine whether each bill was good or forged. It was quite clear that there was a combination of various persons in the wicked design of forgery and deceit, and any person who should make discovery of the counterfeiters so as to cause the conviction of any or all of them would be given immunity from punishment and a reward of £50 from the public treasury.

By 25 July the counterfeit plate and press had been seized and four of the gang had been jailed. The prisoners were two blacksmiths of Boston, Peregrine White, Jr. (the son of Peregrine White, *Mayflower* baby and first-born New Englander of English parentage) and his son, Benoni White, as well as a carpenter named John Brewer and Daniel Amos, a winecooper. The principal actor in the villainy, Thomas Moyran, alias Morton, alias Odell, who was also suspected of making and passing coin, eluded the authorities. It was thought, and so stated in the newspaper, that he had made for New Hampshire with most of the false notes, supposed to amount in all to less than £100. Despite the hue and cry after him he had not been taken up by 8 August, when Governor Dudley offered a reward of £30 for his capture and described him as of middle stature, slender and straight of body, with black hair and thin visage. The fugitive was said to hold his head somewhat on one side in his walk.

Two days after the proclamation of this reward, Moyran — or Odell, as he was called in the newspaper — was apprehended at Stonington, Connecticut, for putting several cheats upon some persons, and was confined in the local jail. The prisons of that day were notoriously insecure and the one in Stonington presented no problem for Odell, who broke out and made his way to Philadelphia. In that city, apparently in May 1705, he was discovered and captured by Jonathan Cawley, Nicholas Thomas Jones, and Robert Sanders. The lieutenant governor, Colonel John Evans, had Odell placed on a sloop owned by Jones and bound for Boston. During the voyage, however, a storm drove the vessel ashore at New York, where the prisoner was locked up in jail until the weather permitted the boat to set out again.

The *Derick Adolph,* on which he was being transported in irons, touched at Newport, where Odell, on the night of Thursday, 31 May, somehow loosened his fetters, got ashore, and lay concealed in a barn two miles out of town until 6 June, when he was again taken up and this time safely conveyed in the sloop to Boston. He was tried on 6 November at the superior court of judicature, court of assize and general gaol delivery, and convicted of having forged the twenty shilling bills, a crime which he had perpetrated at Exeter, New Hampshire. He was duly sentenced to pay a fine of £300 and all costs and charges and to suffer a year's imprisonment. Like many other counterfeiters, Odell was an incorrigible offender, and it is recorded that he broke jail in Massachusetts in 1708 and again in 1714, on which occasions he was also charged with counterfeiting.

One of his accomplices, Daniel Amos, broke jail soon after his arrest in 1704 and apparently made good his escape. Another, Benoni White, pleaded guilty and prayed the mercy of the court, whereupon he was accepted as queen's evidence to testify against all concerned in the crime with him. His father, Peregrine White, Jr., was the other witness who was used to secure the conviction of Odell and Brewer and, since Peregrine was the one who originally gave away his accomplices, he in consequence claimed the reward of £50. Since, however, he was also charged with passing several false gold coins, he was tried and convicted of this crime and was sentenced to pay a fine of £30, to suffer imprisonment for three months, and to pay costs of prosecution. The authorities, taking no chances, deducted the £30 fine from the £50 reward, so Peregrine's betrayal netted him only £20.

The carpenter, John Brewer, was convicted by the testimony of the two Whites and received sentence to sit in the pillory for an hour and a half on a lecture day, to have one ear cut off, to be imprisoned for a year, and to pay the costs of prosecution. The lecture day, probably a Thursday, when a lecture on some religious theme was sure to bring a crowd to town, was a favorite time for the publishing of marriage banns and the punishing of criminals like Brewer. The governor, however, was moved to remit the cropping of Brewer's ear. The trial is important, as it set the pattern for others: the testimony of two or more accomplices, who turned evidence for the crown, was used to convict their associates, a process which appears to have been the surest way of obtaining a conviction.

A matter of no little import to the would-be counterfeiter was the colony in which his crime would be committed, and it was well for him to weigh carefully the punishments in that government for making coin or bills. New York was one province which would brook no tampering with its bills of credit, for the act for the emission of its first paper currency in 1709 provided that any person convicted of counterfeiting the bills should incur death without benefit of clergy, a provision included in two further acts of the same year and in one of 1711 authorizing the printing of further paper money.

The first convictions in New York for such an offense were in 1713, when in June of that year an engraver named James Mark and Joseph Berry, a tailor, came into the clutches of the law. They had recently come to the city from Boston and Rhode Island and they were charged with counterfeiting the four pound New York denomination, of which, it was believed, they had struck off not more than thirteen bills. Berry was arrested in New York (an accomplice betook himself to Maryland), while Mark was apprehended in Philadelphia. Mark claimed that their plate had been broken and then lost in Pennsylvania and he freely confessed his wrongdoing when he was arraigned in the supreme court of judicature on 4 September. Berry, however, pleaded not guilty and was tried and convicted by a jury, which, incidentally, found that he had no lands, tenements, goods, or chattels at the time the felony was committed. On 5 September the court sentenced the engraver and the tailor to be hanged on the following Wednesday between eleven in the morning and one in the afternoon, a favorite time, during the colonial period, for the infliction of punishments in public.

Before Berry and Mark had paid for their crime with their lives, on the Tuesday before the day appointed for their execution, most of the gentlewomen of New York waited upon his excellency the governor, addressing him earnestly with prayers and tears for the lives of Berry and Mark, whereupon his excellency was graciously pleased to pardon them. The pardon, however, was actually issued on 13 October, and on the 17th of that month, being brought to the bar, the two were asked what they had to say for themselves as to why execution should not be awarded against them. At this they produced Queen Anne's pardon and prayed that it be allowed them, to which the court acceded and ordered that they be discharged on payment of their fees. Thereupon Berry, in accordance with a custom dating in England from the reign of Edward IV, presented gloves to each of the judges. Mark, however, because of his extreme poverty, was excused by the justices from the ceremony.

The wide diversity in the laws against counterfeiting in the various colonies may be illustrated by comparing the death penalty in New York with the punishment prescribed at about the same time in Connecticut, which first emitted paper money in 1709. In May of the next year the Connecticut Assembly passed a law providing that persons convicted of counterfeiting the bills of the colony should pay all damages and suffer imprisonment for six months, as well as any other penalty or corporal punishment that the court might inflict.

The first person found guilty under this law was Ebenezer Seamore of Farmington. In June 1710, one Joseph Shepard of Hartford took to William Pitkin, assistant, a Connecticut three shilling bill altered to ten shillings which he had lately received from Seamore. The assistant immediately issued a warrant for the suspect, who was seized and brought before him for examination. Seamore at first made a pretense of innocence, all the time admitting that he had passed a ten shilling bill to Mr. Shepard on the previous day. A night in jail, however, worked wonders, for the next morning the prisoner made the following confession: he had of late been at expense in court and, being therefore in want of money, had decided to try his hand at altering bills; he first approached his cousin, John Woodruff of Great Swamp in Farmington, who at first cautioned him against the business, expressing the opinion that alteration of bills was a cheat, but presently he was overpersuaded by Seamore; the two went to work, and a two shilling bill was made into a forty shilling bill, a five shilling to a forty shilling, a two shilling to a twenty shilling, and a number of other small bills to ten shillings each. But Woodruff soon had qualms of conscience, or perhaps apprehensions concerning the possible consequences of his actions, for he passed none of the bad bills and tried to induce Seamore to drop the matter. All to no purpose, however, for Seamore continued to scrape the numbers off small bills, alter their denomination, and then pass them away. After his examination Woodruff turned queen's evidence, and by his testimony Seamore was convicted and sentenced to serve six months in prison and to pay a fine of £35, prosecution costs of £14.14s.7d., and all prison fees and charges. Woodruff was let off on payment of £6.15s. and prison fees, while a certain Zacharias Seamore, who was found to have gone, on the night of 17 June, at the desire of his brother, Richard Seamore, to the house of Ebenezer Seamore and there searched among Ebenezer's bills and, having found one counterfeit, to have burnt it, was not indicted for his destruction of evidence but was dismissed by the court on payment of 50s., presumably his costs in the matter. All the persons who had suffered loss through receiving the altered notes were reimbursed by the colony, which had collected Seamore's fine of £35 and with it could make losses good.

It has been seen that Robert Fenton over a long period of years and in at least three different colonies had busied himself with counterfeiting either coin or bills and had been in touch with many others who were similarly occupied. Examinations, arrests, and sitting in the stocks had not put a check to his nefarious activity. Likewise Ebenezer Seamore, once he had had a taste of counterfeiting, could not leave it alone and he eventually established contact with other offenders. Even at an early date there was a marked tendency for money makers to form relationships with others of their kind and for the various gangs to exchange intelligence and to co-operate throughout the same colony and with like bands in other provinces.

Thirteen years after his first conviction Seamore was again found to be up to his old tricks. Daniel Tuttle, a farmer from Wallingford, Connecticut, was arrested in Boston on 25 October 1723 for having passed off a false five pound Rhode Island bill to one Elizabeth Ellis. At first he told the justices a yarn to the effect that a certain Francis Brown of New Haven had given him the note and asked him to purchase with it handkerchiefs in Boston. When the constables were ordered to search Tuttle, he quickly tried to chew up a bill and managed to reduce it to pulp before it was forcibly removed from his mouth.

His successful attempt to destroy evidence did not impress the magistrates favorably and he was committed to jail, where a few days of prison fare and discomforts caused him to change his account to the following story, which must in the main be accurate: Ebenezer Seamore had that summer returned from a trip to the Jerseys and brought back false five pound and forty shilling Rhode Island bills and the plates for making them; the plates in question had been engraved by Ovid Rushbrook, a notorious scoundrel and known counterfeiter. Tuttle admitted that he had kept the plates concealed under straw in his barn as a favor to Seamore. On 13 December Tuttle was tried in Boston but was acquitted by the jurymen, who reached their verdict on the remarkable grounds that his putting the bogus money into the hands of Elizabeth Ellis was not 'uttering' it. This is, indeed, one of the many cases which reveal the extreme difficulty of securing the conviction of a counterfeiter.

By the end of December Tuttle was back in Connecticut and ready to give evidence against Seamore and his associates, John Wyard and a French refugee named James Poisson, all three of whom were under arrest. Poisson lied glibly and so did Wyard, although the authorities offered Wyard a reward of £20 and all possible favor if he would reveal the principal actor and give the location of his press. Tuttle, however, was not backward and related what is probably the true story: in the spring of 1723 Seamore hired Tuttle to pilot him through the woods to Guilford, where Seamore said that he was going to find John Blyn, a man who had formerly been associated with Ovid Rushbrook and who had been prosecuted as a money maker. In Guilford Seamore found his man and tried to induce Blyn to journey to Springfield and fetch Rushbrook, in order that Rushbrook might accompany Seamore to the Jersies to make plates and money there. Blyn refused and made the valid objection that Rushbrook would have no truck with him, since he had some time before betrayed Rushbrook to the authorities.

The upshot of the matter was that Seamore went himself

to Springfield and persuaded Rushbrook to join him in Wallingford, whence the two rogues, in the company of John Wyard, set off for the Jerseys. In New Haven, Seamore stopped long enough to purchase at the shop of Joseph Atwater half a pint of linseed oil with which, as he said, to do the flourishes of the bills on the back side. Seamore and Wyard had promised Rushbrook a horse and clothing for his services and Seamore also presented him with a watch and £4 in New York money. Somewhere on the road, Rushbrook, unmindful of the code of honor among thieves, was so ungrateful as to give his employers the slip, so that they arrived in Philadelphia alone. In time they got wind of the fact that Rushbrook too was staying in the city and hastened to the house indicated as his place of abode. The residents of the place stoutly denied that he was there, so Seamore and Wyard departed, only to return half a day later and see their man dashing up the stairs. They followed and cornered him, reproaching him for his villainy in taking their gifts and then leaving them in the lurch.

Rushbrook excused his reprehensible conduct on the grounds that he was fearful of the law, but the two men presently persuaded him to go with them to Egg Harbor and there make plates for counterfeiting five pound and forty shilling bills of Rhode Island. They struck off some of their money 'near Thirty miles from any place,' cutting a hole in a hollow tree and inserting a pry to press the bills.

Wyard and Tuttle turned king's evidence, a fact which made convictions possible. Poisson, a shopkeeper of Hartford, was charged with passing false bills and after his examination was released on bail of £200 put up by one Jonathan Easton for his appearance at the September session of the superior court in Hartford. At this court he was indicted, tried, convicted, and sentenced to serve six months in prison, to stand an hour and a half in the pillory in Hartford, to have the lower part of his right ear cut off, and to pay costs of £9.10s. Poisson, not liking the way things were going, at some point in the proceedings simply decamped and left Easton with his bond forfeited. The whole business was more or less normal in Connecticut; if a criminal could secure bail and then skip, the colony was, as a rule, quite content to collect the forfeited money and leave the convicted offender in peace.

In this instance Poisson merely removed himself to New Haven, where he lived unmolested and with the full knowledge of the authorities. In the normal course of events his bondsman would have been the only one to suffer for his gullibility in trusting Poisson. As it transpired, however, Easton was so inconsiderate as to die before the £200 were safely in the coffers of the colony. Action was taken to collect the money from Easton's widow, who appealed to Peter Pratt, the king's attorney. Pratt, in October 1725, went before the General Assembly and pointed out that Poisson was 'like wholly to escape punishment for his flagitious crime, and the innocent widow and fatherless made the only sufferers.' The lawmakers were impressed and had a warrant issued for the immediate apprehension of Poisson. They voted that the sentence of the court against him was to be executed unless he paid, by the last day of December, the whole £200 in addition to sheriff's fees. Poisson, with no alternative save to let justice take its course, loosened his purse strings and paid up rather than lose his ear, sit in the pillory, and face the extremely unpleasant and unhealthy sojourn of six months in the Hartford jail.

Seamore, the promoter of the affair, fared even better

than Poisson, unhappily for justice. He had been arrested
and was to have been tried at Hartford on 10 March
1724, but he broke out of the jail and fled. Bail for his
appearance in court had been furnished in the amount of
£150 by Samuel Seamore. When Ebenezer, after being three
times called, did not appear, the court declared the bond
forfeited, which probably pleased everyone except Samuel
Seamore. Ebenezer now would have been quits with the
law and would probably have again turned to farming and
counterfeiting on the side, had it not been that he was
charged with a crime committed in another county, namely
Fairfield, since he had passed off one of his spurious five
pound Rhode Island bills to Samuel Starr in Danbury. For
this offense he was taken up and tried at the superior court
in Fairfield on 25 August 1725, was convicted, and was
sentenced to suffer in the pillory, to serve six months in
prison, to have his right ear cropped, and to pay £9 in
costs. Ebenezer, however, was determined and resourceful,
while the Fairfield jail was notoriouly weak, so he promptly
broke out and vanished, very likely shifting his residence
and activities to some other colony where his police record
was not known.

Rushbrook, some time before he had had dealings with
Seamore, had been arrested in Springfield, where he confessed to the magistrate where he had hidden his two
plates, one for making the five pound bills of Massachusetts and the other for counterfeiting the ten shilling notes
of Connecticut. As chance would have it, one Samuel
Chapin of Springfield, who was born in 1699, the son of
Samuel and Hannah (Sheldon) Chapin, was present and,
on hearing Rushbrook's confession, slipped out and found
the plates. He may or may not have originally intended
to deliver them to the authorities, as he later claimed, but

in actual fact he showed them to his cousin, Abel Chapin. Together the cousins repaired to a swamp in the neighborhood and there printed twenty of the five pound bills which they thought would be passable, using a lever to make the impression and resting the plate on a block. They did not use the other plate because it had a crack in the middle and was therefore not serviceable. On the other hand the Massachusetts plate was nicely cut and was supposed to have been made in England. Abel either signed the twenty bills or got them signed, whereupon the kinsmen set off in May 1723 for Newport, Rhode Island. There on the twenty-second of the month Samuel tried to pass a bad five pound bill, was arrested and brought before Governor Cranston and the Council. He had, however, managed to slip his wallet to Abel. Cranston suspected something of the kind and ordered that Abel also be searched by the constables. Between Abel's shirt and his skin was found a pocketbook containing ten counterfeits, while his pocket contained a second purse with nine false notes in it. The cousins were committed to jail, where Samuel, to whom the authorities apparently held out some hope of a pardon, finally made a full confession. Both Chapins went on trial at Newport at about four o'clock in the afternoon of Wednesday, 11 September, Abel for making the five pound counterfeit and Samuel for uttering it. The trial continued until night, and the next day the jury brought them in guilty. They were sentenced to be set in the pillory on 20 September, to have both ears cropped, to pay double damages to all who had been defrauded by their bad money, and to pay all costs of their prosecution. In case their estate or effects should not suffice to meet these terms, the sheriff of Rhode Island was to sell the Chapins for such time as their labor would pay the charges against them.

It may be assumed that proper financial arrangements were made, for Abel, at least, was back in Springfield before long and married Hannah Hitchcock there on 8 January 1724.

Another person who apparently was acquainted with Rushbrook or at least knew much about him and was on good terms with Dr. Whipple of Tolland and John Blyn was Ephraim Shevie, alias John Rideout, who was arrested by Benjamin Judd on 13 December 1723 and taken, along with Thomas Stedman and Israel Scias (or Sias), to Major Talcott, assistant, in Hartford. The three men were closely questioned by Talcott, who ordered Shevie confined in jail.

Shevie was by profession a maker of sundials, though he had probably also taught school and apparently felt qualified as a teacher. During his examination he admitted that he had hidden tools some thirty rods from his lodging, but he was full of excuses and lies and, when charged with having boasted he would make a plate for counterfeiting, maintained that he had done so only in jest.

Stedman and Scias told a different story, for Stedman said that Shevie had asked if he could have a private room at his house and had confided to Scias that he would make the room in question into a mint for striking bills. Their account was that Shevie asked Stedman for a new ten shilling bill and boasted that he would make a plate for this denomination. He also desired Stedman to have ready for him some thirty and twenty shilling notes, telling Stedman and Scias that he had executed plates for five pound, three pound ten shilling, and three pound currency, that he had struck off bills from them, and that they were the best ever made. When they asked him to show the plates, he said they were in the woods some two miles away. He also promised to make £300 in bills for Scias and asserted that the best place to finish his plates would be in the chamber of one Joseph Butler.

The authorities now began to question other persons thought to have knowledge of Shevie's money making, among whom was Abigail Conwell of Middletown. It was indicated that she had interested Israel Scias in trying to benefit by Shevie's work. Upon examination she declared she had heard Shevie and one Daniel Martin talking of making false money and that Shevie had affirmed he could turn out £1,000 in bills that would not be suspected.

As Shevie had for some time boarded at the home of Nathaniel and Hannah Barnes in Middletown, Constable Thomas How of that place now brought them before Justice Hamblin of Middletown to be questioned. The statements of the couple were to the effect that Shevie had boasted he could engrave a plate for making money if Barnes would give him new bills. Barnes provided him with a five shilling Connecticut bill, and a short time thereafter Shevie showed him a plate for printing such money and also another plate with flowers engraved on it. Barnes claimed that he took the plates away from Shevie's work-shop and hid them under the roots of a tree, whereupon the maker of sundials became angry and protested that the plates were worth £50. On one occasion Shevie tried to persuade Barnes to ride to New York to bring him 'Indian black' and 'Linset oyl' for making bills. Mr. and Mrs. Barnes admitted that they had passed off half of a five shilling Connecticut bill to Captain Nols, the tailor, but that when he declared it false they had taken it back. This note, they explained, they had received from Jonathan Prat, a shopkeeper in Weathersfield.

At his examination on 20 December Shevie admitted

that he had engraved letters on a plate and also an escutch-
eon, but only to try his skill. Toward the end of the month,
however, the cold and the poor food in prison seem to have
had an effect, for the prisoner sent a jailer to Assistant
Talcott to indicate that he was willing to make a confession. Talcott, accompanied by Justice Cook, visited the
jail and heard from Shevie that Nathaniel Barnes had
persuaded him to make the five shilling plate, since Barnes
wanted to make money with which to redeem his mortgaged
land. Shevie further declared that when the bills came
off blotched he burnt them, while Barnes carried away the
plate.

Shevie had been extremely indiscreet, for it was disclosed that once at the house of Obadiah Allyn he 'bragged,'
in the presence of Daniel Marcom, to one Thankful Baker
that he could make five pound bills and pulled some out
of his pocket. At this the persons present said they would
complain of him, so he threw the currency into the fire.
On another occasion, at the home of John Williams of
Middletown, when Ebenezer Hubbert, Joseph Starr,
Ebenezer Robind, Moses Bidwell, and Williams were there,
Shevie pulled out about £10 in bills and asked Williams
if he could change one of £5, £3, 40s., or 20s.

The evidence was so strong that at the superior court
held in Hartford in March 1724 Shevie, described as
formerly of Middletown but lately of Weathersfield, was
indicted for having made a plate with which to print
five shilling bills of Connecticut. He was tried, convicted,
and sentenced to be imprisoned, to stand in the pillory,
and to have his right ear cropped. The same month, writing
in jail, he addressed to the judges of the superior court a
petition in which he pointed out that he had already spent
sixteen or seventeen weeks in a dark, stinking, nasty prison,

with only a little straw for a bed and with poor clothing on him in winter weather, so that his bodily and mental health had been impaired. He requested that he be not maimed by cropping so as to be debarred from earning his daily bread in any honest employment of schooling or other labor. What town, he asked, would receive him as a schoolmaster with a cropped ear? He begged to be released from payment of fines or costs and to be allowed to take an oath in secret never to counterfeit and also to act as an informer and agent to seek out counterfeiters and denounce them to the authorities.

The judges turned a deaf ear to his plea and by May he had stood in the pillory and had had his right ear cropped, whereupon he then petitioned the Assembly, asking to be released from jail and complaining that he now had no straw on which to lie, that he was always in iron chains, that it was bitterly cold, and that there had been no fire in the prison in March and April. His outer coat had not been off at all, and, of late, he had received a short allowance of food, so that he suffered gripes within his body and in his mind anguish. It seems probable that Shevie was exaggerating when he wrote of the prison fare; in any case James Henderson, keeper of the jail in Hartford, said that he spent seven shillings on Shevie for food and drink instead of the two and sixpence allowed.

In September, Shevie directed a last desperate appeal for mercy to the Assembly. He had been, he wrote, a prisoner in the Hartford jail for nearly eleven months in close confinement, all the time in iron chains; his sufferings were more than tongue or pen could express; he had received his public punishment in May and ever since March had been given only bread and water, supplemented by a little food sent to him by charitable persons;

he had no bed on which to lie; his breeches were nearly worn off him; his strength was weakened; his understanding was impaired; he was perplexed with vermin. This time the Assembly hearkened to his prayer and ordered his release on condition that he leave the colony of Connecticut within one month and with the understanding that he was to be imprisoned again if he did not depart within the appointed time or if he again came into the colony.

Israel Scias had the effrontery to ask for the reward of £20 as an informer, but his request was denied by the Assembly and the money was given, properly enough, to Benjamin Judd. As for Nathaniel Barnes, he was indicted in March at a session of the superior court held in Hartford for having printed a five shilling Connecticut bill from a plate made of pewter, but there is no record that the king's attorney ever prosecuted the case.

# Chapter 3

## WOMEN MONEY MAKERS

In general, counterfeiting was a man's business, but upon occasion women tried their hands at the game, usually in a rather petty way. Before bills were issued in the colonies four residents of New York City were charged with clipping silver coin and passing it: early in 1701 a grand jury found a bill against a widow, Susannah Elliot, for such an offense, but there is no record of the disposal of the case in the minutes of the supreme court; Sophia Thomas and Anna Vanderspiegel, accused of the like wrongdoing in 1703, got their indictments quashed, while Mary Barnes, a 'victualler,' who was alleged 'fraudulently deceitfully and craftilly' to have clipped and uttered Spanish silver pieces, was acquitted by a jury.

Only three other women figure in the records of counterfeiting in the Province of New York: Catherine Johnson, Margaret Haynnie, and Polly Lewis. Mrs. Johnson's husband, Joseph, a journeyman printer and bookbinder, who probably was employed by William Bradford, publisher of the *New-York Gazette,* early in 1735 struck off counterfeit ten shilling New York bills, was detected, and fled at dead of night to the Jerseys, leaving behind him Catherine and a six-year-old son, Joseph, Jr. The boy was apprenticed by the court of quarter sessions to William Bradford to learn the printing trade but Catherine was tried on a charge of passing bad money, was convicted, and given twenty-one lashes on the bare back. It was probably a good thing that Joseph, Jr., was in the hands of William Bradford, for Catherine did not mend her ways, as is evidenced by court records: in 1766 she was convicted of stealing a piece of checked linen from William Kirby, pleaded her clergy and was burned in the left thumb in the presence of the court, while seven years later she was indicted for keeping a disorderly house.

Margaret Haynnie in 1739 was caught in the act of passing a milled dollar made of pewter and paid for her cheat by receiving twenty-one lashes at the public whipping post and serving a term of three months at hard labor in the house of correction.

As for Polly Lewis, she is mentioned in the confession made by a notorious counterfeiter, Joseph Bill Packer, alias Joseph Bill, just before he was hanged at Albany in 1773. He related how William Hulbert and Daniel Lewis made New York bills from plates which he, Packer, had engraved for them. Hulbert struck off the bills, Daniel Lewis signed them, while 'his sister, Miss Polly, an active, accomplished young lady, distributed the ink upon the plates when the impression was struck.' There is no further mention of Polly, so it may be presumed that she took French leave or perhaps turned king's evidence, thus escaping the gallows as a reward.

In Boston a woman of more than fifty years of age, who had aided in counterfeiting and passing Massachusetts bills, in 1723 was sentenced to stand one hour in the pillory and have one ear cut off; in the same town, nine years later, a young lady was arrested when she tried to utter three unsigned counterfeit five pound Rhode Island bills of

the long sort of the emission of 1737. A search ordered
by the magistrate revealed sixty-five other counterfeits
concealed on her person and she was promptly committed
to jail.

Connecticut had but two women counterfeiters, unless,
of course, there were others who escaped discovery. When
the superior court met at Fairfield on 3 September 1717,
it had the task of determining who had altered a Rhode
Island bill of 2/6 to 10/6. There were two suspects: Lieutenant Richard Higgenbotham and Ann Lockwood, the
wife of Gershom Lockwood, Jr., of Greenwich. Higgenbotham was cleared by proclamation, and it was ordered
that the charges of his prosecution be paid out of the public
treasury, an unusual circumstance, since persons convicted,
acquitted, or released without trial were as a rule all alike
forced to pay costs.

The real culprit was Ann Lockwood, and it came to light
that about the beginning of July 1717, Mrs. Richard Higgenbotham set out from her home in Cos Cob for Greenwich with four pairs of homemade stockings for sale. While
in Greenwhich she disposed of one pair to Joseph Knapp
for some Indian corn and of another pair to a Mr. Jessup
for 4*s*. As Mrs. Higgenbotham was anxious to secure some
wool for her knitting, she left the two unsold pair, together with the 4*s*., in the keeping of Ann Lockwood.

A few days later Lieutenant Higgenbotham and his wife
went to Mrs. Lockwood's and gave her a two shilling Connecticut bill and a two shilling sixpence Rhode Island bill,
requesting her to add this amount to the four shillings she
had already received and with it all to purchase some sheep's
wool for them. As soon as Ann saw the two shilling sixpence bill she remarked that because of a blank space in
the paper there was a fair opportunity to alter the 2 to a

10. The lieutenant remonstrated with her and she hastily promised that she would do no such thing.

Temptation, however, proved too strong; Ann was evidently unable to neglect such an attractive and easy way to make a profit, for she altered the bill and paid it out, together with three bills of 2/6 each, to Benjamin Hobby for nine and a quarter pounds of wool. Hobby presently showed the counterfeit to others, found that it had been altered, and returned it to Ann.

She was by now thoroughly frightened, for the stir caused by the appearance of the altered bill was sure to move the authorities in Greenwhich to action, so on Saturday, 13 July, she betook herself with the bill in question to the Higgenbothams in Cos Cob. There the three — the lieutenant, his wife, and Ann — sat under a 'green tree' and talked for about an hour. Perhaps the green tree was an apple tree and served as an inspiration, for Ann told the couple that it was all the way 'the apple tempted Mother Eve' and that she would never do such a thing again. Her chief concern was to induce them to take back the altered bill and stretch the truth by saying that they had received it of a stranger. If they would accede to her request, she promised to give them £20 and permission to live at one end of her house and have the use of her cows. Her husband, she added, knew of her crime, as did his brother Joseph, who had told her that he 'had a good mind to knock her on the head' because her husband was like to be ruined by her 'confounded tricks.' The most she could wheedle from the Higgenbothams was their reluctant consent to take custody of the bill and to say, if questioned, that they had it of a stranger. They made it clear, however, that if they were called before a magistrate and examined they must tell the whole truth.

Gershom Lockwood, Jr., stood by his wife and twice besought Lieutenant Higgenbotham to burn the bill and say nothing of what Ann had confessed. The lieutenant refused. The persons to whom Hobby had tendered the money denounced him, and he in turn swore the bill on Ann, for whose arrest a warrant was issued. She was apprehended by Constable Joshua Reynolds, jailed, and tried at the September sessions of the superior court. Upon her conviction she was sentenced to stand in the pillory on three lecture days — days of public meeting — for half an hour each day, to be disenabled from giving evidence before any court, magistrate, or justice of the peace, and to pay costs of prosecution amounting to £6.13s.6d. Her husband informed the court that he feared for the welfare of his family, since some of the children were ill, and besought the judges to be speedy in permitting him and his wife to return home, so in September Ann was discharged on bail provided by her spouse and was under necessity of appearing in Fairfield on the public days appointed by the deputy governor to receive such parts of her punishment as had not yet been executed.

The colony's other woman counterfeiter, if indeed she was guilty, was a poor young woman of New London named Grace Edgcomb, who on 18 February 1763 was arrested on the charge of having altered two Connecticut bills by changing with a pen one of five shillings to forty and one of one shilling to ten and then passing both. Justice Daniel Coit had her committed to jail but she secured her release when Robert Douglass and Daniel Reynolds furnished bail of £50 for her appearance at the superior court to be held in March at Norwich. When the time for her trial arrived, it transpired that she had come down with the smallpox and had been removed by the selectmen of the town to a place provided for persons afflicted with that malady. Obviously she could not appear in court when summoned but the judges accepted no excuse, her bond was declared forfeited, and judgment was given against her sureties, who in 1764 made a vain appeal to the Assembly for relief. Grace, at least, was beyond punishment for, as was usual in cases where the bail bond was forfeited, there was no further prosecution.

Although she herself was no counterfeiter, mention should be made of Mrs. John Abbott because of the part she played in effecting the escape of her money maker husband. A dispatch from New London printed in the Boston newspapers reported that on 25 November 1731 a certain Abbott had been committed to jail for counterfeiting the last emission of the five pound bills of Rhode Island and that a few days later the plates from which the bills had been struck were found. As no bail was provided, Abbott was kept in irons in close confinement, but his wife frequently had the liberty of being let in to visit him. On the evening of 7 February 1732 she was admitted as usual. As soon as the keeper left husband and wife alone, the pair managed to get off John's fetters and then exchanged apparel. After some time the prisoner called to the jailer to let out his wife and, when the door was opened, Abbott himself in feminine attire came out and went through a room where several persons were sitting, making them 'the usual Complements of a Woman,' and then departed from the prison undetected. The next morning, when the fugitive had a good start on possible pursuers, Mrs. Abbott summoned the keeper and expressed a desire to be released from confinement, with which request the astonished jailer readily complied. No unpleasantness apparently befell Mrs. Abbott, though there seems to be no reason why she could not have been prosecuted for assisting a prisoner to escape, and her husband for a time dropped out of sight.

The two months and more that Abbott had spent in jail had not brought about a change of heart, for in April he was heard of again, once more as a counterfeiter and this time in the company of Joseph Waterhouse of Saybrook, who was master of a sloop then lying near 'Eles Neck.' Waterhouse, it developed, employed Thomas Monk and Samuel Suard to buy for him two quarts of rum, some pork, and three pounds of sugar, to pay for which he gave Suard a forty shilling Rhode Island bill. Suard turned the money over to Monk, who, apparently in good faith, bought the sugar and rum from Hannah Hull, wife of Captain Josiah Hull, and then gave the change to Suard, who in turn handed it over to Waterhouse. Waterhouse busied himself with passing, for one night he bought from Lydia Lockwood, wife of Lieutenant James Lockwood, a barrel of cider, which he took away in a cart. He paid for the cider with a counterfeit forty shilling Rhode Island bill and received twenty shillings change in good money; at about the same time he uttered another forty shilling counterfeit to Joshua Raymond of Norwalk.

Abbott in the meantime was about the same nefarious business as his associate, for Elizabeth Hoyt, wife of Daniel Hoyt, told the authorities she was paid a bad forty shilling bill of Rhode Island by a stranger, a short, well-set man with a broad, flat face, a short neck, and a brownish complexion, whose name she was later told was Abbott. It was not long before the nature of the forty shilling bills was discovered, and on 19 April a warrant was issued at Greenwich by Joshua Knapp, J.P., for the arrest of Waterhouse and Abbott. Samuel Miles, Sr., of that town seized Waterhouse and searched his sloop, finding in the master's chest on board the boat two copper plates from which the bills had been made, as well as six or seven bills not yet finished. It seems that Waterhouse quickly escaped, for two days later he was picked up in Norwalk by Constable Joseph St. John and confined, first in Norwalk and later in the jail of Fairfield County, until his brother, Abraham Waterhouse of Saybrook, foolishly put up a bail bond of £300. When Joseph failed to appear at the next session of the superior court, his unhappy brother was required to pay the bond, which was eventually chancered down to £150 by the Assembly. As for Abbott, he eluded a hot pursuit by Samuel Miles and a posse of eight men and disappeared, along with his wife, from the annals of crime in colonial Connecticut.

There seem to have been no women counterfeiters in the southern provinces, but there were at least seven in Pennsylvania. Two, whose names are not recorded, were seized in 1774 in the company of five or six men who were making counterfeits in a log house in a remote part of the Jerseys and were imprisoned in Philadelphia. In 1751 Margaret Thomas, accused of passing bad dollars, was acquitted, and Rebecca Johns, convicted three years before of uttering false pieces of eight, got off with a fine, for which she might count herself lucky, for there was a great variation in the severity of the sentences imposed, as is well illustrated by the cases of Ann Tew, Alice Richards, and Martha Hunt.

Ann Tew, a spinster, was found guilty at a court of quarter sessions held at Lancaster in 1765 of having altered a two shilling Pennsylvania bill to ten and then passed it to one Abraham Rinehart. Ann stood for an hour in the pillory, had both ears cut off and nailed to the pillory, was given thirty-one lashes, and was required to pay a fine of £100 and costs. So severe a punishment, it might be thought, would have taught her a lesson, but such was not the case, for exactly a year later she was charged with altering a one shilling bill to ten and putting it off to a certain Wendal Gilbert. She received the same sentence as before, which makes one wonder how the executioner solved the problem of cutting off ears which he had already removed in 1765.

Some twelve months after Ann's second conviction Alice Richards counterfeited and passed in Philadelphia two Virginia bills of credit and in the supreme court was tried and convicted of passing bad paper money. For her wrongdoing she was sentenced to serve six months in the county jail and to pay costs. The lightness of her sentence in comparison with that imposed upon Ann Tew may probably be explained by the fact that the money involved was that of a province other than Pennsylvania and that the conviction was merely for passing rather than for both counterfeiting and passing.

The harshest sentence, however, which was pronounced upon a woman counterfeiter in the colonial period was in the case of Martha Hunt in Philadelphia. Her husband, Edward Hunt, a silversmith, had a bad record, for he had been taken as a rebel at Preston and transported to Antigua, whence he made his way to Pennsylvania. In 1720 he was charged with having made Spanish coin, which was current in the province. His wife had passed some of it. Edward was convicted of treason and put to death, while Martha was found guilty of misprision of treason, was fined £500, and was imprisoned for life. The cruel punishment of the couple was in accordance with the law in England for just such offenses — the counterfeiting and passing of foreign coin current in the kingdom.

New Hampshire seems to have had but one woman counterfeiter, Tamsen Meserve. In 1704 she married Joseph Ham of Dover, and some two years after his death in 1723, became the bride of a widower named John Tibbits, also of Dover. It chanced that in 1731 William Byrn, described as a painter or laborer, came from Rochester, New Hampshire, to Dover, some of whose inhabitants desired him to keep school and, as he put it, 'learn their children to write.' He accepted the offer, and the new schoolmaster was at first boarded at the home of John and Tamsen Tibbits. Tamsen, discovering that the boarder could draw flowers and write, decided to put such talent to work, so she brought a twenty shilling Massachusetts bill and other notes to Byrn and at length prevailed upon him to copy them.

Tidings of Byrn's skill somehow reached the ears of John McVicker and Samuel Styles, who formed a partnership with the gifted penman. Indeed, McVicker and Byrn were so foolhardy as to deliver to Styles two documents bearing their signatures. In one of them they promised to give Styles one fifth of the money he should pass and also to bear his expenses, while in the other they swore 'by the Living God' to betray him neither by signs nor word of mouth.

Tamsen Tibbits put off a thirty shilling New Hampshire bill to Sarah Pitney, while Styles passed a three pound ten shilling note to Hannah Bradford of Portsmouth and another to Sarah Croftswait. Styles fell under suspicion and was arrested and searched by order of a magistrate. In his pocket were found nine counterfeit three pound ten shilling bills, together with much more incriminating evidence in the form of the two documents given him by McVicker and Byrn. Warrants were speedily issued and Styles's accomplices were arrested and committed to jail, where they were soon joined by the Tibbits, who also appeared to be implicated. It was reported that the gang had a plate and that the bills were so nicely struck that nothing but the signings could reveal the cheat.

At a court of general sessions at Exeter on 7 March Byrn was convicted of forging and Styles of passing some three pound ten shilling New Hampshire bills of the emission of 1727. Each was given the same sentence, namely to pay a fine of £14, to stand one hour in the pillory at Exeter at one o'clock on Thursday, 9 March, to have one ear cut off, to be imprisoned for a whole year without bail, and to pay costs. As the court did not have the time to try the other prisoners, McVicker was returned to jail, while the Tibbits were released on recognizance of £500.

Byrn, moved perhaps by repentance but more likely by the hope of obtaining some mitigation of his sentence, now made a full confession, in which he stated that the bills were not made with a plate at all but by his own hand and pen. He claimed that at the instigation of Tamsen Tibbits he made and gave her a thirty shilling Massachusetts bill, of which denomination he made and burned two more. He also executed four forty shilling bills of the same province, of which Tamsen received one and Styles the rest. His total output of New Hampshire three pound ten shilling notes amounted to ten, which he maintained that he had made through the persuasion of McVicker and Styles. He was probably rather bitter against Styles, whose carelessness in carrying the covenant on his person had brought about Byrn's downfall, for he informed the authorities that he had several times seen Styles utter halfpence made of pewter and that Styles had told him that he always had £15 or £20 of these counterfeit coins on hand.

Tamsen and her husband were charged with counterfeiting and passing, but at a court of general sessions held at Hampton, the king's attorney could not get a grand jury to indict them, so they were dismissed on payment of costs. McVicker, on the other hand, was convicted and sentenced to pay a fine of £7 and costs, to be pilloried for one hour, to have one ear cropped, and to serve a year in prison.

Most of these women counterfeiters seem to have been weak characters who yielded to the temptation of making some trifling gain, or individuals who became involved through their menfolk. Such, however, was not the case with two New Englanders of the early days of paper money, Freelove Lippencott and Mary Peck Butterworth.

Freelove has the somewhat doubtful distinction of being the first known woman counterfeiter in New England and the first woman ringleader of a band of counterfeiters in the colonies. Her husband, Robert, was a mariner who in 1712 was supposedly teaching navigation in Newport. His wife sent to England, probably by him, and there had engraved six plates for making the following bills: a £3 of Rhode Island, a 10s. of Connecticut, and a 3s., a 3/6, a 20s., and a 50s. of Massachusetts. Her chief assistant was Edward Greenman, son of John Greenman of Newport, and she also induced her brother, George Lawton, and apparently a Henry Cooke, to pass bills for her. The roll which she used was eventually lost in the Lippencotts' well. Before long her bogus money attracted attention and she, her husband, and Edward Greenman were apprehended. While out on bail and waiting for the next session of the general court to be held in Newport, Freelove, it seems, made the most of the opportunity to strike off some more currency, and then entrusted her plates to the keeping of Captain Edward Greenman of Kingstown, an uncle of her associate, all of which was to cause much woe to the government of Rhode Island and to Captain Greenman and his family.

At the court held in September Freelove and her associates had their indictments returned ignoramus by the grand jury. The court, dissatisfied with this result, on the advice of the General Assembly ordered the accused held to appear at the next sessions in March 1714. Because of the winter season and the coldness of the prison, bail in the amount of £1,000 each was permitted and was furnished by the two Lippencotts but not by Greenman, who presently broke jail and escaped. At the sessions in March the Lippencotts were not prosecuted, probably because the grand jury again would not indict them. Greenman, to be sure, was presented by the grand jurors and was faced with a fine of 40s., all of which was of little moment, since he could not be found.

After her dismissal by the court Freelove remained for some time in Newport with her husband, who was still teaching navigation, but she had by no means abandoned her interest in counterfeiting and probably still had a financial stake in the plates now in the keeping of Captain Greenman. One evening, when alone with her husband and one of his pupils, Joseph Atwood, a nephew of Captain Greenman, she brought the conversation around to the counterfeiting of paper currency and finally asked Atwood if he would be willing to take some bad bills and pass them off. When he readily consented, she gave him a letter directed to Silas Greenman of Kingstown, a son of the captain. Atwood delivered the message and shortly thereafter met Silas at the captain's home. Silas told him to bring a clean skin with which to wipe the plates, and when he had done as was directed, Atwood watched Captain Greenman and his two sons, Silas and Edward, Jr., strike off some bills, using Freelove's plates and a roll made by the captain. As the result was unsatisfactory, Atwood went away empty-handed, but later, on at least two occasions, Silas, who signed the currency, brought him considerable amounts of currency, some of which Atwood burned and some of which he passed off successfully at Ipswich for silver money.

Because of the notoriety she had achieved, Freelove went in 1715 to stay in Branford, Connecticut, in the home of Thomas Banks, a tailor, and it is known that she was quite ill there for some time. Probably her husband went to sea when she left Rhode Island, and he died in the Barbados on 2 April 1718. Freelove told Banks of her reason for leaving Newport and said that if he would go to Silas Greenman he could obtain from him the plates, which were concealed in a hole in the cellar wall at Captain Greenman's.

Banks acted on her suggestion and later came under the suspicion of the authorities because of his carelessness. On Saturday, 6 July 1717, he lodged at the house of John Hill, an innkeeper and justice of the peace, and shortly after he had set out for Stonington on the following morning the innkeeper's eleven-year-old daughter picked up a piece of paper dropped by the departing guest and gave it to her father. It turned out to be a letter, dated 21 June 1717, written by John Lovel, a tailor, to his wife, from whom he requested eight or nine pounds. He was a servant for debt at the time to a tailor in New London named Thomas Farrand, whom he wanted to pay off that he might be released and join his wife and child. So far there was nothing amiss, but inside the letter was found a counterfeit ten shilling bill, neither numbered nor signed. Lovel apparently was never required to explain his connection with the bill, for, not receiving the money for which he had written, he ran away from Farrand and disappeared.

On Thursday, 11 July, John Austin and a fellow traveler named Aply stopped, on their way from New London, at Justice Hill's 'in Naragansett country.' Hill was not at home but his wife showed them the counterfeit dropped by Banks, and when on the following Saturday Austin again stopped at the inn, Hill gave him the bogus bill to be delivered to Assistant William Pitkin. Austin carried out the commission and reported to the assistant that people said Banks 'was very great with Leepincutts Wife' and that a certain Meergratt, keeper of a coffee house in Rhode Island, had told him that he and his wife suspected Banks of being 'naughty.'

Banks was arrested and examined at Branford on 20 July by Pitkin and two justices of the peace, without benefit of having legal counsel. The prisoner readily admitted dealings with the Lippencotts but he maintained that the only money he had had of them was an insignificant sum for boarding Freelove. At the October sessions of the superior court held in New Haven he was charged with passing a bad ten shilling Connecticut bill to Mrs. Savell Latham at Groton. The grand jury, however, returned the indictment ignoramus and the tailor's activities would have escaped detection had it not been for the arrest of one John Andrews by the constables of Milford, and of Joseph Jones in Boston.

Jones, who after his apprehension confessed himself a member of a band of counterfeiters, was sent to Con-

necticut, where he made a deposition involving Andrews
and Banks. He claimed that when he tried to collect a debt
of some £4 from Banks, the tailor told him that he, Banks,
and Andrews had gone with a letter from Freelove Lippencott to Silas Greenman to get plates and a press, which
Greenman agreed to hand over to them for £20. Andrews
eventually gave Banks a dark bay horse, which was then
surrendered to Greenman in lieu of the £20. Banks, having
completed the transaction with Greenman, joined Andrews
and showed him the plates, wrapped in flannel, which he
was carrying in his pocket, and a press in his portmanteau.
The implements were taken to Jones's house, to which
Edward Greenman, Jr., presently came to instruct the
partners in the forging of bills. Jones added that when
Banks was arrested, Edward Greenman, Sr., came to him,
Jones, and besought him not to testify against his son or
Thomas Banks.

Andrews, when he was arrested on 11 August and a press
found in his custody, told the examining magistrates in
Milford, Justices Eells and Law, that Banks, who owed
him money, had sent him the press and some plates and
bidden him make bills with them. Nevertheless he maintained that he had never used the plates but had thrown
them in a well, from which he and an officer sent with him
actually recovered them. Upon his indictment in September he was moved to make a full confession, which was to
the following effect: once at the house, apparently a tavern,
of Samuel Miles in Milford, Banks showed him a letter he
had received from Silas Greenman of Kingstown, in which
Greenman wrote that he had a horse for sale for £20. Banks
then explained that by 'horse,' Greenman meant 'paper
money,' and by '£20,' that he would furnish £100 in bills
of his own making for £20 of good money. When Banks

proposed that they become partners in procuring and passing counterfeits, Andrews consented, whereupon the tailor saw Captain Greenman, who promised that one of his sons would meet Banks between the New London ferry and Edward Dennison's at the bridge.

The rendezvous was kept by Edward Greenman, Jr., who delivered only £40, explaining that his brother Silas, who signed the money, had been appointed justice of the peace and was now unwilling to sign any more bills. Because of Silas's squeamishness, the captain and Edward, Jr., finally disposed of the plates to Banks and Andrews, as has already been recounted. In time Banks left the plates with his associate and moved to New York, whence he later wrote and asked Andrews to send the 'things' to New York. Andrews, indeed, admitted that he had received £29 in counterfeits and had passed them off, but because of his confession and his surrender of the plates he was given an extremely light sentence, namely, to pay a fine of £50 and to serve a term of six months in prison. As a matter of fact, the governor and council were moved by a petition from the prisoner to order his release if he could provide surety that he would pay costs and £30 of his fine.

The outrageous violation of the law by the Greenmans was aggravated by the standing of the captain and his sons. The captain had been a member of the House of Deputies from Kingstown in 1700, 1704, 1705, 1709, and 1710, assistant in 1701 and 1702, and Speaker of the House in 1704. Silas was a deputy from Kingstown in 1716 and in 1718 was made a justice of the peace. The situation called for vigorous action, and Massachusetts, Rhode Island, and Connecticut concerted their efforts in an attempt to secure conviction. To this end they induced three of the gang to turn evidence for the king: Jones, who was sent by Massachusetts to testify against the Greenmans, was rewarded with £150; Joseph Atwood of Newport was presented with £50; Banks, who was sent to the trial as a witness from Connecticut, at least had his expenses paid.

The Greenmans, confronted with the wrathful determination of the authorities and the evidence of three accomplices, spared the government the expense and bother of a trial by pleading guilty. The captain was sentenced to stand an hour in the pillory, have both ears cropped, pay costs and a fine of £600, and give a bond of £700 for the payment of double damages to those injured by the forged currency of his making. As for Silas and Edward, Jr., each was required to stand in the pillory, lose both ears, pay costs and a fine of £300, and put up a bond of £400 for the payment of double damages to every person injured by the counterfeits.

Had it not been for his death from natural causes, Samuel Vaughan, a cordwainer of Newport and member of the Greenman gang, might also have suffered through Freelove's villainy. Vaughan's widow, Mary, made deposition that her late husband and Joseph Atwood had been associated in the money making. On one occasion Vaughan had told his wife that Atwood 'went to school to Mrs Lipincut to get information about making bills & that they Laid the bills against Glass &c to take the Impression.' On his deathbed Vaughan bemoaned his having been concerned in the wicked practice and prayed his brother Daniel to reveal the affair in a letter to the governor. Daniel, indeed, planned to write such a letter and drop it in such a way that it would reach the proper hands; he delayed taking the step, and his good intention came to naught through his accidental drowning in Virginia.

In 1715 a far more talented woman than Freelove Lippencott set up in the counterfeiting business at Rehoboth, Massachusetts, across the river from the town of Providence in Massachusetts Bay Colony. This newcomer in the money making field was Mary Peck Butterworth, daughter of the innkeeper of the 'Sign of the Black Horse' and wife of a well-to-do housewright named John Butterworth, Jr., who after his marriage was generally known merely as 'Mary's husband.' Mary holds something of a record, for she made and sold more than £1,000 of forged bills over a period of seven years without being detected and, when her skulduggery came to light, escaped punishment with the rest of her gang. She died at the age of eighty-nine in the year 1775.

Mary was thirty years of age and rearing a family of seven children when she opened her workshop in her kitchen. Her methods were extremely simple and effective and as efficient as her management of her husband, children, and the band of helpers and passers which she organized: first she placed a piece of damp starched muslin on top of the bill she intended to imitate and then lightly ran a hot flatiron over the cloth, causing the material to pick up the printing from the money; next she would iron the muslin hard to transfer the pattern to a blank piece of paper which was to be the counterfeit bill. The cloth, having served its purpose, was immediately thrown into the fireplace and consumed to ashes, so that no plate was left to be seized and used in court as damaging evidence. Mary had doubtless observed that the possession of a copperplate for counterfeiting was a risky business and one which might readily bring about the conviction of its owner.

As her next step, she would with a fine crow quill pen trace over the impression on her new bill and after that go over the letters to reproduce the exact thickness of the letters on the true bill. Her most valued helper was one of her brothers, Israel Peck, who was an expert at fashioning the pens and became a specialist at filling in the background on the bills. Her manufactory was, indeed, a family affair, for two other brothers, Stephen and Nicholas Peck, often lent a hand, while Nicholas' wife, Hannah, under Mary's tutelage, in time became as expert as Mrs. Butterworth herself.

The product consisted of Rhode Island bills of £5, £3, 20s., and 10s., Connecticut bills of £5, and Massachusetts bills of £5, £3, and 40s. The quality of workmanship was high and Mary sold her bills at half their face value — she never passed them herself — whereas the Greenmans had been content to obtain 20 per cent of the face value for their inferior product. Eight of Mary's gang of customers or passers are known: her brother Nicholas, Hugh Betties and Arthur Noble, both young Irish carpenters recently come to America who were Mary's husband's hired men, two Chaffees, Nicholas Campe and his sister, and Daniel Hunt, a deputy sheriff and innkeeper in Rehoboth.

In the course of time the authorities noted with alarm the steady stream of carefully executed counterfeits and in 1722 a court of quarter sessions went so far as to issue a warrant for a search for counterfeit plates in the house of one of its own judges, Daniel Smith. The result of the search was, of course, negative, for the only 'plates' involved were scraps of muslin burned as soon as used in Mary's fireplace. One emission of five pound Rhode Island bills, that of 5 July 1715, had to be recalled, largely, no doubt, because of Mrs. Butterworth's operations, and the evil might have continued for years if there had not been a slip on the part of one of her passers, Arthur Noble, Butterworth's young carpenter.

The nineteenth of July, 1723, was to be a gala occasion in Newport, for a pirate ship, the *Ranger*, had recently been captured by His Majesty's 20-gun ship the *Greyhound*, and twenty-six of the freebooters from the *Ranger's* crew were to be hanged at Bull's Point, opposite the town. Noble decided to see the spectacle, so the day before it was to take place he rode off to Newport on a horse probably borrowed from his master and with a supply of Mary's counterfeits on his person. The next day, as luck would have it, Arthur encountered three young women from Rehoboth, also in town for the execution, so nothing would do but that he treat them and pay the score by passing one of the false five pound bills to Elizabeth Weir, probably the wife or employee of the tavernkeeper. The cheat was discovered and Noble, after being taken to Bristol and examined, was presently locked up in the jail which had so recently housed the twenty-six pirates, who had now paid their debt to society.

Governor Cranston of Rhode Island speedily laid hands on another of Mary's passers, Nicholas Campe, who turned king's evidence and related the story of Mary's operations in great detail. As a result, on 15 August three deputy sheriffs appeared in Rehoboth with warrants and arrested suspected members of the band, all of whom, save Mary, were dismissed after being questioned or were released on bail. Mrs. Butterworth was confined until the next session of the court was held in Bristol but apparently neither she nor her accomplices were convicted: there were no damaging plates to be discovered and brought into court. The only advantage secured by the government was that Mary's workshop was put permanently out of business.

Perhaps the success story of Mary Butterworth inspired two imitators in the same colony. A woman of Tivertown about 1740 made bills with her pen and had her son pass them whenever she needed money. Once, however, she made the mistake of giving some of her handiwork to her brother to put off; he got drunk, explained how the bills were made, and thus put an end to his sister's productivity. Another woman counterfeiter, who lived in South Kingstown, forged bills of credit with her pen but lacked Mrs. Butterworth's ability and was quickly discovered, pilloried, and cropped for her pains.

It was all but impossible to secure a conviction unless some member of a counterfeiting gang turned king's evidence. This was doubtless the reason why counterfeiters sometimes drew up solemn covenants in which they pledged themselves not to betray their associates. Such a pact was found in the pocket of Samuel Styles when he was arrested in New Hampshire, and a similar document was signed in Rhode Island in January 1729 by three men and two women. In the first part of the latter compact Nicholas Otis, a tailor, Samuel Hallet, a mariner, and David Richards, Jr., a merchant, agreed to make and put off a quantity of paper money. The articles of agreement were to the effect that damnation should be the portion and inheritance of anyone who made their proceedings known; that no partner should be taken into the undertaking without the consent of all concerned; that each partner should have an equal share in the plate and other counterfeiting materials; that Nicholas and Samuel were to print and utter such bills as were judged passable by the company; that David should use his utmost skill in signing the bills; that on demand each should render an exact account and divide produce and money received in equal shares; that no partner should pass more than 20s. a week without special permission and anyone found cheating in this respect was to pay a fine to the others of £50 out of his own stock of paper currency; that if one of the gang should be betrayed and imprisoned, the rest should bear their proportion of the loss in defraying his charges and should use all requisite means for his relief. The interesting paper concluded with these words: 'God save the King Prosper our Progress herein and Preserve us from all Traytors,' to which was added the following, 'Then each and every one of us taking the Bible in our hands Swore by the Contents thereof to Observe these Articles of Agreement and Fullfill the same. . .' Somewhat later in the same month Hannah Hallet and Joanna Otis signed an appendix to the above by which they stated that they had been concerned in the affair and would act for their husbands if the two men were absent, and they bound themselves to secrecy.

It was the misfortune of the confederates that they lacked the technical skill to make their own plate and so were forced to employ John Brown, an engraver of Newport, who, as a matter of fact, had actually engraved plates for genuine bills of the colony. Brown executed their plate but, tempted no doubt by the prospect of the reward of £50 usually paid informers against counterfeiters, immediately notified the authorities of the mischief that was afoot. Nicholas Otis was arrested and had the misfortune to be carrying the covenant on his person. All five of the gang — a sixth person, 'Phineas Chace of Tiverton,' was said to have been on the point of joining the band — were tried but only two were convicted, Nicholas and Joanna Otis. The husband was given the choice of paying a fine of £150 and costs or standing in the pillory and having both ears cropped, and, when the money was not raised, he endured the corporal punishment; the wife was sentenced to stand in the pillory and have both ears cut off or in lieu thereof to pay all costs and a fine of £50. Her relatives came to the rescue, paid the fine, and thus saved her ears and spared her the merciless pelting which was usually the lot of those who stood in the pillory.

Counterfeiters were often popular with their neighbors, which may well account for what transpired in the cases of Richards and Samuel and Hannah Hallet. Richards first found a flaw in his indictment — the 'Jr.' had been omitted after his name — and got it quashed, but was promptly presented again. The jury, however, seemingly was determined not to convict him and the two Hallets, for in the trial of each a verdict of not guilty was brought in; in each instance the court expressed dissatisfaction and sent the jurors out again, only to have them return once more with a verdict of not guilty. At this the king's attorney gave up in despair, and the three wrongdoers escaped unscathed.

# Chapter 4

## COUNTERFEITS FROM GREAT BRITAIN AND
## IRELAND

Engraving a plate for counterfeiting called for technical skill, so it was natural enough that Freelove Lippencott and others should send sample bills to Europe to have the plates engraved by competent craftsmen. There was, moreover, a distinct advantage to having plates or bills made in Ireland or England, for there was little if any danger that the authorities would interrupt the work. A crime was being committed, to be sure, but it was against a province in distant America and was an offense that would be punishable only in that colony. Passers of the false currency or owners of counterfeiting plates would incur a risk in America alone, while the engraver or printer in Europe was not likely to have any difficulties. There is, indeed, no case where an engraver or printer in Europe was actually punished or even arrested for counterfeiting provincial bills of credit.

Under such circumstances the authorities in Massachusetts must have felt no little anxiety when on 13 January 1719 a sailor named Peter Woodin was arrested in Boston and brought before two justices of the peace, John Clark and Samuel Checkley, on a charge of having put off false twenty shilling Massachusetts bills of the latest emission which were signed by four hands. At his examination fifty-eight such counterfeits were found on his person. Nine hundred and four counterfeits and the plate and roll were found on board the ship *Providence,* on which he had arrived at Cape Cod from London about a fortnight before. Woodin made a clean breast of the matter, admitting that he had already passed about a dozen of the notes. While in London he met a certain Briant, an engraver by trade, in George Yard on Tower Hill, who told him that if he was a New Englander he had a commodity that would suit him well and showed him a counterfeit twenty shilling Massachusetts bill. The sailor purchased for a guinea a bundle containing more than a hundred such notes and later obtained for a guinea and a half the copper plate, a roll, and a thousand bills, with the understanding that when he next came from America he would give the engraver a further gratification. Briant worked off the thousand bills in the sailor's presence but the magistrates could not discover who signed them, for Woodin either could not or would not tell. The sailor doubtless had counterfeiting in mind even before he set sail for England, for he carried with him as samples one twenty shilling bill and two of five shillings, which he sold to a Captain Clark for half a guinea, apparently for no honest purpose. The *Boston Weekly News-Letter* referred, justifiably, to the detection of Woodin before he had put off most of his notes as 'a favourable smile of Providence to this Province.'

The government of Massachusetts must have had forebodings that the arrest of the sailor would not be the end of the danger to the currency of the province. On 2 November of the following year Governor Shute addressed the legislature as follows: 'The Vile practice of Counterfeiting the Province Bills, is carrying on not only in many parts of these Provinces; but also in Great Britain, which if not timely prevented must prove very fatal to most of the American Settlements, whose Medium of Trade are Bills of Credit.' To put an end to such evils he recommended legislation to make the offense a capital crime and urged the strict enforcement of any act to that effect. The Assembly complied with his request and in December he gave his consent to their action.

New York, like Massachusetts, had a lucky escape from being flooded with counterfeit twenty shilling bills which were apparently struck off from plates made in England. Thomas Lynstead, a freethinker who had belonged to such a sect in England, from which he had lately come, was boarding at a house in Hempstead, Long Island, in May 1723. He was described as 'a Man of bright Parts, and great Learning, in good Credit at Long-Island' and was engaged to be married on 9 May. As chance would have it, a young woman, who was probably Sarah Albertsen, at the place where Lynstead was lodging, ventured to open a bundle of papers he had left there and found them to be twenty shilling bills of credit. She took seven of these to New York City and tried to pass them but was soon detected, since none of them was signed.

When word reached Lynstead that his counterfeits had been discovered, he went home and hanged himself on the very day on which he was to have been married, leaving behind a memorandum about £3,000 in these bills and a paper signifying that he had met with a great deal of trouble, of which this was the greatest. A search brought to light some £250 in false twenty shilling notes tied up in his handkerchief, whereupon the government left no stone unturned in what proved to be a vain quest for the rest of the money. His acquaintances, one Sherrard, a tailor, Thomas Kable, and Samuel Burcham, all of

Oyster Bay, Thomas Pullen, a merchant of New York City, Samuel Burdsell, Sarah Albertsen, and Deborah Wright (probably his fiancée) were strictly examined. It appeared that Lynstead had delivered a number of bills to the Albertsen woman and had once sealed up a parcel of counterfeits in the presence of Burcham. Much investigation by the sheriffs of Queens and New York counties produced no further evidence, nor, apparently, did Captain Walter, Mr. Harrison, and Dr. Colden, a select committee appointed by the governor and council, have any better luck.

It soon became obvious that Woodin and Lynstead were but an advance guard of counterfeiters who were obtaining plates or bills in England, Germany, Holland, and especially Ireland. Some months after Lynstead hanged himself, Captain Michael Kent, lately arrived in Massachusetts on a ship commanded by Captain West, was arrested and jailed in Boston on suspicion of having imported a number of counterfeited Massachusetts bills. The whole story was never revealed, for the captain, while in prison awaiting his trial, broke out on Sunday night, 12 April 1724, and made his escape.

The danger to the currency occasioned by counterfeiting done in Ireland was brought to the attention of the colonists in March 1728. Patrick Gordon, lieutenant governor of Pennsylvania and the counties of New Castle, Kent, and Sussex, addressed the members of the Assembly of Pennsylvania in these terms: 'We have seen large Quantities of *Counterfeit Bills* of our Neighbouring Colony issued in this Province to the great loss of its Inhabitants, and I am credibly informed, the design has been laid to pour in upon us a flood of our Own Bills Counterfeited from *Ireland,* where they have so artfully imitated most of those of Jersey, that it requires more skill to distinguish them, than is to be expected amongst the common, and especially amongst Country People.'

Gordon's speech was prompted by the arrest on 4 March 1728 in New York City of David Wallace and David Wilson on a charge of passing counterfeit New Jersey currency. Wallace, when examined by the mayor and other magistrates, told the following story: in Dublin, Ireland, a certain Thomas Morough, who had previously lived at Elk River in Maryland, had caused to be printed and signed some £3,000 in counterfeit bills, of which Wallace took £1,000, paying £10 in good money for them and promising something more whenever Morough came back to America. Wallace himself, in November 1726, brought over his counterfeits to Philadelphia in the ship *Richmond* from Dublin. He then repaired to Maryland, where, after burning some five shilling Pennsylvania bills because they were badly signed, he secured Wilson to help him pass his currency by promising him that he might retain four or five shillings in the pound. Together they made their way to New York City, where, upon their arrest, they were found to have on their persons the following counterfeits: 183 New Jersey bills of £3 and ninety-three of 3s.; twenty-three Pennsylvania bills of 5s. and one of 1s.; 646 New York bills of 4s. and three of 15d. It was discovered that the day before their arrest they had passed £100 in Jersey money and one four shilling New York note.

Some of their bills were carelessly executed, to put it mildly; in many of the Jersey notes Parker, the name of one of the signers, was written Parher, while the paper was coarser and thinner than the true currency; further, in the three pound Jersey bills the B was left out of PUB-LICK; in the twelve shilling denomination the flourishing at the top was handsomer and finer and the letter T blacker than in the genuine; in the six shilling bills the words SIX SHILLINGS at the top and the figure 4 in 1724 were larger and the down stroke of the great T narrower than in good money; the figure 4 in 1724 was also too large in counterfeit Jersey eighteenpenny and four shilling bills and in New York fifteenpenny bills.

Wallace and Wilson were tried in October and were acquitted on charges of counterfeiting and passing New York money, thus escaping the penalty of death. On the other hand, they were found guilty of a cheat in uttering forged Jersey bills, and in December in New York County were pilloried, carted, and flogged, Wallace with thirty-nine lashes and Wilson with twenty-eight; in January they received the same punishment in Kings County and in February in Queens; in March in Westchester County they were pilloried and flogged, Wallace with twenty lashes and Wilson with ten, after which they were transferred to Manhattan to serve terms in jail, Wallace for six months and Wilson for three.

The Pennsylvania Assembly was so impressed by the information laid before it by Lieutenant Governor Gordon that some of the first impression of the province's bills were to be brought in counterfeited from Ireland, that it was proposed to have the Loan Office call in the remainder of the money outstanding. New Jersey, too, in alarm because of Wallace's activities and confession, struck new bills to exchange for those of the issue dated 24 March 1724, which had been so widely counterfeited. The currency of the old bills was to terminate in November 1728, and Samuel Keimer, who printed the money which was to replace the former emission, took pains to make the new bills in such a way that it would be difficult to

counterfeit them. The sum issued, £24,760, as Governor
Burnet explained in a letter to the Lords of Trade, made
no increase in the paper money in circulation, for the
bills merely replaced the emission which had been counterfeited in Ireland.

The new bills, however, could not have been long in
circulation before a sample eighteenpenny bill was taken
to Dublin and forged. Fortune, at least, favored the government in this instance, for when, on 30 July 1729, the
sloop *Charming Sally* from Dublin arrived in Philadelphia,
one of the passengers immediately gave information that
a quantity of false Jersey bills had been found in the chest
of Thomas Eanon, who had died during the crossing. Mayor
Thomas Lawrence and the magistrates ordered an investigation made by the sheriff, who found in Eanon's
chest 118 unsigned eighteenpenny notes of the new emission. It was supposed that a greater sum of bad money
had gone to Burlington on the *Woodside Galley,* on which
Eanon had originally booked passage and shipped goods
but on which he himself had failed to sail.

Further light was shed on the doings of the deceased
counterfeiter when on Friday night, 19 September, William
Scott was apprehended in Woodbridge, New Jersey, for
passing eighteenpenny counterfeits, of which he admitted
he had five on his person and which he claimed he had
obtained from a person unknown to him in exchange for
some ribbons he sold on Long Island. Between eleven
o'clock and midnight the prisoner was stripped and questioned at the jail in Perth Amboy, whither the magistrate
in Woodbridge had had him taken. The following morning
the mayor and aldermen of Perth Amboy examined the
captive and then reported to the governor, who at once
dispatched a certain John Thompson to New York City

to make a search of Scott's lodgings. Thompson found that the prisoner had passed bad bills on the road, discovered some counterfeits in his quarters in New York, and braced his chest and bedding to be put on board the *George and John,* commanded by Anthony Adamson, and transported to Amboy. On 22 September the authorities in that town boarded the ship and found in a false bottom of Scott's trunk 476 counterfeit bills, signed but not numbered, and 106 more that were neither signed nor numbered. Next the magistrates visited the prisoner in jail and informed him of their discovery, whereupon he broke down and related the following story: Captain Adamson had carried a Jersey eighteenpenny bill as a sample to Dublin, where he persuaded Scott and Thomas Eanon to have imitations printed. They agreed and paid a printer, whose name they were sworn not to divulge.

Captain Adamson and his crew were now examined and lied, swearing that they had seen Scott only at Salem, Massachusetts, where the passengers from Ireland were landed, and again at New York when his belongings were put on board. Despite their affirmations Adamson was imprisoned and he and Scott were tried at a special court of oyer and terminer held at Perth Amboy. Both men, having been convicted of counterfeiting and passing, soon received their punishment: Adamson was carted through the streets of Perth Amboy with a rope about his neck, was pilloried there for an hour, and was carted to Woodbridge, first to the meeting house and then to the square before Mr. Herd's door, where he stood in the cart for a quarter of an hour, having a paper fixed on his back and breast declaring his offense and with one of the counterfeit bills affixed thereto. Then he was confined in jail until all fees and charges should be paid. Scott received the same punishment save that he was carted to Piscataway.

The officials of the colonies could not attack the evil at its source in England or Ireland but, as has been seen, they could punish passers once they were apprehended in America. The risk of arrest and the rigor of the laws in many provinces seem to have exercised little restraint on enterprising criminals. A few years after the carting and pillorying of Adamson and Scott, on a Monday evening in early December 1732, three men entered the Indian Prince Tavern in Philadelphia and called for liquor, in payment for which one tendered a twenty shilling Pennsylvania bill. The proprietor, Mr. Brockden, suspecting the money to be counterfeit, pretended to go out for change but instead took the note to Mr. Hamilton of the Loan Office, who caused the three men to be arrested. Upon examination two of them seemed innocent, but on the third were found two false bills, which he stoutly maintained that he had received in the market from an unknown woman who had purchased his hogs. The examination of the suspect was continued at another inn where it was learned that the prisoner had left his horse. A strange woman in an outer room of this public house was observed to be concerned, whereupon she was called in by the officers and, when questioned, admitted that the man was her brother. When she was asked if she had any money about her, her brother was observed to wink at her. She replied in the negative but a search of her person revealed twenty-three twenty shilling counterfeit bills in her pocket.

Upon this discovery her brother decided that a full confession was indicated and declared that a certain Grindal, having taken a true note to Ireland as a pattern, had caused 600 imitations of the twenty shilling bill of Pennsylvania to be struck off, all of which he had brought to

Pennsylvania in the ship commanded by Captain Blair in the summer of 1732. Grindal then set off to pass money in the Jerseys, altering his name to Thomson, 'lest a wife he had married at New-Garden should hear of him.' Before departing, however, he took Joseph Watt into partnership, leaving bills for him to pass in Pennsylvania and proposing that they should meet at Christmas in Philadelphia to divide the profits. The self-styled porkseller claimed that Watt had given him twenty-seven bills to pass on commission and had told him it was no sin, for it would 'make money plentier among poor people.' The porkseller did not know the whereabouts of Grindal but revealed that Watt was at Eastown in Chester County. At this, officers rode all night, surprised Watt in bed about daybreak, and brought him to Philadelphia. The porkseller was doubtless accepted as king's evidence, for Watt was tried, convicted, and sentenced to be whipped, pilloried, and cropped on 10 January 1733, a market day. It is recorded that Watt behaved in such a fashion as to arouse the compassion of the mob, so that the people did not fling at him, as had been expected, snowballs or anything else. After the infliction of corporal punishment Watt was confined in the jail in Philadelphia, but on the night of 13 June he broke out and made his escape. In an advertisement inserted in the press he was described as being about forty years of age and having long, straight brown hair and a scar at his throat where he had attempted to cut it. Grindal, the importer of the bills, was taken in the Jerseys but presently escaped. In his pocketbook was found a memorandum of costs for having the counterfeits made, including the amount paid the engraver and the printer and the charge for the paper.

In August 1734 it was found that spurious twenty shilling

Pennsylvania bills, the paper of which was thinner and the ink paler than in true notes, were circulating, and on 20 November several counterfeit New Castle bills were also detected. The passer of these, whose name is not recorded, having been pursued and apprehended in Chester, was taken to Philadelphia, where he revealed the names of his associates and the fact that £5,000 of the false currency had been imported. The public was at once advised through the press how the bad money might be detected: in the first line of a bill the word 'Indented' stood too high; toward the bottom the words 'of this' were placed too close together; and all the lines were more uneven than in genuine bills.

The importer and the signer, Robert Conway and a certain Sherwin, were taken, apparently near Salem, New Jersey, while their counterfeits, consisting of twenty and ten shilling New Castle and twenty and fifteen shilling Pennsylvania bills were found hidden on an island in the middle of a great marsh. The two men were transferred from the Jerseys to New Castle, where Conway pleaded guilty and Sherwin was tried and convicted, presumably through the testimony of their associate who had been arrested in Chester. In March 1735, Conway and Sherwin were whipped, pilloried, cropped, fined £100 each, and required to pay double the damage caused individuals who had accepted their counterfeits.

New England was not spared the plague of imported counterfeits. In September 1735, the operations of a gang that was passing bills printed in Ireland came to light through the arrest in Providence, Rhode Island, of one Forrest Dalzel on a charge of passing false Connecticut bills. The prisoner, who seems to have come from Wells, in what is now Maine, confessed that he had received the

£100 in counterfeits which were found on him from William Mortimore, who had promised him the half for passing them. As he stated that Mortimore was in Boston, the authorities in that town seized the suspect at night in a public house near the town dock and took him before Justice Savage, who examined him and had him searched. Four false ten shilling bills were found in his pocketbook, while in the foot of a stocking in his portmanteau were discovered one bad five pound note and eight ten shilling bills, which he maintained that he had received in trade and believed to be genuine. The justice of the peace, however, had him committed to the jail in Boston, whence, before he could be brought to trial, he escaped on the night of 29 January 1736, in company with a burglar and a deserter, John Hayes and John Joyce. They left behind a fourth prisoner who was too corpulent to squeeze through the hole they had dug underground in order to get out. A reward of £10 which was offered for his capture brought no results.

The government of Massachusetts took energetic measures, for it was found that £100,000 in counterfeit notes of £5, 40s., 20s., and 10s. had been struck and signed in Ireland and then brought to the province in a chest which was now seized. At the time of Dalzel's arrest some £10,-000 or £12,000 of this money had already been uttered. Doubtless through Dalzel's confession the authorities had learned of Mortimore and also of John Davis, master of a coasting sloop, who was then in Boston. Shortly after he was taken into custody Davis made, on 18 September 1735, a confession in which he related how, about 23 November 1733, he met William Patten, a blacksmith of Wells, at Patten's shop. The smith gave him ten twenty-five shilling New Hampshire counterfeits to pass, with the understanding that he might keep half the proceeds. Somewhat later Patten confided in him that John Macdonald had gone to Ireland to get five pound bills and that upon his return Davis might have some to utter. In the autumn of 1734, Davis met Patten in Boston and later received at his house Patten, Macdonald, and Mortimore. The upshot of this gathering was that Davis took Mortimore in his sloop to Wells and there secured from Patten and Macdonald a quantity of false five pound and ten shilling Connecticut bills, which he subsequently carried with him in a wig box to Boston. He heard, apparently from one of his associates, that Joseph Bragdon, a miller in York, also had a considerable supply of the forged bills. In August, at least as he claimed, Davis became alarmed and threw overboard all his counterfeits, tied up in a piece of bunting with a brick, save for six five pound bills, which he passed in Newport.

As a result of Davis's disclosures Joseph Bragdon and Jedediah Prebble, both of York, and William Patten were apprehended and, along with Mortimore and Macdonald, indicted at a court of assize held at York in June. Presumably Davis or Dalzel or both were accepted as evidences for the king. Mortimore could not be tried, since he had escaped, and Bragdon and Prebble were not tried because the king's attorney felt he might obtain more evidence later. Patten was acquitted, while Macdonald alone was convicted. When he pleaded his clergy he escaped execution thereby and was burnt in the hand and ordered to suffer imprisonment for six months and pay costs, all of which shows how unwilling the courts often were to bring counterfeiters to the gallows. Juries, indeed, were as a rule loath to convict a counterfeiter when the penalty was death, so that, in order to obtain a conviction, there very likely was an understanding in this case that the culprit would be allowed to plead his clergy. In the case of Macdonald the justices ordered that he make good all loss suffered through his counterfeit twenty-five shilling New Hampshire bills that had been passed by him or others, if the injured persons brought the forged currency to the clerk of court within the next six months.

No doubt the authorities in port towns kept a close watch for counterfeits imported from England and Ireland. Late in October 1738 a ship from London commanded by Captain Homans put in at Boston and shortly thereafter bad paper money appeared in circulation. One of the passengers who had arrived in Homans's craft was arrested, and in his possession were found a number of New Hampshire ten shilling bills of the latest emission and the plate from which they had been struck, while another passenger, evidently his accomplice, fled. After Governor Jonathan Belcher reported the matter to the New Hampshire Assembly, that body passed a law setting death without benefit of clergy as the penalty for counterfeiting its bills and those of the neighboring provinces.

At approximately the same time a certain Whitesides, lately arrived from Ireland in a vessel under the command of Captain Grieves, was apprehended at New Castle for passing counterfeit twenty shilling bills of that government, dated 1734, and a search of his person brought to light 1,029 of them. Whitesides was convicted, pilloried for one hour, and fined £100.

New York, where the penalty for forging or passing counterfeit bills was death, was by no means free of the scourge, for in June 1737 the governor and council were alarmed by the results of the arrest and examination of a mariner named Garrit Van Voorhees, who arrived in

New York City from Dublin on 21 June in the snow *Eagle,* Jacobus Keirstead master. Van Voorhees, on the Friday following his landing, passed three false forty shilling New York bills, printed on much worse paper than the genuine and with the signatures of the signers all written by the same hand. Thirty-nine such notes were found on him, which he claimed he had obtained from a fellow passenger from Dublin, Samuel Mames, who, Van Voorhees asserted, had a roll of the bills as large as the small of his leg. Mames was supposed to have boarded a sloop for Albany but he was never located and very likely was a fictitious character. Van Voorhees broke jail one night and vanished, so that the affair was never cleared up.

In Boston the officers presently arrested two importers of forged bills. One, Thomas Mellony, an Irishman who had lately come from the Emerald Isle, was taken up in 1741 for passing counterfeit £5 bills of the Rhode Island emission of 1737 numbered 137, 138, and 140. The plate had presumably been made in Ireland in a rather blundering fashion, so that the passer was quickly detected and committed to jail. The following year, however, a far more serious attempt on the currency came to light, when Robert Neal, a mariner of Salem, who had lately come from London in a ship commanded by Captain Fones, was taken up in Boston and examined by two justices of the peace on suspicion of being concerned in procuring counterfeiting plates and uttering bad bills. The justices ordered him searched, and the officers found five false notes of the Rhode Island emission of 1740, four of 10s. and one of 1s. Then, upon further examination, Neal confessed that he had imported about £1,000 in the bills, made and signed in London, and had hidden them, together with the plates, in a rocky place in Salem. The constables, taking their prisoner with them, went to Salem, where, after turning over many large stones, they located the box they were seeking under a rock and removed its contents to Boston. It contained plates for making twelve and seven shilling Connecticut and ten and five shilling Rhode Island bills, as well as 800 sheets of currency struck from the plates on extraordinarily good paper but all unsigned. The *Boston Gazette* commented that the whole was 'nearer the Originals, and better printed, than any we have ever seen before,' while the *Boston News-Letter* called it 'a most seasonable Discovery; for the Engraving so near resembles the Original (except the Back-side of the Connecticut Plate) that if he could but have obtain'd an accurate Signer, they might have been soon spread all over the Country to the great Damage of the Publick, which is now prevented, not one of them being out.'

In all these cases little or nothing was discovered of the operations abroad, partly no doubt because prosecution of offenders depended upon the efforts of provincial authorities in America. As it happens, two notorious affairs of about this time do reveal details of counterfeiting attempts in London. The first was concerned with William Bodie, who had lived in Pennsylvania and had married the daughter of a certain Houston who lived near Dobbs Ferry, about thirty miles from New York City. In the summer of 1736 Bodie embarked at Boston on a vessel bound for London. On board he became acquainted with William Franklyn, Jr., son of a brewer of Bednall Green, and when they reached England young Franklyn introduced his American friend to Robert Savory, a gardener of about forty years of age, who lived in Bednall Green and for some years had served Franklyn's father. Bodie and Savory soon became intimate and frequently met at a public house in Spittlefields which was kept by John Parker. One day Bodie told his new acquaintance and Parker that he had received orders from the proprietors of Pennsylvania to have some money bills printed in London, showing them at the same time a half crown Pennsylvania note and a crown note of the Counties on Delaware, which he had brought with him to serve as patterns. Parker suggested that Savory was just the man to show him the town and also to find for him proper persons to cut the plates and print the bills. Accordingly, taking Bodie along, Savory visited several places in London and finally settled with William Pennock, a woodcutter in Jewin Street, to cut wooden dies for the half crown bills, while one Halfhide, an engraver in the Minories, was engaged to cut a plate for the crown notes.

About Christmas, when Savory and Bodie had become still better acquainted, the American confessed that the bills were really for his own private profit and once they were signed by some experts at that business in New England they 'would be equal to so much money.' When Bodie then offered to let him in on the deal, Savory agreed and together they took the wooden dies made by Pennock to a printer in Aldersgate Street, who obligingly made some £700 of the half crown notes. None of the crown bills, however, were struck, for Halfhide refused to let Bodie have the plate unless he would give security to keep the engraver free from harm in case any improper use should be made of the plate, and such security Bodie declined to furnish.

Savory by now had given up his business and sold most of his possessions in order to accompany his friend to America, so now the two men set out for Bristol, where they planned to take ship for the colonies. While in Bristol

Savory became very uneasy about the venture and discussed the matter with an acquaintance there, named Joseph Allen, an employee of the East India Company, who dissuaded him from his design. Thereupon Savory told Bodie of his change of heart, but, since he was ashamed to return home, he sailed alone on the *Bellinda Hawkins,* commanded by John Cole, for South Carolina, taking with him a bundle of counterfeits, pressed on him by Bodie, but intending only to use them as evidence of Bodie's scheme. In Charleston he fell ill and was attended by a Dr. Killpatrick, to whom he related the whole affair and to whom he entrusted one counterfeit, which the physician promised to forward to the proper authorities in Pennsylvania. Presently Savory himself, leaving his chest which contained several of the unsigned bills with a tavernkeeper named Thomas Lamson, made his way to Philadelphia, where he revealed the design and delivered a parcel of the bills to Andrew Hamilton, one of the trustees of the General Loan Office in Philadelphia. Nothing further is recorded of the matter save that the government of Pennsylvania took all possible steps to check the veracity of Savory's account and to apprehend Bodie.

The other case which shed light on the making of counterfeits in England and explains why there is no record of any forgers of provincial bills being punished there concerns two cousins, Peter Long, a weaver of Greenwich in Gloucester County, New Jersey, and Robert Jenkins, a mariner of Salem in the same province. About 1735 or 1736 Long had taken some paper money to England, had there had counterfeits made to the amount of £6,000, and upon his return, with some assistance from his cousin, had passed off most of it in New Jersey and neighboring provinces. It was later discovered that his feeling of security was so great that he had even dared to display his false money on one occasion at the home of William and Rachel Brick at Piles Grove in Salem County. William Pauling, who was present at the Bricks' abode, had stated his belief that there was no New Jersey money counterfeited, whereupon Long pulled from his pocket a large parcel of paper notes, displayed a counterfeit twelve shilling Jersey bill, and explained the differences between the true and the false.

Long's first venture proved highly successful, so he decided to continue the nefarious business and with that intent, about October 1739, wrote his cousin, Robert Jenkins, who had gone to England in a small ship and was then staying at Letten Chainey in Dorsetshire. In the missive he bade Jenkins find some 'honest printer' and have him make 1,000 twenty shilling New Castle bills and 1,200 each of the fifteen, twelve, six, and three shilling bills of New Jersey; genuine bills of each denomination were enclosed as patterns, as well as a letter of instructions for the printer to the effect that paper, ink, type, and every spot must be reproduced exactly as in the genuine, for otherwise the counterfeits would be of no value. With an eye to future operations Long urged his cousin to arrange with the printer to copy any new bills they might send him from time to time in the wadding of a saddle and to return the false notes to America stuffed in the same saddle. Long wrote that he would soon obtain and send on to be counterfeited certain bills of the new emission of Pennsylvania. By this arrangement he felt that he and Jenkins would be spared the trouble and expense of going back and forth to England to have each new emission forged.

Jenkins, upon receipt of the communication from Long,

approached Abraham Ilive, who dwelt in Bird Cage Alley near St. George's Church, Southwarke, and was a printer at Mr. Reyner's Printing House. He offered Ilive five guineas and a further gratuity upon his return to New England. When Ilive remonstrated that the characters were out of use and hard to match, the American told him how he and Long had passed the £6,000 in bad bills. He explained further that, in order to make the notes look foul from handling in trade, he had put them in a bag with six pounds of shot and ridden with them thirteen miles, after which they looked as though they had been in circulation ever since the date of the emission. Persons, he added, could be induced to sign the money for a quarter of the value, or in case those he had in mind were unwilling, Jenkins himself could sign them and then pass them with ease, since he traded in a shallop of his own from the Jersies to Connecticut and elsewhere. In case the counterfeits were detected, the whole emission might well be called in and new currency printed, in which event Jenkins said that he would immediately send samples of the new bills to Ilive to be copied.

At first the English printer apparently entered into the scheme with good will but after about a week got cold feet, fearing that he might become involved in trouble with the law. He therefore gave information of the affair to the undersecretaries of state, calling the money by mistake New England and New Jersey bills. The undersecretaries, as they later stated, not knowing where New Castle, Kent, and Sussex were, sent for the New England and New Jersey agents in London. As the agent for New England was confined to his bed for about three weeks, some time elapsed before the matter was brought to the attention of Frederick John Paris, the agent of Pennsylvania.

Mr. Paris at once sought advice from attorneys and from the solicitor general, all of whom advised him that the counterfeiting would not be punishable in England and therefore suggested that Ilive furnish Jenkins with the counterfeits, taking care to employ some secret marks by which the false currency might be identified. Then when Jenkins returned home, the provincial authorities, alerted in advance, could seize him. Paris adopted the suggestion and wrote to Lieutenant Governor George Thomas of Pennsylvania, giving him the key to the detection of the counterfeits, namely a dot on the fore shoulder of the lion, another on the unicorn, and a third at the foot of the flying horse in the king's arms. In addition the letter I in INDENTED was unlike that in the true bills and the letter P in PAYMENTS was below the line in the counterfeits.

Jenkins, who had no suspicion that his scheme had been divulged, had been forced, because of the embargo, the press, and the very severe frost, to delay his departure so long that his good money was spent and he could not make the down payment he had promised Ilive. On 21 January 1740, expecting that the weather would soon permit him to sail, he wrote the printer to hurry along the job, offering to give him three gallons of cordial at once and to send him a hogshead of rum by the first ship from America.

In the meantime Lieutenant Governor Thomas of Pennsylvania sent word of the business to Governor Morris of New Jersey, who laid Thomas's letter before the Provincial Council in Burlington on 9 June 1740. It was promptly ordered that two justices of the peace, Clement Hall of Salem County and James Hinchman of Gloucester County, should issue warrants to arrest Jenkins and persons thought acquainted with him and Long and to search the houses

of such individuals. On the previous day, 8 June, Robert
Hunter Morris had issued a warrant for the arrest of
Long, who was taken into custody by Sheriff Samuel Harrison and then released on bail of £500 provided by Long
himself and £250 each by George Cozens and Andrew
Long for his appearance at the next court of oyer and
terminer to be held in Gloucester County.

Governor Clarke of New York was having the mayor
of New York City check the passenger lists of incoming
ships from England. Late one Thursday night in June
a vessel commanded by Captain Gill arrived in port, and
when the mayor examined the list of passengers the next
morning, there was no Jenkins on it. Fortunately, however, Governor Clarke, upon making further inquiries
himself, found that Jenkins had shipped as a sailor and
served as cook on the voyage. The governor had him
arrested, and in a secret compartment in his chest were
found 971 counterfeit bills and certain papers, all of which
were sealed up by the mayor to be used as evidence. The
prisoner, bogus currency, and papers were taken by William Biddle, undersheriff of Philadelphia County, to Philadelphia, where Jenkins was examined by the lieutenant
governor, the council, and Andrew Hamilton, the recorder of the city. As the accused seemed to them to be
guilty, they ordered Biddle to remove him to New Castle
for trial. At this same time the authorities in New Jersey
set about collecting samples of the handwriting of Long
and Jenkins. The counterfeiters were very likely tried by
a special court of oyer and terminer, the records of which
have not been preserved.

Ilive was apparently rewarded by the government of
the Three Lower Counties on Delaware, for on 21 October
1740, the lieutenant governor suggested 'that it were not

amiss that the House would order to be printed in the publick News-papers, Advertisements signifying that a Reward was to be given to the printer in England who discovered the printing of Counterfeit Bills . . . lately brought over by Robert Jenkins, that it would be an Encouragement to other Printers to make future Discoverys; and that if the House would order it he would have it put into all the publick News-papers.'

# Chapter 5

## COUNTERFEITING IN THE SOUTHERN PROVINCES

THE southern provinces were by no means immune to the plague of counterfeiters which was growing to the north. In Virginia, as early as 1698, the justices of Accomack County found Edward Brotherton guilty of possessing counterfeit money, coin, of course. There does not seem, however, to have been any serious problem until 1734–5, the period when the bills of the provinces to the north were so widely imitated, especially in Ireland and England.

Governor Gabriel Johnston of North Carolina, after his arrival in that province, was apprised by several of the leading merchants and traders of the numerous and great inconveniences to trade and commerce caused by 'the great Multiplicity of Counterfeit Bills of Credit issued by Vagabond and Idle people passing from one part of the Government to another.' The governor laid the matter before a meeting of the council, held in the courthouse in Brunswick on 2 November 1734 and attended by Robert Halton, Eleazer Allen, and Roger Moore. Upon deliberation it was decided that Johnston should issue a proclamation commanding all persons to assist in apprehending the counterfeiters and offering a reward of £50 for the bringing to justice of any person who should be convicted of the offense, while he was also to promise a royal pardon to any of the accomplices of such criminals who should discover one or more of them so that they be taken and convicted, provided only that such discovery be made within two months from the date of the proclamation. The provost marshal, moreover, was charged with having the proclamation published at the courthouse door in every precinct in North Carolina and with having a copy affixed to each such door.

On 15 January 1735 Governor Johnston addressed the Council and House of Burgesses, warning the members that the matter of the currency of their bills could no longer be neglected 'without the entire Ruin of the Country.' He pointed out that originally their notes were on a very precarious footing but that now the situation was infinitely worse because of the great number of counterfeits spread into all parts of the province 'by the villanous Arts of wicked and ill disposed persons, and to the utter undoing of many poor industrious Families.' The governor charged his hearers with finding a proper remedy for so great an evil and urged upon them, since the people could not carry on their dealings without a paper currency, the necessity of preserving the credit of the same and preventing the industrious planter from being robbed of the fruits of his labor 'by the Tricks and Frauds of profligate and abandoned persons.'

The House, in replying on 20 January to Johnston's speech, laid the blame for the bad state of the currency on 'the late corrupt Administration,' which neither had the taxes collected in proper fashion nor suffered the 'vile persons' who counterfeited the bills to be prosecuted. An act for regulating the currency had been passed by 13 February, and the governor's proclamation had borne fruit within the two months that the reward was to be in effect, for on 27 February a claim for £100 in rewards for the discovery of two counterfeiters was approved by the House of Burgesses.

Georgia and South Carolina also were alarmed by the appearance in May 1735 of counterfeit fifteen pound bills of South Carolina which were much like the genuine and very hard to distinguish. The *South Carolina Gazette* alerted the public to the danger, pointing out that the first F in the word FIFTEEN in the true bills had a bigger stroke at the bottom and that in the margin the turning round of the flower on the back of the F was very regular, while in the false notes the flower was more straight and irregular; in the true money one part of the heart in the middle of the line just touched the flourishing work above it but in the counterfeits there was more distance. The printer of the newspaper expressed the opinion that the General Assembly would call in all the notes of that denomination to prevent further dispersing of the bad money.

His surmise was correct, for on 5 June it was ordered that, since the current South Carolina bills of £15, £4, and £3 had been forged and passed by 'divers Evil-minded Persons,' all such money was to cease to be legal tender after 7 August, before which date possessors of these denominations were to turn the notes in to the commissioners, Charles Pinckney, Othniel Beale, Gabriel Manigault, John Champneys, and Roper Sanders, who would meet to receive the currency on Wednesday and Thursday, 18 and 19 June, and on every Wednesday and Thursday up to 7 August, at the home in Charleston of the merchant, Othniel Beale. Soon it was discovered that the ten pound bills had likewise been imitated, so on 18 July Governor Thomas Broughton issued a proclamation requiring that this denomination also be brought in to the commissioners within two months, when it was ordered that the legal tender of the bill cease. When the advertisement about the counterfeits of £15, £4, and £3 had been printed for six weeks, it was ascertained that not half of those in circulation had been surrendered, whereupon the commissioners announced that they would sit daily, except on Sundays, to receive these bills until 7 August, and until 20 September to take in the £10 notes.

Two miscreants who were responsible for much of this trouble and expense, Thomas Mellichamp and Richard Turner, were taken and indicted by a grand jury in Savannah, Georgia, on 12 July for having counterfeited the money of South Carolina and passed the same. Turner's two servants gave evidence against their master and Mellichamp and claimed that Turner had made a press and utensils for the nefarious business on Mellichamp's directions. As Mellichamp was not to be found, Turner alone was tried and found guilty of making implements for counterfeiting but was acquitted of all other charges. Because of the high nature of his misdemeanor he was fined £200 sterling and committed to jail until the sum was paid or other instructions came from the trustees.

On 18 August Othneil Beale, one of the commissioners for reprinting, signing, and exchanging the bills, received information from a gentleman in the country that there was a box containing a great number of false bills in Captain Samuel Underwood's barn on Wadmellaw Island and that Thomas Mellichamp and Joshua Morgan had passed several such notes in the neighborhood. Constable William Hamilton, provided with a search warrant from the governor and a warrant for Mellichamp's arrest from a justice of the peace, went to the island, where he stealthily ap-

proached Underwood's barn. There he surprised Mellichamp and Morgan 'cutting and hammering' brass, with a
loaded musket beside them. The moment they caught sight
of the constable and his aids, the men sought to flee, but
Morgan was immediately seized, while Mellichamp, who
took to his heels, was pursued, overtaken, and knocked
down in a cornfield. In the barn were found a roller and
press and in the house a box containing several instruments
and utensils belonging to engravers and printers, together
with plates for making twelve pound ten shilling, three
pound, and one pound bills of South Carolina. In Mellichamp's pocketbook the officers discovered several counterfeit twelve pound ten shilling notes, some signed and others
unsigned, as well as three one pound bills and one of the six
pound five shilling denomination, all false. On Wednesday
Constable Hamilton took his prisoners to Charleston to
Justice Thomas Dade, who committed them to jail, while
at the same time Mellichamp was also committed for
counterfeiting by Justice Lamboll on information lodged
by the magistrates of Georgia.

The turnkey of the common jail in Charleston where
Mellichamp was confined was Thomas Gallway, who, at
the orders of Provost Marshal Robert Hall, put both fetters
and handcuffs on Mellichamp. Some persons soon complained of such harsh treatment of the counterfeiter, whereupon Hall had the handcuffs removed but asked Charles
Pinckney how he should keep his prisoner. Pinckney replied that the law required him to 'keep his prisoners
safely' and added that, 'as Mellichamp was charged with
having been guilty of a very hainous Felony tending to the
injury of every Man in the Province, it behooved him to
take particular Care to prevent his Escape.' At this Hall
said he would run no risks and would have the handcuffs

put on again. Later the provost marshal again visited Pinck-ney, informing him that as the sessions approached his prisoners grew so turbulent that he apprehended it would be difficult to keep them without having a watch set over the jail at night and that he would immediately apply for such a guard to the commanding officer in the town.

True to his word Mr. Hall made such application to the Honorable Joseph Wragg, Esq., who replied by letter that the captain of the town watch said he had so few guards that he could not station a sentry at the prison and could only order the rounds that way every hour. Wragg there-fore advised Hall to hire two guards to keep watch under arms at night in case he feared that the inmates of the jail might attempt to break out.

There was, indeed, cause for apprehension, for on Fri-day, 19 September, Turnkey Gallway reported to Mr. Hall his fears that Mellichamp and other felons intended to try to escape, 'for that there having been some Persons, who the Night before had given a knock against the end of the House under the Criminal Room Window, which this Deponent (Gallway) apprehended to be a Signal, a Pillow-bere tied to a String having been thereupon im-mediately let down out of the Window, and on this De-ponent's going out to the end of the House he saw two Men standing, who on sight of this Deponent instantly ran away.'

Gallway, on orders from Hall, tried in vain to hire persons to keep watch and even went a second time to implore the captain of the watch to send a sentry to the jail, all to no purpose. Then on Sunday, 21 September, between ten and eleven o'clock at night, Mellichamp and three other prisoners attacked Gallway. Three persons who dwelt near the jail gave accounts of the affair: one, Joseph Fidler, an upholsterer, was sitting in his house near the prison when he heard the jailer's wife cry out that the prisoners were murdering her husband. Fidler immediately ran to the jail, where he picked up a musket which he saw standing in the entry below stairs. With this weapon he rushed up the stairs, when he 'heard a great knocking on the Stair head-door.' When he asked who was making the noise, someone on the other side replied that it was Thomas Mellichamp. Fidler told him he could not come down that way, whereupon Mellichamp at once went to a window, broke the bars, and in company with three other prisoners jumped out. Fidler hastened down the stairs and out into the garden, where he took aim at Mellichamp and tried to fire but the gun would not go off, so that Mellichamp managed to break through the garden paling and escape.

Two other neighbors, Lawrence Mckoy, a vintner, whose house was next to the jail, and Childermas Croft, whose residence was next but one to the jail, both ran to the scene, arriving shortly after Fidler. Both had been in bed and Mckoy had heard the turnkey call out: 'Help Neighbours, for Godsake help! the Prisoners are risen, and are murdering me!' Mckoy sent his maid to inform Mr. Hall of what was happening, while he himself hastened to the jail. His maid's shouts that the prisoners were murdering the jailer caused Croft to spring from his bed and hurry to give aid to the turnkey. Croft, Mckoy, and Fidler all testified under oath that a few minutes after their arrival, Provost Marshal Hall appeared at the prison 'in his gown and shoes slip'd, without stocking, and a Sword in his Hand.'

For the time Mellichamp was at large, but Captain Samuel Underwood, on whose premises he and Morgan had been counterfeiting, was taken into custody and then released on bail. On 16 October, however, he was brought before the general sessions of the peace in Charleston and was committed to jail on suspicion, since the commissioners for restamping the paper bills of credit had secured evidence that he had been helping Mellichamp and Morgan in counterfeiting the currency. Underwood's fate is not recorded but Morgan was tried at the same sessions on one indictment. Although the evidence was considered very full, the petit jury found him not guilty. At this the counsel for the king postponed action on two other indictments until the next sessions, in the hope that another jury might find the evidence sufficient to convict him. As there is no account of what happened to him, it is quite likely that the crown failed to prosecute, especially since he may have turned king's evidence against Mellichamp.

Mellichamp did not remain at liberty for long, for there is a record that by order of two members of the council several Swiss were paid £175 'for bringing down Mellichamp.' Then, about four o'clock on the afternoon of 12 March 1736, the prisoner was brought to the bar at the court of general sessions for South Carolina. Constable William Hamilton had, by direction of the commissioners for exchanging the current bills of credit, served subpoenas on witnesses to appear against Mellichamp. He was indicted for both counterfeiting and passing and when he was asked to plead thereto he first begged the court for a copy of the indictment and an hour's time to see if he could 'find something therein to quash it.' The favor was granted, and, at the insistence of the court, he selected as his attorneys Mr. Rutledge and Mr. Lewis. He pleaded not guilty to this indictment as well as to another found against him for forging twenty shilling bills. At nine the next morning he was tried and convicted but probably got

off with a fine and perhaps a short term in jail. As a result
of his operations the Assembly in June passed an act for
emitting money with which to exchange the bills of credit
and for 'making them less subject to be Counterfeited.'

By the end of July word came from Charleston to
Savannah that Mellichamp was coming to Georgia, where
a reward of £10 was offered for his arrest. A grand jury in
that city had found an indictment against him for forgery
and he had been convicted. The reward produced results,
for on 4 August he was apprehended at Savannah 'together with a Gang of Men of very vile Characters, upon
some of whom stolen Goods were taken.' Mellichamp was
committed to jail, while his family and his mother, being
concerned in the doings of the gang and in conveying away
goods, were expelled from Georgia.

By 14 October Thomas Mellichamp was no longer in
custody. Perhaps he had been banished from the province
or he may have made his escape. In any event, when some
rogues had been pursued and captured, it was ordered
by the magistrates on the morning of 14 October 1736 that
William Gough take the captives 'to the house (in Savannah) where Tom Mellichamp lately had been a prisoner,
his chains still remaining on the premises,' and there to
chain and fetter them. With this notice Mellichamp disap-
pears from the records of the day. It may be noted that
Thomas Mellichamp — unless there was another man of
the same name — had an influential connection in England, a brother, the Reverend Elisha Mellichamp, who in
1734 contributed £12 for the establishment of the Colony
of Georgia, and whose letter, requesting that two servants
be sent to his brother Thomas in Georgia, was read before the palace court on 16 April 1735.

Mellichamp's associate, Richard Turner, had been fined

£200 but was either unwilling or unable to pay it and
somehow managed to secure his release, so that he was
probably at home when some of his friends got into trouble
under his roof. A certain William Watkins of Abercorn
had married the widow of James Willoughby and then,
when she was already with child by him, discovered that
his own wife was alive in England. Thereupon he got the
woman married to one Richard Mellichamp but apparently
continued to consort with her himself. Shortly before 20
November 1735, Watkins and the woman were one night
at Richard Turner's, when her new husband, Richard
Mellichamp, came and desired her to go home. She was
unwilling, and Mellichamp, exasperated, said he would sell
her 'for a Groat at any time.' One of the company present
then bid a shilling for her and others entered into the
sport until she was finally declared sold to the highest
bidder for £5 sterling. Mellichamp said that he was satisfied, while the woman 'declared she would go with the
buyer and behaved Immodestly.' A Mr. Langford then in
the company at the couple's desire conveyed them to his
lodging, where they were bedded in public, and the £5
was paid and accepted. When the authorities heard of the
affair, those concerned were arrested and a grand jury
found a misdemeanor against Watkins and Langford.
Watkins was whipped and then jailed for want of surety,
Langford was bound over to good behavior, and the woman
was charged with bigamy and confined to prison.

Turner escaped trouble from this incident but it doubtless served to keep him under the scrutiny of the government. In December 1737 he was again in difficulty, as is
recorded in the journal of Colonel William Stephens,
secretary to the trustees of Georgia. An execution under the
town seal was granted 'against one Turner, a Carpenter,'

for payment of a debt of £5 or £6 and was put into the hands of a tithingman to execute. When this person arrived at the home of the Turners, husband and wife 'shuffled away betwixt them what Goods were of most Value' and sent the official away with blows. He, aggrieved, complained to the magistrates, who promptly issued a warrant for Turner's arrest. Turner, somehow getting notice of all this, hid in the house of a certain Scot, a gunsmith and notorious dealer in spirits, who soon secured a boat and attempted to carry off his friend in it. It chanced that Mr. Christie, the recorder, was near the guardhouse and saw the boat putting out with Turner in it. Christie at once ordered the sentinel to fire his piece as a signal for the officer in command to come and at the same time to hail the boat to come ashore, threatening to fire at them if they did not obey. Turner and those in the craft told the sentinel to shoot or do anything else he wanted and kept on their way till they were soon out of reach. Stephens noted that Turner owed many small sums and lay under a heavy fine imposed for having helped Mellichamp in counterfeiting the currency, a fine which out of mercy had never yet been levied on him. On this account Colonel Stephens opined that Turner would never return, but in this the colonel was mistaken, for early in January 1738 Turner brazenly appeared again in public in open contempt of all authority. This time, however, he had gone too far, for the infuriated magistrates had him taken up and committed to prison.

The early colonists in Virginia took a serious view of the counterfeiting of current coin. When, therefore, in November 1645, they enacted a law that all should leave off trading for tobacco and use a metallic currency, they provided that the counterfeiting of Spanish silver pieces, which were to circulate, was punishable by death. In October 1710 a law which established the foreign silver money which was to be current stated that any person or persons who should 'coin, counterfeit, falsifye, or debase' such coins or should aid, consent, or counsel therein should, upon conviction, be adjudged as offenders in treason and suffer the pains, penalties, and forfeitures mentioned in the act of Parliament of the eighteenth year of the reign of Queen Elizabeth. Not long thereafter, in November 1714, the House of Burgesses specified the gold coins that were to be current and declared the counterfeiting of them to be high treason and subject to the same penalties as in England. Thus, when in October 1737 a certain William Stevenson was tried by the general court in Williamsburg 'for Treason' in counterfeiting and uttering money and was acquitted, he had doubtless been charged with coining.

In the following year a case of clipping, an offense which had been much more common in the seventeenth and early years of the eighteenth century, was discovered in Savannah. On Ash Wednesday, 1738, an Irishman named Smith, who was not a freeholder but who dwelt in that town and was commonly called (for some reason now unknown) 'the golden shoemaker,' paid away a few Spanish bits. The receiver, observing that they were all freshly clipped, went to a magistrate, from whom he obtained a warrant to apprehend the 'golden shoemaker' and search his premises for more clipped coin. The search proved fruitful, for the constables found in Smith's house one bag containing half a pound of new clippings and another filled with newly clipped Spanish bits. The presumptive evidence was so great that the shoemaker was committed to prison to take his trial at the next court for his high misdemeanor. The following day the magistrates notified him that they would admit him to bail if he could find sufficient surety. In any event he was in court on 23 February, had little to say for himself, was convicted, and on the 25th was sentenced to be flogged on the bare back at the public whipping post on three separate days and afterward to be banished from the colony of Georgia. At this the *South Carolina Gazette* ironically commented: 'Hard Sentence!'

# Chapter 6

## JOHN POTTER AND RHODE ISLAND
## COUNTERFEITERS IN 1741

COUNTERFEITERS were by no means restricted to the lowest social and economic levels of colonial society. The Greenmans of Rhode Island were, as has been seen, persons of consequence, as was a Quaker named John Potter, who was born in North Kingston on 3 January 1715, the son of Colonel John Potter. In 1736, at the age of twenty-one, he married Mary Perry and, upon her demise a few years later, he took as his second wife Elizabeth Hazard, a member of a prominent family of Rhode Island.

Potter had acquired a small house in South Kingston known as the John Julian house but in 1740 he started the construction of an imposing mansion which still stands in that section of the town known as Matunuck. He engaged Simeon Palmer, a house joiner of Warwick, who on 14 April 1740 went to live and work at Potter's and completed the job about the end of December 1741 or the beginning of January 1742.

The fact that Potter was appointed to the grand committee for signing the Rhode Island bills of the emission of 1740 may have put ideas into the Quaker's head. In any event his practical experience with the emission and the circumstance of his having numerous workmen engaged in the construction of his new dwelling made it easy for him to try his hand at counterfeiting. Palmer had taken into partnership for the building of the house Ephraim Gardner of South Kingston. One of their journeymen was Timothy Barden of Seaconk, and in addition there were two painters engaged, one named Packard and the other William Heffernan, Jr., of Newport, while William Fairfield, a mason and bricklayer, was also present. Potter's scheme, which was to imitate the twenty shilling bills of the emission of 1740, called for accomplices, so he approached Simeon Palmer, who readily fell in with the plan and went so far as to construct a press for striking the bills. A plate was of course a vital necessity, so William Fairfield, who had joined the partners in crime, recommended that they secure the services of a talented goldsmith named Obadiah Mors, very likely a son of Nathaniel Mors (or Morse) of Boston. Palmer and Fairfield set out to Middletown, Connecticut, to induce Mors to come and cut the plate but found that he had gone to Boston. Sometime later Fairfield alone made a trip to Middletown, taking with him a letter from Potter, who asked Mors to come to South Kingston, ostensibly to paint his house. The goldsmith consented and joined the gang, the numbers of which had been increased by a blacksmith named Ichabod Sheffield and possibly William Potter, a minor.

William Heffernan, Jr., in his examination before the magistrates at Newport on 26 June 1742, told how in October 1741 he had gone to John Potter's to work with Mors at painting the new house and remained there until about Christmas. When he arrived he found that a painter named Packard had finished the outside of the dwelling and sized the inside on instructions from Simeon Palmer. Heffernan then did the chief part of the inside painting, the most elaborate work under the direction of Mors, who otherwise seemed to spend most of his time in the Julian house, where, as he said, he was making buckles for Mr. Potter, Dr. Talman (Potter's brother-in-law), and William Potter and 'a fine thing for John Potter.' Fairfield was often together with Mors in the Julian house, and the room where they worked was kept locked and had the windows covered with paper instead of glass. During the three months he was busy at Potter's Heffernan received only his keep, for the understanding was that he was learning as an apprentice to Mors.

Before long the gang lost Simeon Palmer on account of a bitter quarrel which the house joiner had with John Potter about payment for 'overplus' labor on the dwelling. Ephraim Gardner, indeed, heard his partner threaten that if he were not paid to his liking he would burn down the place over Potter's head and then escape to France. After the utterance of this and other threats Palmer withdrew from the counterfeiting venture, at a time when he had partially completed the woodwork for the press for printing the bills. Fairfield, however, finished it off, after securing the necessary iron parts from a local blacksmith, Joseph Hull. Fairfield came to Hull in April 1741 with some wooden patterns, which he asked him to copy in iron for John Potter. The blacksmith complied with the request, on the understanding that they were for a roller 'to rowl the Green grass with,' and charged them to Potter's account in his book. After his falling out with Potter, Palmer demanded that the press be destroyed, whereupon Potter and Fairfield assured him that they had burned it. Two weeks later, however, he found it intact and complained so violently that they really destroyed it.

Unfortunately for them, they did not abandon their scheme and Fairfield, on Potter's account, went to Southcote Langworthy, a pewterer in Newport, to purchase a piece of copper to use for a plate. When Langworthy turned away Fairfield empty-handed, Potter went in person and convinced the pewterer that the metal was needed for mending a kettle, whereupon Langworthy sold him a piece which was sixteen inches long, eight inches wide, and so very thin that, when Mors saw it, he said it would not serve and employed a sheet of copper of his own, upon which, about 17 July 1741, he engraved a plate for imitating the twenty shilling bills.

Potter, as one of the grand committee for signing the true bills, was in a privileged position, which he did not hesitate to use to full advantage. On 28 February 1741 he went to Colonel John Coddington for bills to sign and secured all that were printed and dry — 300 sheets of the great plate and 600 of the small plate. He studiously asked the colonel why some bills were fairer than others, a difference which Coddington explained by the fact that he could not get Frankfort black ink from Boston and also that when some notes were printed the weather was so cold that the paper would freeze before he could take the bills from the plate. As a final bit of information Potter learned just how the ink was prepared.

Since William Fairfield was to help with the printing of the counterfeits, Potter carried his effrontery to the point of taking Fairfield with him to Coddington's about the end of February. Having secured the colonel's permission, they went to the press room, where they watched the colonel's assistants, Joseph Rogers, James Carry, and John Houtton at work.

Mors, installed in the Julian house with his forge, bellows, and goldsmith's utensils, engraved a plate which was an excellent imitation of the genuine. Potter had found out just how to prepare the ink and had secured suitable paper, for he later admitted that he bought a ream of writing paper from Major Carpenter and also obtained a ream of paper which his, Potter's, brother had had sent from the shop of Abraham Borden in Boston. Naturally he claimed that it was all for his own use or for that of his family.

The false bills were struck off in the Julian house but they still had to be signed. According to Fairfield's confession, the confederates agreed never to see each other do any signing, for thus they could never testify in court to having seen an associate forge the signature of a signer. Any bills that came off the plate poorly printed were burned, while Fairfield partially signed the good ones and then placed them in Potter's counting house in the new dwelling, though upon occasion he delivered them directly into Potter's hands. Potter signed them, and his own signature on them was at least genuine enough, though he also wrote the names of others, for one spring evening Simeon Palmer saw Fairfield and Potter striving for an hour or two to imitate the signatures of Brenton, Dexter, and other authorized signers. In fact, a piece of paper which was seized by the authorities as evidence has been preserved and bears attempts by Potter to copy the names of D. Updike, G. Gardner, and John Julian. Potter usually kept his bills in a little oak desk which stood in a bedroom under his mother's bed.

The counterfeiters lost no time in putting their product into circulation. About 26 December 1741 Potter made to Simeon Palmer as a partial payment on what he owed for the building of his house the sum of £170 or £180, half of which was in false twenty shilling bills. Potter like-

wise passed eighteen of these bad notes to George Babcock of South Kingston, yeoman, seventeen to Job Almy
of Newport, merchant, and six to Joseph Hammond of
South Kingston, shopkeeper. Ichabod Sheffield was no
doubt active in passing, and at the same time the products
of Mors's plate were being circulated by another gang, as
will be shown later. Naturally the flood of spurious currency attracted attention. Joseph Hammond, who had
taken in some of the money as genuine, went to Boston,
where six of his twenty shilling bills were refused by
Edward Brumfield as counterfeit. Upon his return to
South Kingston Hammond showed them to John Potter
as a member of the grand committee. When Potter of
course pronounced them genuine, Hammond passed them
without difficulty.

To forestall serious doubts about the bills Potter hit
upon a clever plan. He went to Colonel Coddington, who
was ill in bed, informed him that people in South Kingston
were uneasy about the paper money and showed him some
of the counterfeits. Coddington, as Potter had hoped and
expected, thought them good and expressed the opinion
that any variations were due to the fact that the plate was
worn and had been engraved over again. Further, the
colonel thought that some bills were wider than others
because one bill would dry more rapidly than another,
so that there would be more printing on one than another. As these explanations were exactly what Potter
wanted, he asked Coddington to write them out and sign
the document. Since, however, the invalid felt unable to
get out of bed and write, Potter set down the explanations
and the colonel signed, promising also that he would inform Colonel Updike, who mistrusted the bills, that in his

opinion they were genuine. But before Coddington actually communicated with Updike it was discovered that the money was really counterfeited.

The heavy hand of the law fell first upon William Fairfield, who was arrested on 23 January 1742 by Constable Martin Howard and lodged in the jail of Newport. A little before sunrise the next morning, a Saturday, William Heffernan, Jr., visited the prisoner and then set out with a letter written by Fairfield to John Potter. At about nine in the morning the messenger was carried on the first stage of his journey to South Kingston by Nathan Nash, who kept the ferry for Warner, and, on Nash's advice, Heffernan told Mr. Slocum, ferryman of the North Ferry upon Conanicut, to make great haste since John Potter was ill. About noon Heffernan found John Potter at Joseph Hull's smithy, delivered the letter, and informed him that Constable Howard and Messrs. Corey and Hazard had apprehended Fairfield and taken him to prison.

Potter asked Heffernan to fetch Ichabod Sheffield, but before he could set out, Mr. Slocum, the ferryman, came up and told Heffernan that he must return with him to Newport at once. Potter then persuaded Benjamin Congdon, the son of William Congdon, who was at Hull's smithy, to take his (Potter's) horse, ride to Sheffield and summon him, telling him that Fairfield was in custody for counterfeiting and that Potter must immediately leave for Newport. The message was delivered, and within half an hour Sheffield arrived and was promptly arrested, for while Potter was awaiting him Jonathan Nichols and William Read arrived with a warrant (signed by Peter Bours and William Ellery, assistants) for the apprehension of John Potter, Sheffield, Mors, and Heffernan. They accompanied Potter to his house and searched his person. Simeon Palmer, who happened to be in a meadow near the blacksmith shop, saw what was up and followed Potter, Nichols, and Read to Potter's new house. There Potter, catching sight of Palmer, managed to get him apart from the others and then promised him the £50 for 'overplus work' which he had previously refused to pay. Nichols and Read now searched the new dwelling and seized various bills as well as a piece of paper on which Potter had practiced the signatures of some of the signers of the bills of credit. Next the group, including Palmer, visited the Julian house, where Nichols and Read discovered two pieces of lignum vitae. Probably during their search Potter managed to ask the house joiner if he had told anything about the counterfeiting and, upon receiving a negative answer, he repeated his offer to pay the £50 for overplus work and also give Palmer a very fine horse. Shortly after this Potter and Sheffield were removed to Newport and turned over to the authorities.

The next day, 24 January, Potter was examined but he denied any knowledge of the counterfeiting of the twenty shilling bills and in general found glib answers to the questions put to him. When he was asked about the letter he had received from Fairfield the preceding day, he maintained that the writer of it had merely stated that he was in custody and wanted assistance, so that he, Potter, considering it of no consequence, had immediately burned it. The sheriff of Newport County, Thomas Potter, took from the prisoner twenty-nine bills, six of which were of the twenty shilling denomination.

After the examinations of Potter and Sheffield, the taking of depositions, and the collection of evidence, Governor Ward and Bours, Ellery, Dexter, and Howland, assistants, sent a mandate to Captain Robert Hazard of South Kingston and Daniel Coggeshall of North Kingston, by which they were required to search for counterfeits, a plate, a press, and counterfeiting utensils. Hazard found a quantity of false twenty shilling notes in the possession of George Babcock, who had them of Potter, and in a desk in the Julian house came upon a letter, apparently of suspicious content, written by Potter to Mors.

On 29 January Fairfield, still in jail, suddenly became loquacious about the part played in the scheme by Benjamin Peckham, Jr., of South Kingston. Peckham, he alleged, asked him if he could not induce Mors to make a plate for counterfeiting and, when Fairfield informed him that one was already prepared, Peckham joined him at the Julian house, where together they struck off ten or a dozen bills, which Fairfield partly signed. Fairfield affirmed that he had seen Peckham forge the signature of Jahleel Brenton on three or four of them and in addition he expressed the belief that John Case of Tower Hill was involved in the counterfeiting.

These statements about Peckham — and surely also about Case — were completely false, for on 1 October 1742 Fairfield sent a letter to Mr. Fleet, printer of the *Boston Evening Post,* requesting that he publish a confession that John and William Potter and Ichabod Sheffield had induced him falsely to accuse Peckham and others. John Potter, he claimed, offered him £500 and all three promised to stand by him, telling him that the only way to save them from utter ruin, to abate the passions of the people, and to moderate the resentment of the government was to accuse Peckham and others and thus puzzle and perplex the prosecution. It would at least, they felt, be the means of getting themselves admitted to bail. Fairfield now desired humbly to ask the pardon of God and of Benjamin Peckham, Jr., for his lying accusations.

Potter did, indeed, mange to be admitted to bail on 12 February in the enormous amount of £60,000, with four sureties, George Hazard in £25,000, James Perry in £15,-000, John Seager in £12,000, and John Bennett in £8,000, for his appearance at the March term of the superior court in Newport. The *Boston Evening Post* of 12 April 1742 reported that at that term of the court fifteen persons were indicted for counterfeiting the paper currency of the colony. Five indictments were brought against John Potter, one for having the plate engraved and the other four for passing bad twenty shilling bills to George Babcock, Job Almy, Joseph Hammond, and Simeon Palmer. Potter pleaded that he would not contend with the king and on each indictment he was sentenced to stand for half an hour in the pillory and have his ears cropped or, instead of corporal punishment, pay fines, costs, and so forth. On the indictment for having caused the plate to be engraved the alternative to pillorying and cropping was to pay a fine of £4,000, double damages to all persons injured by his counterfeits, all costs, and further to give bonds in the amount of £24,000 for exchanging all false twenty shilling bills that had been passed and for paying double damages; the alternative on each of the other indictments was to pay a fine of £1,500, double damages, and all costs.

The total of £10,000 in fines had to be paid before 21 June or Potter must suffer cropping and spend two and a half hours in the pillory. He was willing to loosen his purse strings rather than endure the infamous punishment, so he elected to save his ears at a price that made them easily the most valuable pair in all North America. As he found it impossible to raise £10,000 in cash on such short notice, he petitioned the Assembly to allow him to pay at once half of his fine in gold dust at the rate of £20 an ounce and to give him until 8 October to produce the remaining £5,000. The legislators were in no mood to lose such a sum, which surely was more useful to the treasury than Potter's ears, so his prayer was granted. The lawmakers had no intention of being hoodwinked by the wily Quaker, so Peter Bours was designated to join the treasurer of the colony in examining the gold dust to see that it was merchantable. One may well wonder how Potter had come by 250 ounces of gold dust; it may be that he had acquired it in trade from the East Indies, Africa, or South America.

Little is known of Obadiah Mors previous to his connection with Potter. He was probably a son of the goldsmith Nathaniel Mors of Boston (1685–1748) and himself kept a goldsmith's shop in 1733 on King Street in Boston. Later he had been in New London and Middletown in Connecticut and, it may be surmised, had very likely tried his hand at counterfeiting, for he was favorably known to villains like Fairfield and Henry Bosworth. He was arrested in 1742, doubtless in Massachusetts, and then transferred to the jail in Newport, where he was indicted at the same sessions as Potter for having engraved the plate and struck bills from it. Upon his indictment he prayed the court to admit William Bollan and Henry Bull to be his counsel. These attorneys took exception to the jurisdiction of the court on the grounds that counterfeiting, not being a capital crime, was therefore originally triable at the general sessions of the peace. When this legal maneuver failed, since it was overruled by the court, Mors pleaded not guilty, was tried, and convicted. He was sentenced to stand for half an hour in the pillory before the door of the Colony House on Friday, 28 May, between ten and twelve in the morning and have his ears cropped or pay a fine of £1,000 in bills of any of the New England governments, be imprisoned six months in Newport, and pay all costs of prosecution and fees. For want of sufficient estate to satisfy the same he was to be sold into service by the sheriff of Newport County for any term not exceeding five years.

Mors had neither Potter's money nor Potter's gold dust but he was quite as unwilling as was the Quaker to lose his ears. It chanced that he was well acquainted with a certain Johnson who lived in part of the house of Dr. Norbert Wigneron, a physician of Newport. Possibly through Johnson the goldsmith had come to know Stephen Wigneron, a minor son of the physician. Be that as it may, Stephen was a friend of William Fairfield, frequently visited him in jail, and probably took there tools or disguise to assist in an escape by Mors. On 26 May, two days before the pillorying and cropping were to take place, young Wigneron went about dusk to a point of vantage near the jail, where he engaged in a conversation with Frances and Sarah Clarke, all the time keeping an eye on the prison. Suddenly Wigneron and the two girls noticed a person dressed in a woman's blue riding hood and cloak slip quickly around a corner of the jail. The Clarke girls exclaimed that it was no woman but Obadiah Mors, whereupon Wigneron, apparently for the sake of appearances, tarried for a scant quarter of an hour and then hurried home, where his parents were not in evidence. No sooner was he in the house than Mors appeared at the door and begged him for God's sake to hide him there for the night. After a feeble protest about what his mother and father would say if they discovered the matter the young man conducted Mors to the garret, where the counterfeiter concealed himself in a hole, the existence of which — or so the lad claimed — had been unknown to Wigneron himself. After two nights in concealment Mors left, much to the relief of his uneasy host.

Wigneron had good reason for apprehension, for the day after the jail-break Governor Richard Ward issued a proclamation promising a reward of £1,000 for the capture of the felon, while in June the Assembly passed an act laying a fine of £500 upon every person who should conceal the goldsmith or convey him out of the colony. Half of such a fine was to go to the informer and half to the treasury.

Sometime during the summer Mors was retaken and when in September he was brought to the bar he put himself upon the mercy of the bench. His sentence was that he stand for half an hour in the pillory on Friday, 10 September, between ten and twelve in the morning, and have his ears cropped or be imprisoned for six months and pay a fine of £1,000 and all costs. For want of sufficient estate he was to be sold into service for not more than five years. For his crime in breaking out of the jail he was fined £50 and costs. Stephen Wigneron was tried on a charge of having aided Mors to escape but was acquitted.

There is no mention in the court records of Ichabod Sheffield, who seems to have been deeply involved in the scheme, so he may well have been admitted as a witness for the crown in order to insure the conviction of Potter, though it is possible that he broke jail and escaped. Other associates of Potter were brought to trial. Fairfield was convicted and sentenced to stand for half an hour in the pillory on Thursday, 27 May, and have both ears cropped or pay a fine of £800 and costs and serve a term of six months in jail. He apparently chose to save his ears and, for want of estate to pay his fine and costs, was to be sold for a term of not more than five years. William Potter, apparently a minor son of John Potter, deceased, and a brother of John the counterfeiter, was indicted for having passed a false twenty shilling bill to Christopher Champlin of Charlestown and was tried but acquitted.

Another relative of John Potter, Dr. Stephen Talman, a deputy from Portsmouth and one of the committee of two in charge of distributing his town's proportion of the bills of the emission of 1740, was indicted for passing twelve twenty shilling bills to Ebenezer Morton of Middleborough, Massachusetts. Since the chief witness against him, Sarah Potter of South Kingston, John Potter's widowed mother, was too ill to be present in court, the case was put over to the September, 1742, term and then again to March, 1743, when Talman was tried and acquitted. It is not unlikely that the physician escaped conviction because of the illness and death of Sarah Potter, who had died by 1744.

An incident growing out of Potter's counterfeiting and which occurred quite some years after the stir about the affair had died down was related by Nicholas Hazard, a favorite nephew of Elizabeth Hazard Potter, John's second wife. Nicholas was once visiting at the home of his aunt and uncle when a large dinner party was given to some prominent persons, all of whom were Quakers. It happened that a poor old lady, who was a relative of the Potters and who was occasionally a little out of her mind, was staying at John Potter's at the time and during a pause in the conversation at dinner said, 'Friend Potter, who made money in the Overing house [apparently referring to

Julian house]?' Potter made no reply but started a brisk conversation. The old lady, however, watched for another pause and then repeated her question with like success. Finally, losing her patience, she gave Potter a smart slap on the knee, saying, 'Friend Potter, I asked thee who made money in the Overing house?' Potter, thoroughly irritated, incautiously answered, 'I don't know, unless it was the devil.' 'I always said it was the devil,' replied the old lady, 'but my husband says it was thee, Friend Potter.'

It developed that a gang which was distinct from Potter's had obtained bills made from Mors's twenty shilling plate. In June 1741 Benjamin Force (or Vorce) came to Lieutenant Israel Phillips of Smithfield and told him that Obadiah Mors had promised Henry Bosworth to cut a plate for making Rhode Island twenty shilling bills on condition that Bosworth raise £100 with which to pay for it. Force added that Samuel Thompson of Mendon, a miller, was concerned with him and proposed that he and Phillips go to Captain Israel Arnold of Gloucester to secure him as partner. This was done, and Arnold fell in with the scheme, contributing, together with Phillips, enough money to make up the £100, which was then entrusted to Force. Thereupon Force and Bosworth proceeded to Coventry and showed the money to Mors, who promised to engrave the plate for them. It was agreed that Force, Thompson, and Seth Arnold, who also joined the gang, should repay their share of the £100 to Phillips and to Israel Arnold. Before long Samuel Hunt and Daniel Darling, both of Mendon, apparently entered the partnership, as did Samuel Staples of Smithfield, whom Mors described as 'a comical fellow.'

Staples in turn recruited Daniel Comstock, Jr., of Smithfield, and either Daniel or Staples also won over Daniel's

brother, Azariah Comstock. Before long Jacob Boyce of
Bellingham, Suffolk County, Massachusetts, hearing that
bills were being counterfeited and that Staples was concerned, ventured to approach Staples, who confirmed the
report and told Boyce that if he would go to his cousin,
Joseph Boyce of Salem, Joseph would provide him with
some false currency. Joseph did, indeed, supply him with
one forty shilling and two three pound bills of the Rhode
Island emission of 1738, all signed, as well as £50 in unsigned notes, all on the understanding that Jacob would
pay Staples to sign the unsigned bills and would then keep
half of the profits for himself. Jacob placed the unsigned
bills in a haystack, notified Staples that they were there,
and three days later found them all signed, for which
service Jacob gave Staples a good ten shilling Boston bill.
Staples had done a bad job of signing but Jacob Boyce
nevertheless delivered the £50 in counterfeits to Moses
Bartlett of Bellingham, who in turn gave £5 of the money
to Stephen Ellis of Mendon.

This Ellis, along with Staples and Jacob Boyce, decided
to obtain a further supply of bogus currency, so one Sunday night, 10 January 1742, the three set out from Ellis's
home for Salem, which they reached the next evening.
There they spent two nights at the house of Joseph Boyce,
who gave Staples and Ellis £800 in counterfeits. The three
visitors, accompanied by Joseph Boyce, then proceeded
as far as Bowden's Tavern in Lynn, where Ellis sold a horse
to Joseph Boyce. Joseph, not having enough money with
him, sent his cousin back to Salem to get £150 from a small
box which was concealed under some deerskins in the
garret of Joseph's house. Jacob found the money and took
the sum desired, all in signed three pound and forty shilling
bills, and left still in the box about £300 in the same de-

nominations. Staples presented Jacob with £5 of the money and told him to pass it if he could. Jacob soon attempted to utter the bills in Medfield, but the fraud was detected and Jacob was committed to jail.

Joseph Boyce was not the only source of counterfeits, for Staples and Israel Arnold also were securing for themselves and others some twenty shilling bills of the 1740 emission. They found that Mors had removed from Connecticut to the home of John Potter, where they visited him. Mors told them he had the plate but persuaded them to leave it with him. He supplied them, however, with unsigned currency, on which Staples then forged the necessary signatures. On other occasions Staples, Israel Arnold, or Bosworth obtained from Mors quantities of bills said to be signed by William Fairfield and John Potter, while once Bosworth signed a considerable number himself.

The appearance of so much bad money in circulation did not fail to attract the notice of the authorities, so that not only Potter and his immediate associates but also the others who obtained bills from Mors or Boyce were sought by constables and sheriffs. Some were not easily to be found, for Captain Joseph Borden, with a warrant issued 9 May 1742, pursued Henry Bosworth from Rhode Island through Connecticut and as far as Bateman's Precinct in New York, all to no avail, though before September Bosworth was taken into custody. Others arrested were Daniel Comstock, Jr., and Azariah Comstock, both of whom had passed bad bills in Connecticut and Rhode Island, Israel Phillips, Moses Bartlett, Samuel Thompson, and Seth Arnold, all of whom, together with Bosworth, were indicted, tried at Newport, and sentenced to pillorying and cropping or paying stiff fines, double damages, and costs. For want of sufficient estates with which to pay, they were to be sold into service for terms not exceeding five years.

The colony and neighboring provinces were surely scandalized at the extent of the counterfeiting, especially since at the same time a number of persons were indicted at the superior court in Newport for altering and passing such raised bills, among them Joseph Plummer of Gloucester, laborer, Richard Angell of Smithfield, blacksmith, and Silas Williams of Providence, yeoman. All were tried, convicted, and sentenced to stand in the pillory or pay fines and costs. Because their estates were not sufficient to satisfy the fines and fees they were to be sold for a number of years.

Some of the rogues were not brought to justice and they were probably quite numerous. It appeared, indeed, that Benjamin Boyce, Isaac Richardson, Benoni Benson, Thomas Irons, Jonathan Richardson, Jr., John Mowry, Jonathan Thayer, and Benjamin Wilkinson had played some part in the counterfeiting business. The numbers involved, the importance of persons such as John Potter and Dr. Stephen Talman, the readiness of all sorts and conditions of men to enter such schemes, the adverse effect on the paper money, the widespread co-operation between the counterfeiting gangs — these matters were profoundly disquieting and indicative of a growing evil which was afflicting all the provinces and which the severest legislation apparently could not check.

Rhode Island was put to the expense and trouble of calling in the bills of the new emission of 1740 which had been so widely counterfeited. As a result of the arrests and trials in 1742 an act was passed in the following year providing that persons convicted of counterfeiting bills of credit should be prevented 'from proxing or voting' in the colony or being chosen to any office. Offenders were to be pilloried, cropped, branded with R on both cheeks, imprisoned, and compelled to pay double damages to all individuals defrauded, all costs of prosecution, and double interest during the time of possessing false currency; further, all deeds or other instruments of lands or personal estates made by persons convicted of counterfeiting were to be void.

After the events of 1742 some of the counterfeiters merely transferred their activities elsewhere. Joseph Boyce and Henry Bosworth, for example, were members of the infamous Oblong Gang in Dutchess County, New York, while Bosworth, after that nest of scoundrels had been broken up, moved on to Pennsylvania. Counterfeiting was becoming a vast and highly organized underworld activity which extended throughout the colonies and posed a constant threat to their currency and commerce.

# Chapter 7

## COINING AND COUNTERFEITING IN THE
## JERSEYS

THE 1740's witnessed the rapid growth of organized gangs of counterfeiters who appear to have co-operated and been well informed of each other's activities. When the vigilance of the authorities in one province broke up a group, some of the band frequently would move to another colony and resume their nefarious pursuits. Thus, for example, after the government of Rhode Island carried out wholesale arrests in 1742, two of the rogues, Henry Bosworth and Joseph Boyce, moved to a district in Dutchess County, New York, known as the Oblong or Equivalent Tract, which had been ceded by Connecticut to New York on 14 May 1731. Soon Bosworth and Boyce formed a good-sized band and by the autumn of 1744 their operations attracted the attention of Governor George Clinton of New York and Governor Jonathan Law of Connecticut. Magistrates were alerted, and in January 1745 one of the justices on the western border of Connecticut committed Andrew Nelson to jail for putting off a bad twenty shilling Rhode Island bill and for having seventy-two of the same in his possession.

Toward the end of April Governor William Shirley of Massachusetts learned from Robert Clarke of Uxbridge, Massachusetts, that John Scias, Joseph Boyce, and Henry

Bosworth concealed themselves at and near the Oblong. Clarke had become acquainted with Joseph Verry and Joseph Boyce of Salem, Massachusetts, John Scias of Durham, New Hampshire, and the rest of the gang through their cheating him by means of a bond which he had to pay. When he complained of the cheat, they offered to recompense him with counterfeit Rhode Island and New Jersey bills and sought to recruit him for their band. Clarke pretended to be tempted to join them as one of the many emissaries they were constantly sending out to various places in order to purchase with the counterfeits horses, cattle, and other things of worth. In reality, however, Clarke reported everything to Governor Shirley, under whose sponsorship he proceeded to New York and gave information to Governor Clinton and the council of that province. As a result of this Justice John Hubbard in April took the deposition of Elnathan Smith relative to Daniel Hunt's having passed false money, while another magistrate, Justice Swartwout of Poughkeepsie, carried out further investigations which he reported to Clinton.

Connecticut's governor, Jonathan Law, was likewise keenly interested, and at his initiative Samuel Canfield, a justice of the peace in the western part of that province, co-operated actively with Robert Clarke. Clarke contrived that Joseph Boyce, Jr., and others should be taken in the act of using their counterfeit plates in a swamp in the Oblong. But when Clarke could not induce the New York authorities to take vigorous action, he sent a twenty shilling Rhode Island plate and an incomplete twenty shilling New York plate, together with press cloths and other implements which he had found, to Justice Canfield in Connecticut. Then he managed to decoy young Boyce and a certain Hurlburt over the line into Connecticut, where they were promptly seized and committed to jail in New Haven. There Hurlburt made a confession in which he implicated no less than twenty-two confederates, most of them in New York. A third person taken with them was released on bail, while sometime between 18 July and 21 August Boyce and Hurlburt broke jail and escaped. Boyce was described as good looking and strong, wearing his black hair short, branded with the letter T, and also burnt in the hand for having counterfeited bills.

When the activities of the Oblong gang were at least temporarily broken up, Henry Bosworth moved southward, for in September 1746 he was indicted at the court of quarter sessions in Bucks County for passing a false twelve shilling bill and discharged when the grand jury returned his indictment ignoramus. He seems to have spent some time in New Jersey, where he counterfeited pieces of eight, and then to have returned to Bucks County. About July 1747 the sheriff of that county, by virtue of a warrant issued by the supreme court at the instance of the chief justice of New Jersey, took Bosworth into custody. President John Reading of New Jersey thereupon applied to Anthony Palmer, president of the Council of Pennsylvania, to have Bosworth delivered to Samuel Burrows, undersheriff of Middlesex County, that the prisoner might be removed to the Jerseys for trial. Palmer, indeed, was inclined to grant the request for the extradition of the coiner but Chief Justice Kinsey of Pennsylvania intervened and had Bosworth sent to Bucks County, where in September he was indicted for having passed a false twelve shilling bill to James Simson. The counterfeiter, however, secured bail and prudently failed to appear to stand trial when called at both the September and December sessions. Although Bosworth was never brought to justice for forging Spanish coin in New Jersey, his activity was an indication of a vast counterfeiting operation in that province. Other evidence of what was afoot was obtained when in August 1747 Francis Kelly was committed to jail in Philadelphia on suspicion of making French pistoles, and various others were apprehended there for coining dollars. It became evident that a considerable number of persons were engaged in the work, among them good artists who could make the copper white and tough and prepare molds and dies. The counterfeits were like true coins in all respects save that they would not withstand testing in fire, so that country folk could not be warned about them, though persons who knew silver well could detect them and would refuse to accept them. As a result the poor, simple people would have to bear the loss both from the copper dollars and from dollars made of pewter and coated with silver.

Two of these coiners, John Thomas Jones, a smelter lately come from Bristol, England, and Stephen Barnes, a blacksmith from Greenwich, Morris County, New Jersey, were tried at the supreme court in Philadelphia and convicted of having stamps for making pieces of eight. Each was sentenced to stand in the pillory on two market days, to be imprisoned for six months, to pay a fine of £50, and to give security for good behavior for six months after release from jail. With the hope of escaping punishment they petitioned the Provincial Council in September 1747 to remit the sentences on condition that they serve in the army anywhere in the king's dominions. Since the members of the council believed there were great numbers concerned in 'this most pernicious Practice of coining,' it was resolved that mercy might be shown in case the prisoners discovered all their accomplices and made a full confession.

To this end Chief Justice John Kinsey examined Jones and Barnes and extracted information about persons who counterfeited money in the Jerseys.

One such individual was Thomas Dote, who in 1744 had been a constable in Morris County, had in partnership with Folker Folkerson and Anthony Hutchinson purchased for £120 a pair of dies for making pieces of eight from James Bruff of Elizabethtown, and had sought to employ Barnes to assist him in coining. Folkerson, it was revealed, had made a set of dies for Peter Ulrich of Philadelphia, while others involved in the shady business were a younger brother of Folkerson, John McNeal, and Hans Davacutt, who had offered Jones £20 if he would make some base metal malleable.

The confessions did not impress the council and Jones and Barnes would have been pilloried, had it not been ascertained that the scribe who took down their examinations had omitted the fact that they revealed the place where they had thrown their dies into the river, and had not the sheriff then fished out the dies and produced them in the council. As it was, the pillorying was remitted and, when the rest of the sentences had been performed, the two men were released from jail in June 1748 on condition that they enlist in the army.

According to Barnes, Thomas Dote in his capacity of constable, on orders from Justice John Anderson of Morris County, in 1744 went to the house of Edmund Robinson in search of John Bellamy, who was suspected of counterfeiting Spanish pistoles. It is not clear whether Dote apprehended Bellamy but he at least secured his pocketbook, in which he found, among other money, four counterfeit pistoles, about £80 in false Rhode Island bills, and a bogus New York five shilling note.

Bellamy, indeed, was no novice at counterfeiting. In 1735, when he was working as a blacksmith in his shop in the Parish of Horseneck in Greenwich, Connecticut, it was suspected that he was coining Spanish half pistoles of brass and other mixed metals and passing the same. Abraham Todd, it was learned, saw iron dies for counterfeiting in the possession of the smith, remonstrated with him about his conduct, and told him what grief he would cause his father, Matthew Bellamy. Before long Solomon Close, a grand juryman, made a complaint against young Bellamy; the blacksmith was arrested by Constable William Reynolds and then examined and committed to jail by Justice Nathaniel Peck. Thomas Hill, however, the sheriff of Fairfield County, was foolish enough to release his prisoner on bail and, when Bellamy failed to appear in court in February, Hill was fined £100.

The blacksmith, nevertheless, did not get off so easily, for Constable Reynolds complained of him to Justice Ebenezer Mead, who issued a writ and had the suspected coiner arrested. This time Bellamy was freed on bail of £500 and appeared in court in August, at which time the grand jury returned his indictment ignoramus. Yet he was still in difficulties because of his failure to appear in court in February and he therefore petitioned the General Assembly to allow him to give a bond of £100 and have the sentence against Sheriff Hill declared fully satisfied, a request which was presumably granted. But Bellamy, like a large percentage of the colonial counterfeiters, could not refrain from making bad money, once he had started. Early in 1739 Samuel Darling of New Haven traced a bogus New York five shilling bill back to Bellamy, who was then residing in Wallingford, and the evidence indicated that the blacksmith was both the forger and the passer. Darling therefore complained to Joseph Whiting, assistant, on 27 February, and a writ was issued directing either the sheriff of New Haven County or the constable of Wallingford to search for bills, plates, or counterfeiting materials and to arrest Bellamy or anyone else concerned. Bellamy was apprehended and then released on bail of £300, furnished by himself and his father, for his appearance at the superior court to be held in New Haven in August. He was present in court on the second day of the sessions, when he was indicted, but the following day he was called three times and failed to appear. His bail was declared forfeited, while Darling, as the informer, received a reward of £20. No doubt at this time Bellamy left the province, very likely for the Oblong, where so many other counterfeiters were soon assembled, and when the business of that gang received a temporary setback it is probable that Bosworth, Bellamy, and others moved on to New Jersey to help in promoting the worst epidemic of counterfeiting that province had ever experienced.

As far as coining goes the Jerseys had been little troubled in the seventeenth century and forty years or so of the eighteenth century, during which there is record of but one conviction, that of Duncan Campbell in 1731 for clipping. On the other hand New Jersey bills had been widely counterfeited, chiefly abroad, which fact made for the safety of counterfeiters, since the forging of New Jersey currency within the province was punishable by death. Obviously such a situation called for remedy, so in 1730 the Assembly, in passing an act for the emission of £20,000 in bills of credit, sought to correct matters. It was provided that the prosector should allege the crime to be committed where it actually was done and if upon the trial it appeared that the fact was done in the place alleged or in any other place, then an offender should suffer in the same manner as if the crime was alleged and proved to be done in some county of New Jersey, while the juries for trials of all such foreign issues should be drawn from the bodies of the counties of Burlington and Middlesex or one of them. The act was duly confirmed by the king in council on 4 May 1732, seemingly without opposition.

Such, however, was not the case when in 1733 an act for emitting £40,000 in bills was passed by the New Jersey Assembly and carried with it the same provision as the act of 1730 with regard to the counterfeiting of any bills already current or which would be made current by the act of 1733, for in England a group of Bristol merchants secured the services of a solicitor named John Sharpe to act for them in an attempt to have the law of 1733 disallowed by the king. Sharpe addressed his arguments to Secretary William Popple, then some thirty years of age, who had entered the cofferer's office in 1730, was later appointed solicitor and clerk of the reports to the commissioners of trade and plantations, and finally was made governor of the Bermudas. Popple, something of a man of letters, had published a volume of poems and in 1733–4 was engaged in writing his first comedy, *The Lady's Revenge, or The Rover Reclaim'd*. To this personage Sharpe protested that by the act of 1733 anyone who did anything to lessen the value of the bills would be liable to the same penalties as one who refused them altogether or even counterfeited them. As for the provisions about foreign counterfeiters, Sharpe argued that this was unjust and directly contrary to the laws of England, since by them no person was liable to be tried for an offense of this nature committed out of the kingdom. Besides, he maintained, it was unreasonable for a person charged with committing a crime in one place to be punished if it were proved that he did it elsewhere. Further, it seemed to be quite unreasonable for a person to be tried except by a jury of the county in which the fact was charged to have been committed.

Reply to Sharpe's arguments was made by a Quaker, Richard Partridge, born in 1681 in Portsmouth, New Hampshire, the son of a wealthy merchant and ship-builder, William Partridge, who had served as lieutenant governor of that province from 1697 to 1703. Richard had gone to England at the age of twenty-one, had married there and settled down as the agent for various colonies. He was shrewd, resourceful, and genial, and as the brother-in-law of Governor Jonathan Belcher of Massachusetts, had considerable influence in official circles. He had just become agent for New Jersey in 1733, and it fell to his lot to defend the recent act of the legislature of that province.

In 1735 he presented to the Board of Trade his answer to the objections of Solicitor Sharpe and the Bristol merchants. It was, he argued, the duty of every legislature to preserve the credit of the public money and to restrain persons from bringing it into contempt by counterfeiting, refusing in tenders, or extending the prices of commodities beyond the usual markets. Counterfeiting of bills, he explained, was a kind of transitory crime, which might be committed with more secrecy out of the province than in it. If only persons who forged the paper money within the province should be liable, this would in effect give license to counterfeit the bills in another province. Then if money makers were to come and utter their notes in New Jersey and could be indicted only in the place where they counterfeited them, they would pass with impunity. As for Sharpe's

point about the laws of England, Partridge cited a law
of 1 and 2 Philip and Mary, chapter 11, to the effect that
if any person counterfeits money out of the realm and
brings it to England, it is treason for which the offender
is triable by commissioners or the king's bench. In short,
Partridge concluded: 'Counterfeiting is the Substance of
the Indictment; the Manner, the time and the place are
mere Circumstances; and if the Party is clearly convicted,
Place & Every thing Else are quite immaterial.' Either the
colonial agent's arguments or his influence prevailed, for
the law was confirmed by the king in council in 1735 and
the pattern set for dealing with counterfeiters of New
Jersey bills who did their work outside the province.

As luck would have it, the early importers of New Jersey
paper currency, such as Wallace, Wilson, Scott, and Adamson, were speedily detected and punished. Counterfeiters
who did their job in America at first caused little trouble:
in 1724, to be sure, Richard Wilson of Woodbridge, a
peddler, and Miles Foy of Middlesex County, a yeoman,
were indicted for counterfeiting twelve shilling New York
bills and passing them; in 1730 a schoolmaster on Staten
Island with his pencil cleverly forged a number of thirty
shilling and three pound bills of New Jersey and passed
off £10 or £12 of them before he was detected and arrested; Jeremiah Brewer of Burlington, yeoman, on 3 August 1740, it was charged, passed a false New Jersey note of
the emission of 1733, but the grand jury returned his indictment ignoramus; in 1742 Jacob Ebbermann of German-
town, Pennsylvania, a butcher, was arrested for raising
paper money of the Jerseys and escaped from the clutches
of Christopher Ottinger, the constable who was taking
him to jail; this fugitive, for whose capture a reward of
£5 was promptly offered, was described as from the Pa-

latinate, short of stature, with jet black hair and a pale complexion, a very large mouth, and teeth wide-set in front, and when he fled he was wearing a felt hat and linen jacket and trousers. So far there had been little cause for anxiety on the part of the New Jersey authorities, who must have looked upon these few incidents as of trifling importance and must have been somewhat complacent until a veritable epidemic of counterfeiting commenced in 1744.

One of the trouble spots was Morris County, and it will be recalled that in 1744 Justice John Anderson had sent Thomas Dote after John Bellamy. Anderson must have been hampered in his courageous attempt to detect money makers by having to use the services of a constable like Dote, who was soon involved in counterfeiting himself. Still worse was the shocking conduct of a fellow justice of the peace, Henry Stewart of Greenwich, to whom Anderson applied on 1 August 1744 for aid in apprehending Josiah Pricket, Jeremiah Wright, and Joseph Field. These men, Anderson informed his colleague, met in Pricket's house in Greenwich and were thought to be collaborating with others in coining gold and silver and forging New Jersey paper money. Stewart not only refused his aid but secretly hastened to warn the money makers, so that they concealed themselves and their instruments. For the time being Justice Anderson was thwarted with regard to these particular rogues, but he may have had a hand in investigating a case which was brought to the attention of the authorities in Philadelphia in this same month by one Tom Bell, a former Harvard student and notorious rogue, who for some time had been going from province to province, taking to himself the names of important persons and practicing every sort of swindle. It seems that a gang had set up a mint in a log house in a remote part of the Jerseys — perhaps Morris County — and there had begun to counterfeit New York five shilling and forty shilling bills of the emission of 1737. One of the band made the mistake, natural enough, of soliciting the aid of Tom Bell in signing the money, but Bell, for once not running true to form, betrayed the affair to the Pennsylvania authorities, who in some fashion must have lured part of the gang into Pennsylvania, for they seized and committed to jail in Philadelphia five or six men and two women of the band.

The following year there were signs that all was not well in Morris County, for at a court of oyer and terminer held there in March the grand jury indicted Daniel Price for altering a three pound New York bill and passing it. His case came up in July but apparently the crown decided not to prosecute, and in 1748 it is recorded that he was granted a license to keep a public house and inn in Hanover, where he lived. The same grand jury which indicted Price also presented Caleb Osborn for passing false money, but he too appears to have escaped punishment, at least for the moment. In March 1749 Osborn was convicted of an assault on Nathaniel Wheeler and was fined 20s., but the court, taking into consideration the circumstances of the defendant's poor family, reduced the fine to 5s. Osborn had pleaded not guilty to the indictment for passing false money. In September 1750 he was in court on an old indictment, probably the one for passing, but he then withdrew his plea of not guilty, threw himself upon the mercy of the court, and was fined 20s., which would indicate that he had uttered paper money of some other province than New Jersey. He was frequently in hot water, for in December 1751 he was presented by a grand jury for assault and battery, to which charge he pleaded not guilty. When, however, his case came up for trial in March 1752, he withdrew his plea and got off with a fine of 10s.

It is possible, to be sure, that Osborn had passed a New Jersey counterfeit, despite the amazingly mild punishment, for though by law the counterfeiting of New Jersey bills of credit was punishable by death, it is recorded that at the May 1745 term of the supreme court, James Tylee was presented by the grand jury for passing a counterfeit New Jersey bill and at the November term threw himself upon the mercy of the bench and was merely fined 40s. and ordered committed until fine and court fees were paid. There may have been, indeed, extenuating circumstances, such as a confession involving accomplices or a promise to testify against counterfeiters, though there is no record of any such thing.

Early in January 1747 the House of Assembly of New Jersey was gravely concerned by the discovery of extensive counterfeiting of New Jersey bills of credit and Spanish pieces of eight and requested Governor Jonathan Belcher to direct the attorney general and all other officers of the colony to be vigilant in apprehending those suspected of such crimes and strictly and vigorously to put into execution the laws against such offenders. A month later Mr. Nevill and Mr. Stelle introduced a bill for punishing coiners and counterfeiters of foreign coin. The act comprised a clause calling for the pardon of persons guilty before the publication of the act provided they should voluntarily surrender and confess what they knew about the counterfeiting of foreign coin of gold or silver passing current in the province. In a letter written on 11 February 1747, the governor signified that it would be well pleasing and agreeable that the bill should pass into law provided there be nothing contained therein that might be construed to pardon any species of high treason. The assembly, in accordance with Belcher's wishes, inserted such a proviso and passed the act, which was duly signed.

In addition to a flood of false Spanish coins the province had to contend with quantities of counterfeit Jersey bills. In April 1747 it was reported in the Philadelphia press that two men who went by the names of Maynert Johnson and William Casway and who came from the Jerseys were traveling about and passing forged twelve shilling bills of the emission of 1733. Their money was poorly printed and signed, the lines very crooked, the letters and figures misshapen and disproportioned, the flourishes and arms very dull, and several words scarcely legible.

One passer of such bills, a New Englander who went by the name of Jeremiah Carpenter but whose true name was thought to be Amos Fuller, was taken up and committed to the jail in Burlington, from which he broke out on 19 September and escaped. Sheriff Joseph Hollinshead offered a reward of £10 for his capture and described him as about six feet in height and of a pale complexion. When he fled he had on a gray homespun jockey coat with brass buttons, old leather breeches, yarn stockings, a linen cap, and an old felt hat. Amos Fuller, for such was the man's real name, was a native of Lebanon, Connecticut — a fact which apparently was unknown to the New Jersey authorities — and he must have returned to his own town, for early in 1749 he was arrested as a member of a counterfeiting gang headed by Joseph Bill and Isaac Jones, was convicted by the superior court, and savagely punished in accordance with the law of Connecticut. In October 1749 he petitioned the Connecticut Assembly for his release from the jail of Windham County, stating that his health was endangered in jail and that he

was willing to give evidence against the money makers if
he were set free. The legislators granted his request on
condition that he pay all costs and charges, find sureties
in the amount of £500 for his good behavior, and remain
within the limits of the town of Lebanon. Eight years later
he again memorialized the Assembly, desiring that his full
rights of a freeman be restored to him in order that he might
recover some debts owed him before his conviction, but
his prayer was denied.

Besides the counterfeits of the twelve shilling bills of
the emisison of 1733 two new varieties of bad currency
had appeared by October 1747. One was in imitation of
the fifteen shilling note of the emission of 2 July 1746.
The paper of the counterfeits was thin and smooth and,
when looked through in the light, appeared fair and free
from knots, while the paper of the true bills was thicker
and rougher and, when looked through in the light, appeared clouded and uneven. The counterfeits were wholly
done from a copperplate, but the genuine money from
common printing types. In the counterfeits the three crowns
by the side of the arms were unlike each other and rounder
than those of authentic notes; the flowers above and below
those crowns in the counterfeits were not at all like those
in the true money, while the letters in the word SHILLINGS
in the counterfeits were too large. The other denomination of the same emission which was forged was that of six
shillings. In these counterfeits the s in SILVER was larger
than the other letters, while the s in GRAINS was very
badly made. There was a great difference in the border
of flowers around the sage leaf on the back of the bills and
the flourishing was more open, loose, and irregular in the
counterfeits than in the genuine money, while the strokes
representing the fibers of the leaf in the counterfeits were

not as naturally rough as in true bills. At the top of the bill in counterfeits the s in SIX was much smaller than the IX and the letters in the word SHILLINGS at the top were very crooked. These counterfeits were also entirely done from copperplate, while the true six shilling bills were made with printing types.

Governor Belcher was aware of this situation and toward the close of the year he was sent a quantity of forged New Jersey bills through the kindness of Mr. Hopkins, a magistrate of Rhode Island. He reported to the Assembly his belief that a knot or combination of villainous persons was making a trade of forging New Jersey money. Two who were prominent in such counterfeiting activities had been seized about 1 December in Hackensack for passing false Jersey money. One was John Lummis, a native of Narragansett, a blacksmith, and the other claimed to be 'Dr.' Joseph Bradford of New London, though he also went by the name of James or Joseph Bill. It is, indeed, quite possible that they had been masquerading earlier in the year as Maynert Johnson and William Casway. In any event they had on them when taken 102 false fifteen shilling bills of which thirty-six were signed, 142 twelve shilling bills of which eight were signed, and eighty-nine six shilling bills of which twenty-seven were signed. Bill now managed to escape from the jail of Bergen County and continued his career of counterfeiting, which finally brought him to the gallows at Albany, New York, in 1773. There is no court record of Lummis, so it is not unlikely that he too escaped from jail before he could be brought to trial.

At this time most of the jails in the colonies were extremely weak, so that a determined and ingenious prisoner could escape, particularly at night. Reasonable caution required a guard around the prisons at night but this cost money, which as a rule was not available. To make matters worse, it happened that in 1748 some of the counties of New Jersey were practically in a state of open rebellion over land, so that the local authorities were often intimidated or even sympathetic toward their prisoners, whether rioters or counterfeiters. Under the circumstances Governor Belcher earnestly desired to have the Assembly vote money for guarding the jails. In this he was disappointed, for on 7 March the Speaker of the Lower House in a formal address informed him that the present condition of the colony would not admit the raising of money for guarding the prisons, though the House would not be understood to discourage the officers from putting the existing laws into execution against both rioters and counterfeiters of money, whose evil practices were productive of many very pernicious effects.

The extent of the counterfeiting activities which were brought to light in 1748 must have been shocking in the extreme. In March, Joseph Linn of Basking Ridge in Somerset County was arrested and indicted in the superior court for having passed a false New Jersey bill of the emission of 1746 to Jacob Weyser of New Brunswick. Evidence for the king consisted of the prisoner's confession and a Mr. Schuyler, one of the members of the jury, which returned the indictment *billa vera*. The prisoner pleaded not guilty and was bound over to the August term of the court to be held at Perth Amboy. His bail was in the amount of £300 and his sureties, each in the amount of £100, were Alexander Linn, John Hoey, and Bryant Leferty, all three of Basking Ridge. These gentlemen nearly lost their money, for at the court, when Linn was called three times, he failed to appear. Within a short time, however, Linn showed up and was committed to the custody of the sheriff. The next day, 10 August, by consent of the attorney general the defendant was released on bail to attend *de die in diem* during the term and on 16 August he was continued on his bail until the next session of the supreme court or the next court of oyer and terminer in Middlesex County, whichever should first be held.

As it transpired he was brought before the supreme court in Perth Amboy in April 1749, when he retracted his plea of not guilty, put himself upon the mercy of the court, and then produced two witnesses to prove his endeavors to apprehend the person who, he alleged, had induced him to commit his crime. His witnesses attested to his general good character, with the exception of the trouble in which he was then involved, and the attorney general prayed judgment. The court, however, decided to take more time to consider the matter and bound him over in bail of £200, with Alexander Linn and Matthew Sharp as sureties in the amount of £100 each, from term to term until in March 1750 he was fined £10 and required to give security for his good behavior for three years, a sentence scarcely calculated to discourage counterfeiting!

Linn's wrongdoing came to the attention of the authorities in March, and two months later, doubtless as a direct result of the publication of the act of 1747 which promised pardon to counterfeiters who gave themselves up and made a full confession, Houghton Mershon of Maidenhead in Hunterdon County surrendered to some person in authority, very likely Chief Justice Robert Hunter Morris of New Jersey, and stated that he had been concerned with three other inhabitants of Maidenhead, Robert Wild, Abraham Anderson, and Job Rosell, in counterfeiting Spanish cobs. Wild was the one who provided, prepared, and compounded copper and other base metals and various ingredients for blanching copper. Mershon was taken before Justice John Allen in Burlington upon the order of the chief justice and then committed to the jail in Trenton. Wild, Mershon, Anderson, and Rosell were indicted by a grand jury of Hunterdon County, and Rosell and Mershon pleaded guilty. A warrant was issued to David Martin, high sheriff of that county, to arrest Abraham Anderson and bring him before the supreme court at Perth Amboy in March 1749, but the counterfeiter was not found. As there is no further record concerning Mershon, it is almost certain that he was pardoned in accordance with the law, since he had voluntarily surrendered. Since Rosell and Wild are not mentioned again in the files of the superior court, it is quite possible that they were prosecuted at a special court of oyer and terminer.

By July it was reported that some persons had been apprehended and committed to the jail in Newark on suspicion of counterfeiting New Jersey money, while at about the same time several others were in jail in Trenton for the same offense. One of these, a printer named Heinrich Jaeger, admitted that he had made £40 in counterfeits but had passed only a fifteen shilling bill. He was tried at a court of oyer and terminer, was convicted, and was hanged in Trenton on Saturday, 16 July 1748, leaving behind a wife and nine children, most of whom were small. Further, at the gallows, a fine of £50 was imposed upon his wife. One of the gang, who had turned king's evidence against him at the trial, was no sooner released than he bought a horse with counterfeit money; he was quickly overtaken and imprisoned. It is small wonder that the government now expressed its determination to exert itself in detecting and punishing this growing evil.

The hanging of Jaeger doubtless induced a large number of counterfeiters to attempt to save their necks by the one sure method of surrendering themselves in order to take advantage of the pardon offered by the terms of the law of 1747. In the forefront of the scramble were Zorobabel North, Joseph Marsh, Daniel Perine, Richard French, John French, and John Roll, all of whom presented themselves, very likely in a body, on or before 1 August to John Stiles, a justice of the peace of Essex County, declaring themselves guilty of counterfeiting coin or assisting therein. Justice Stiles turned over his voluntary prisoners to William Chetwood, sheriff of the county, who was ordered to bring his charges before the supreme court at Perth Amboy on 12 August.

At about the same time that Justice Stiles was waited upon by the counterfeiters, two other justices of Essex County, Samuel Woodruff and John Ross, were visited by another gang of coiners who deemed it prudent and timely to give themselves into custody. Those who surrendered voluntarily were James Bruff, Josiah Winans, and John Radley, all of Bound Brook in the township of Bridgewater in Somerset County, as well as Daniel Clark, Jr., Andrew Miller, and Aaron Miller. All were entrusted to the custody of Sheriff William Chetwood, who delivered his prisoners on 12 August to the supreme court in Perth Amboy. Bruff and Aaron Miller confessed that they had made molds and stamps for coining pieces of eight; Clark, Winans, and Andrew Miller said they were guilty of procuring such stamps; and the story of all was that Radley, Winans, and John Joline, all of Bound Brook, together with John McNeal, Thomas Doty, and others had secured molds, stamps, and instruments from Bruff and had confederated to make pieces of eight. At the August term of the supreme court the following were released on bail to appear at the next court of oyer and terminer to be held in Essex County: James Bruff and Aaron Miller in £300 each; John Radley in £200; Andrew Miller, Daniel Clark, Jr., and Josiah Winans (or Winants) in £100 each; Zorobabel North, Daniel Perine, Joseph Marsh, John Roll, John French, and Richard French, each in £50. Inasmuch as all had voluntarily surrendered, it may be presumed that they were pardoned in accordance with the terms of the law of 1747.

The law of 1747 specified that counterfeiters who surrendered and confessed must also disclose the names of all their accomplices. The extent of their disclosures may be gauged by a warrant issued on 17 August 1748 by Robert Hunter Morris, chief justice of the province, just five days after the counterfeiters who had surrendered were brought before the supreme court in Perth Amboy. The warrant, directed to the high sheriff of Somerset or his lawful deputy, required him to arrest Jacobus Vanetta, Robert Levingston, David Brant, Court Timery, John McNeil, Joshua Robins, Isaac Woortman, Ebenezer Doud, Abraham Anderson, Peter Salter, and Abraham Southerd, all of whom were reported to have been engaged in counterfeiting the bills of New Jersey or in making plates for that purpose or in passing the counterfeit notes.

Further action taken by Chief Justice Morris is revealed by a report which he made on 21 October to the governor and council in Burlington. In it he informed these gentlemen that he had committed eleven persons to the jail of Morris County on suspicion of counterfeiting, as well as one each to the jails of Somerset, Middlesex, and Essex Counties, while in addition there were some individuals whom he had not yet examined committed to different jails.

From letters sent he learned that ten of the eleven persons whom he had committed to the jail of Morris County had escaped and, through the great remissness of the sheriff and magistrates, had continued in the county, in and about their own homes, and were not apprehended, so that some of the justices and freeholders of Morris County had petitioned that a special court be appointed for the trial of the money makers. The ten prisoners who had been committed on or about 20 September and had broken jail on 25 September were Timothy Conner, Seth Hall, Jonathan Hathaway, John Pipes, Job Allen, Andrew Morrison, Abraham Southerd, Samuel Blackford, Sylvanus Totten, and David Brant, all of Morristown. Of these Hall, Hathaway, Pipes, Allen, and Morrison had been taken up on a warrant issued by Chief Justice Morris on 20 August to John Kinney, a sheriff of Morris County. The same warrant also included the names of Abraham Hathaway, Jacobus Vanetta, John McNeal, Joshua Robins, Abraham Anderson, Robert Levingston, Court Timery, and Isaac Woortman.

The wholesale arrests of counterfeiters and coiners were reported to the Assembly by Governor Belcher, and on 16 November the House of Representatives expressed to him the hope of the members that the discoveries would soon put an end to the vile practice and that the punishment of the authors of it would prevent the like for the future. The representatives moreover professed their belief that every honest and good member of the community would assist in the further discovery and detection of this villainous combination, for it was the duty and interest of all honest persons to aid in so good a work.

On 23 November the Provincial Council, meeting in Perth Amboy, appointed a committee to consider the money coiners, and the next day the council referred to that committee a representation of the attorney general. He informed them that John Lindsley, Jr., and John Kinney, to whom the eleven counterfeiters taken in Morris County were delivered to be carried to the county jail, had suffered one of the delinquents to escape from their custody. This fugitive had then been received and protected by Thomas Darling and Seth Crowell, although they knew full well why he had been committed. As for the remaining ten prisoners, Caleb Fairchild, then high sheriff of the county, had committed them to jail but afterward suffered them to make their escape. Although the attorney general may not have known it at the time, it was subsequently revealed that John Kinney, who by 1750 had become high sheriff of Morris County, had persuaded two of the prisoners, Hall and Morrison, to break jail. The attorney general requested that the council order him to prosecute Lindsley, Kinney, Fairchild, Darling, and Crowell in the supreme court, 'as he had found it impracticable to Cause any Delinquents for Crimes Committed in the said County of Morris to be apprehended and prosecuted to Effect in the Courts there by the ordinary proceedings of the Law.'

It has already been noted that the chief justice of New Jersey on 21 October had notified the governor and council that he had committed a person to the jail of Middlesex County and another to that of Essex County for counterfeiting. The one in prison in Essex County was probably James Bruff and the other, who was jailed in Middlesex County, was James Marshall, both of whom — Bruff by 30 November and Marshall by 7 December — petitioned the governor and council that special commissions might issue for holding courts to try them.

This the governor and council were not inclined to do for excellent reasons, as is shown by the deliberations of the council. The affidavits and papers concerning the money makers were first studied by a committee of the council, and Mr. Morris then reported for the committee that it was almost impossible to convict any counterfeiters in Morris County, where it appeared that very great numbers were involved. Further, since Essex County and some of the other counties were in a state of rebellion, it would be dangerous to hold courts of oyer and terminer in them, for to do so would subject the judges and officers to the insults of a rebellious mob. At the suggestion of the committee, therefore, the council instructed Robert Hunter Morris and James Hude to prepare a bill providing that the governor or commander in chief, on the advice of council, during two years, might issue commissions for trying suspected counterfeiters in such county and by juries of such counties as the governor or commander in chief, on advice of council, might think fit. Since there would be much expense for transporting, guarding, and trying the prisoners and since there was no money appropriated for paying the contingent charges of the government, it was ordered that Mr. Morris request the lower house to appoint a committee to confer on the subject of the counterfeiters with a committee of the council, which would consist of Mr. Morris, Mr. Antill, and Mr. Kemble, assisted by the Speaker. These gentlemen were to explain the proposed bill and the reasons for it to the lower house, to urge that body to vote the necessary funds, and to lay before its members the affidavits, examinations, and papers relating to the business.

The following day, 9 December, a bill was introduced in the council for the more speedy trial both of counterfeiters and of persons guilty of the late treasons and riots. The council thereupon reported to Governor Belcher the steps which had been taken, informing him also that some of the magistrates and officers of Morris County, where much of the villainous business was carried on, had greatly contributed to the growth of the villainy there through their remissness and negligence. Furthermore, despite the discoveries already made and the numbers arrested, there was reason to believe that the affair had not yet been fully uncovered.

If the council expected co-operation from the lower house, it was sadly mistaken. The representatives tartly informed the governor that the existing laws, if only carried out, were quite sufficient to deal with counterfeiting, as had recently been demonstrated in Trenton. The defect, if there was any, must be in the conduct of the officers. To this Governor Belcher countered that it was the duty of the legislators to vote money to secure men for guarding the jails and protecting civil officers. They should, moreover, pass legislation for bringing the counterfeiters and rioters to such punishment as might be adequate to their heinous crimes.

There was, to be sure, no lack of agreement between the council and the governor, for on 10 December Belcher thanked the members of the upper house for their zeal for suppressing the outrageous offenders who were 'so openly trampling under their feet the King's name, Authority and Laws.' Then he intimated that if the lower house failed to co-operate he would represent to the King the wretched state to which his government and loyal subjects in the province were reduced 'by a Lawless Seditious Crew, who seem to be just upon the Brink of an open rebellion.'

Two days later the council loyally supported the governor by approving his refusal to issue commissions for trying the criminals in Morris County, where the counterfeiters then discovered had many relatives and where there was reason to believe that the persons unknown who had been involved in the mischief were many more in number than those already known. Under such circumstances it was impossible for the sheriff to know that many of the jurors he would return to try the criminals were equally guilty of the same offense or were relatives of those who were so. Hence it was the unanimous opinion of the special committee of the council that it would tend to defeat justice to try any of the miscreants either in Morris County or by juries of that county. Furthermore, as long as the counties of Essex, Hunterdon, and Somerset continued in their present state of rioting and breaking jails, it would be exposing the judges and officers to great danger and contempt to try the counterfeiters before a sufficient force could be raised to guard the jails, the judges, and the officers.

The members of the council went doggedly ahead with their proposed legislation but the lower house made no reply to their request for a conference, so that the council ordered Mr. Morris and Mr. Antill to inspect the journals of the lower house to see what had been done. It developed that the representatives had refused to take part in the requested conferences, so that on 15 December the council passed a resolution condemning that refusal as 'a Breach of that Harmony which ought always to subsist between the branches of the Legislature,' while subsequently the council formally reported to the King the neglect of the lower house in relation to the traitors, rioters, and counterfeiters.

The council had expressed the belief that all the counter-feiters had not been detected, and in the disturbed status of the province it was only natural that some time elapsed before further criminals could be prosecuted. One small nest of coiners — though it may be suspected that there was correspondence between all these various gangs — consisted of Samuel Jaquess, Andrew Brown, and Jonathan Campbell, all of Middlesex County. The prime mover was apparently Campbell, who induced Jaquess to prepare molds with which the three then made pieces of eight. On 17 August 1748, the day when Chief Justice Morris issued the warrant for the counterfeiters in Somerset County, Jaquess voluntarily surrendered to Samuel Nevill, a justice of the peace, while Brown, presumably at about the same time, gave himself up to James Hude, a member of the Provincial Council. All three criminals were indicted at the April 1749 term of the superior court, but Jaquess and Brown could not be prosecuted because they were protected by the terms of the law of 1747, and they were therefore discharged on payment of fees, though Jaquess had to furnish bail for his appearance at the next term of the superior court to testify against Campbell. Campbell, indeed, was in court in August 1749, and again in March 1750, when his attorney, Mr. Ogden, pointed out that several terms had passed without a true bill being found against him. To this the attorney general had to agree, so that Campbell too was discharged on payment of costs.

Since in 1749 most of the offenders were still unpunished or had been set free because of having voluntarily surrendered, it is not surprising that other persons were willing to take their chances with the law. Thus on 17 October Zebulon Cook of Burlington County passed a counterfeit New Jersey bill to Elizabeth, the wife of Thomas Moore of Chester. He was soon detected, arrested, and taken before the superior court in November, when Elizabeth Moore, Hugh Hollingshead, and Samuel Wickward gave such damaging testimony against him that the grand jury returned his indictment *billa vera*. As there is no further mention of him in the records of the supreme court, he may have been tried by a court of oyer and terminer, as perhaps was also the case with Andrew Chichester, who in March 1750 was indicted for passing a false bill but whose name then disappeared from the minute books of the supreme court.

It was not until July 1750 that the authorities were able to take resolute action against the counterfeiters in Morris County. The sheriff's calendar of prisoners at a special court of oyer and terminer held for that county on 2 July lists Samuel Blackford, Abraham Hathaway, Job Allen, John Pipes, David Brant, Seth Hall, Sylvanus Totten, and Andrew Morrison, all charged with coining Spanish pieces of eight, while since the sitting of the court three more persons, Josiah Pricket, Jeremiah Wright, and James Vanetta, had been committed 'for counterfeiting money.'

Coiners of Morris County indicted at the July term of the supreme court for having made pieces of eight were Ebenezer Doud, Abraham Southerd (or Southward), Timothy Conner, and Peter Salter. True bills against Doud and Southerd were returned by the grand jury. Salter, specifically charged with making eleven pieces of eight, pleaded guilty but explained that through forgetfulness he had omitted giving an account of some such counterfeits, though he had subsequently sent them to a magistrate. The court took this into consideration and fined him, though his sentence may have included other punishments not mentioned in the records of the court. Conner was presented for having had molds and stamps for making pieces of eight and also for having purchased from Andreas Wortman a quantity of unsigned counterfeit New Jersey bills of credit. His indictment was returned *billa vera,* but there is no mention of his trial. He was also charged with breaking out of the jail of Morris County on 25 September 1748, to which he pleaded guilty.

Typical of the general sympathy for the counterfeiters in Morris County was the conduct of John Kinney, an undersheriff in 1748 who had become high sheriff of the county by 1750. In September 1748 he had persuaded Seth Hall and Andrew Morrison to break out of the jail, for which crime he was presented by a grand jury in July 1750. Hall and Morrison both appeared as witnesses against him, as did Keziah Hall, Gilbert, Elizabeth, and Priscilla Heading, and Mary Darling. The indictment was returned *billa vera* but it is not recorded whether he was further prosecuted.

The attorney general at this same term of the supreme court charged David Brant of Morristown with having aided Conner, John McDaniel, and other criminals in forging New Jersey bills and passing them. To this Brant pleaded guilty and was apparently held in jail until 5 October, when he was released in bail of £200 for his good behavior for a period of seven years, beginning 2 July 1750 — an amazingly light sentence for a crime which called for the penalty of death! Perhaps he surrendered in accordance with the terms of the law of 1747, though in that event it is hard to understand why the court required a bond for his good behavior.

The justices on the bench at this term of the supreme court were Samuel Nevill, Timothy Tuttle, Ebenezer Byram, David Cooper, and John Anderson. Anderson, it will be recalled, had been balked by Henry Stewart, a fellow justice of the peace, in an attempt to apprehend Josiah Pricket, Jeremiah Wright, and Joseph Field in 1744. Now at last Anderson had the satisfaction of seeing Pricket and Wright indicted for having joined with Field and Lemuel Washbourn, both of Greenwich, in counterfeiting both New York and New Jersey bills. Lemuel Washbourn had been accepted by the crown as an evidence against his accomplices, and also testifying against them were Samuel Grant, Jr., Walter Cahoun, Thomas Hutchinson, and James Hanna. The grand jury found a true bill, but since there is no mention of the trial in the minute books it is likely that the men were brought before a court of oyer and terminer for trial.

Frequently it was dangerous for a magistrate to take action against counterfeiters, for he was then exposed to retaliation by the malefactors, their relatives, and their friends. Justice Anderson was the object of a plot hatched against him on 1 June 1750 by Josiah Pricket, Henry Stewart, William Henry, and Joseph Warford, all of Greenwich. At that time, falsely representing themselves as acting on specific orders from Governor Belcher, they applied to Jonathan Pettit, a justice of the peace, to examine persons evilly disposed toward Justice Anderson, whom they accused of giving judgments partially. Their aim, of course, was to take away his good name and have him removed from his office of justice of the peace. Their scheme failed, and the four men were indicted for conspiracy. The case was continued until September 1751, when the attorney general decided not to prosecute them further. At the same court, however, Henry Stewart, on the evidence of John Anderson and the convicted counterfeiter Stephen Barnes, was indicted for having 'tipped off'

Pricket and his accomplices concerning their imminent arrest. The grand jury returned a true bill, but the end result is not recorded.

Even while the authorities were taking action against so many coiners, two residents of Little Egg Harbor in Burlington County, Samuel Denyke and Joseph Palmer, commonly known as 'Indian Jo,' prepared a mold made of cedar wood, beaten earth, and chalk, with which they turned out pieces of eight. Denyke was soon apprehended and apparently examined by John Matthews, justice of the peace, at Little Egg Harbor. Denyke and 'Indian Jo' Palmer were indicted at the supreme court in 1751 on the testimony of Jacob and Abel Gale. Palmer, it seems, was not taken, but Denyke was to be tried at the May 1752 term of the supreme court.

Justice Samuel Nevill, a prominent attorney and author of *The Acts of the Assembly of the Province of New Jersey*, which was published in this year, 1752, by William Bradford, was to be one of the judges at Denyke's trial. Nevill sent word by Daniel Matthews that his father, Justice John Matthews, should be sure to be present at the next supreme court in Burlington with all the recognizances concerning the money makers. Young Matthews chanced to deliver the message to his father when a Quaker named Hannaniah Ganntt, a tailor, and Charles Loveland, a mariner, were present. The justice of the peace, enraged at the message from Nevill, exclaimed: 'Samuel Nevill may kiss my arse; I know my business as well as he doth.' Such at least was the sworn testimony of the Quaker, though Loveland claimed he heard no such disrespectful remark.

In any event the papers and the justice of the peace apparently were in court as required. Denyke pleaded that he was not guilty of the misdemeanor with which he was charged but he was tried and convicted. The foreman of the jury which brought in the verdict of guilty prayed the bench to be merciful 'considering his youth and the good character he bore from the time of his Infancy to his acquaintance with Indian Jo Palmer who they had good reason to believe had seduced and corrupted him.' The judges were apparently moved by the recommendation to mercy, for they merely sentenced Denyke to stand one hour in the pillory in Burlington on the coming Tuesday between the hours of eleven and four, to pay a fine of £5, and to give recognizance for his good behavior for three years.

Many of the counterfeiters of Morris County were still unpunished. Nine of them, Abraham Hathaway, Sr., Jonathan Hathaway, Job Allen, Andrew Morrison, John Pipes, Timothy Conner, Sylvanus Totten, Seth Hall, and Samuel Blackford, were presented by a grand inquest at a court of oyer and terminer held in Morristown in September 1752 for having been concerned in providing and making molds and stamps and in procuring material for counterfeiting pieces of eight and in making the same. Abraham Hathaway was likewise indicted for having a mold and making with it pieces of eight, an indictment which was returned *billa vera* when one of his accomplices, Seth Hall, gave evidence against him. Just a year later Samuel Blackford was presented for making pieces of eight and in his case also an accomplice, Sylvanus Totten, turned evidence for the king, so that the grand jury returned a true bill against Blackford.

As far as the records reveal, this marked the close of the great wave of counterfeiting in New Jersey in which such large numbers were involved. Money makers by no means ceased their activities, but the fact that 'the

heat was on' in New Jersey led the professional counterfeiters, who constituted by this time an organized underworld throughout the colonies, to turn their attentions
elsewhere. The masterminds of the counterfeiting game
to be sure drew heavily on persons of all walks of life
who were all too easily persuaded to forge bills or coins
and pass them. The leaders in the industry, such as Joseph
Bill, Isaac Jones, the Boyces (father and son), Glazier
Wheeler, Owen Sullivan, Henry Bosworth, John Scias, to
mention but a few, moved as seemed expedient from colony
to colony, corresponded with others of their ilk, exchanged
intelligence, recruited personnel, and actually turned
counterfeiting into a big business that was a constant
threat to the currency of the province and hence to its
trade and commerce.

# Chapter 8

## SAMUEL WEED AND THE DERBY GANG

WHEN the activities of the Oblong Gang were at least temporarily broken up in 1745, Henry Bosworth and probably others of the band removed to the southward. Some of the group were prosecuted by Connecticut. Andrew Nelson, who was taken up for passing a false Rhode Island twenty shilling bill, was released on bail to appear at the superior court to be held in New Haven in August 1745, but he escaped almost certain conviction when Captain Leonard Hoar, acting on orders from Colonel John Stoddard, impressed young Andrew and his father's firelock gun for the king's service in guarding the western frontier. Two other rogues from the Oblong, Thomas Cooper and Jeremiah Thornton, made the mistake of passing Rhode Island counterfeits in Colchester, Connecticut. They were immediately detected, tried, and convicted at the March 1745 session of the superior court in Hartford. In accordance with a Connecticut law of 1724 they were sentenced each to have his right ear cut off, to be branded on the forehead with C, to forfeit his estate, to be forever debarred from any trade or dealing within the colony, and to be committed to a workhouse and there confined to work under a master until the day of death. The corporal punishment was inflicted but on 9 May 1745, encouraged, no doubt, by previous action of the Assembly in similar cases, they petitioned for release from life imprisonment in case they could find someone to pay their expenses and charges. It cost the taxpayers money to keep these offenders in jail, so the legislature granted the prayer on condition that they pay all costs and charges and £20 each — the rewards given to the informer or informers against them — and with the understanding that if they were ever found in the colony after the ten days following their release had elapsed they were to be returned to the workhouse for life.

In addition Joseph Boyce, Sr., and John Scias had been taken up through the efforts of Robert Clarke and lodged in the Hartford jail. In May Clarke requested of and received from the Connecticut Assembly aid in having the two offenders transported to Hampshire County in Massachusetts. Seth Sherwood, Joseph Plummer, Samuel Thompson, a certain Hurlburt, Israel Keith of New Sherburn, and Joseph Boyce, Jr., escaped punishment through breaking jail, forfeiting bail, or other means.

Young Boyce seems to have been instrumental in promoting a new gang in Derby, Connecticut. Public knowledge of their operations came about when in October 1746 Daniel Grant of Newtown became suspicious of a twenty shilling new tenor bill of Connecticut which had been paid him by Samuel Sherman, also of Newtown. Grant took the note to New Haven to George Wyllys, who pronounced it a counterfeit and had Sherman arrested. Sherman was soon released on a bail bond of £300, furnished to Sheriff Thomas Hill by Samuel and his brother Benoni, and he told the following story to the authorities: in April 1746, he and Dr. George Weed talked one day in Newtown about counterfeit money, and on 11 May they went together to Woodbury, where Sherman obtained some false Connecticut money from the doctor and passed it successfully in Woodbury. The doctor informed him that his brother, Samuel Weed, who lived in Derby, signed the bills and could imitate any man's handwriting. Later George Weed at Sherman's house showed him a counterfeit Connecticut bill that was not printed on the back and subsequently passed off the same in Norwalk, incidentally remarking to Sherman that the gang in Derby had a plate for making forty shilling old tenor Rhode Island notes. So far there had been no trouble, but on the night of 13 October Dr. Weed came to Sherman's home and gave him three twenty shilling Connecticut bills — which he said were good — and Sherman gave him credit for them. It was one of these which Sherman passed to Grant and which landed him in the jail of Fairfield County, where on the night of 26 October he was visited by George Weed. The physician, who was let in by John Whitear, secured a mug of flip, which he shared with Sherman and a Negro prisoner. Dr. Weed said that he had passed on that very evening to a tavernkeeper in Stratford a twenty shilling bill which came from the house in Derby and he urged Sherman to break jail. Sherman replied that he could easily get out in a quarter of an hour but he decided against it on the grounds that he expected to get bail the following day, when he was actually released.

As soon as he was at liberty Sherman set about winning favor with the government by running down the counterfeiting gang. His first move was to secure the arrest of Dr. Weed, who promptly broke away from the grasp of the constable and made good his escape. Next Sherman sent to Derby to have Samuel Weed and the rest of the band apprehended, but he himself failed to appear in court when summoned and his bond was declared forfeited. On 20 May 1749, however, he asked the Assembly to cancel his bond on condition that he pay all costs and charges, a request which was denied. But later, in large part no doubt because of the recommendation of Justices Thomas Tousey and Job Sherman given on account of his full confession and his instrumentality in bringing the Derby gang to justice, the Assembly ordered the court to chancer the bond down to such an amount as would cover the charges and the reward allowed to Grant as informer.

Proceedings against the counterfeiters in Derby apparently began when, on 16 November, Samuel Riggs, a justice of the peace, issued a warrant for the arrest of Samuel Weed, who was apprehended the next day by Constable Samuel Tomlinson. In Weed's house were found a press, two bottles of red ink, and a sheet of paper from which it was judged that a bill had been cut. Weed himself apparently was soon released on bail, for about the end of February 1747, on an information lodged by Elihu Hall, he was again taken into custody and jailed in New Haven.

His wife, Sarah, soon set about planning his escape, for which she enlisted the services of their son, David, their Negro slave, Zadock, Samuel's brother, Joseph Weed of Waterbury, and Joseph Trowbridge, also of Waterbury. Zadock was promised his freedom for his part in the undertaking, while Trowbridge, who felt that Samuel had been wrongfully imprisoned, was promised a reward and was strongly encouraged by Ephraim Washborn. Sarah set about procuring suitable tools for an attempt on the jail and to this end gave Trowbridge money, with which he purchased a file and a gimlet in Milford; Sarah herself went to Daniel Tucker, a blacksmith in Derby, and had him make her a burning iron three inches wide with a cutting edge, and this she took, together with a cold chisel and a file, to be used in the projected jail break.

On Saturday evening, 30 March, Trowbridge, Zadock, and David and Joseph Weed set out for New Haven, separating in order to avoid attracting attention and then meeting again near the jail. Joseph went first to the prison and when he came back he reported that Samuel already had his irons off. Zadock had brought along a shoe knife and a tap augur, Joseph an iron, and David another iron. While Trowbridge kept watch, these three bored a hole in the stud, then inserted a spike and pried the stud out. At this a cry was raised, and they fled and did not see Samuel when he actually escaped. All this took place between midnight and four o'clock in the morning. On the way back from New Haven, Trowbridge stopped in Derby and took with him to Waterbury two cows for a debt owed him by Samuel Weed, while Samuel Weed, Jr., drove some of the family's cattle to the house of Trowbridge's father to be cared for by John Weed, all in the hope of avoiding their loss if Samuel's estate should be forfeited. The fugitive made for Waterbury, hid out there for a short time, but was seized by Constable John Blakeslee and conveyed back to the jail in New Haven, where he was indicted at the superior court on 29 April 1747, pleaded guilty to the charge of counterfeiting twenty shilling bills of Connecticut and forty shilling notes of Massachusetts, and was sentenced in accordance with the law of 1724.

As was to be expected, action was taken to investigate the jail break and to punish those responsible for it. David Weed, perhaps because of his youth, was not apprehended but Trowbridge, Joseph Weed, and Zadock were arrested on 4 April and examined by Justice John Hubbard, to whom Trowbridge and Zadock confessed their guilt. At first Joseph Weed protested that he was innocent but on 10 April he too admitted his guilt. Bail for each of the three was set at £5,000 and they were committed to jail. At the April term of the superior court in New Haven, Joseph Weed was fined £100 and required to find surety for his good behavior in the amount of £200 and pay costs amounting to just under £38; Zadock was given twenty stripes on his naked body but Trowbridge, who apparently was accepted as king's evidence, was not prosecuted.

The authorities, of course, were also interested in discovering the confederates of Weed and bringing them to justice. On 23 December 1746 Samuel Bassett, a justice of the peace, had Edward Washborn of Derby arrested and examined him both on that day and again on 26 December at the home of Captain John Riggs. After the questioning Washborn was committed to jail in New Haven but soon released on bail of £500 which he and his brother Ephraim furnished. Constable Tomlinson had informed the justice that Silvester Wooster of Derby had made a press for Edward Washborn for counterfeiting bills, and it was suspected that Edward had passed six false Connecticut notes. From the silence of the court records it may be guessed that Edward somehow escaped prosecution, as seems to have been the case with another suspected member of the gang, Jonas Tomlinson, who, on a warrant issued 29 April 1747, was arrested by Ebenezer Lines, a deputy sheriff, examined by Justice John Hubbard, and committed by him to the jail in New Haven. He was subsequently released on bail of £500.

Other associates of Samuel Weed were less fortunate. On 15 April Nathaniel Wooster of Derby was examined at an inferior court in that town. He pleaded not guilty to a charge of passing but admitted that he knew about the counterfeiting, that he had had in his possession two false twenty shilling Connecticut bills, and that he had seen Robert Lennox make plates and Sam Weed and Edward Washborn strike six or seven of the twenty shilling counterfeits. At length, however, he broke down and confessed that he had struck off one bill himself at the desire of Lennox. He was committed to the jail in New Haven, where he was indicted in April 1747, tried, convicted, and sentenced in accordance with the harsh provisions of the law of 1724.

Another accomplice, Daniel Tucker, a blacksmith of Derby, was taken into custody on a writ signed 8 April 1747 by Captain Samuel Riggs, justice of the peace, and was examined the next day by Justice Hubbard. He at once made a full confession, which gives the clearest picture of the whole affair. One day in August 1745 on the Town Street of Derby he met Gideon Washborn, who asked Tucker if he would shoe his horse for him. In the course of their conversation Gideon took out his pocketbook and showed the blacksmith a forty shilling new tenor Massachusetts bill, saying that they could have as many of them as they wanted.

Later on Gideon Washborn had Tucker make some steel pens, and told him that Boyce had gotten out of jail, that Boyce was in Derby, and that he was going to make some plates for himself, Edward Washborn, and Samuel Weed. Young Boyce, it will be recalled, had been jailed in New Haven, along with one Hurlburt, and both had broken jail either in July or August. In Derby Joseph Boyce, Jr., apparently assumed the alias of Robert Lennox. Since Samuel Weed and his confederates needed copper for their plates, they sent Jeremiah Ocain toward New York to buy some of the metal for their purpose, and he returned with a copper teakettle, which they brought to Tucker and had him cut into the form of a plate. Further, with money supplied by Sarah Weed, Tucker bought a copper pot at Mr. French's and also fashioned it into a plate. For ink the counterfeiters first tried to use lampblack and oil but these did not serve at all, so Weed sent to Boston by William Clark, who brought back for them nut galls and ivory black but reported that he could get no Frankfort ink. The press was set up in Edward Washborn's house, where Weed, the two Washborns, and Tucker struck off a number of bills. Tucker received from Edward Washborn two counterfeit twenty shilling Connecticut bills, one of which he burned and the other he returned to Washborn. Edward Washborn also gave him a false two shilling note and some quarters of two shilling bills, and Tucker passed two of the quarters to a Mrs. Clark.

The others were active in passing away their bad money. Weed and Gideon Washborn told the blacksmith that they paid out nearly £20 in Stratford, and the tailor, Nathaniel Wooster, told him how he uttered some quarters of two shilling bills to Mrs. Clark. The tailor, indeed, had taken an active and important part in making the plates, for he described to Tucker how he pressed a twenty shilling Connecticut bill and a twelve shilling bill 'with his Tailors Goose on the Backside to press down the Letters that are stamped on the Same with a Card in Order to prepare the Same for a Plaister of Wax on ye Plate to take the Letters out of the Backside of the Bill in Order to cut the Plate by.' Tucker related that at Mr. Clark's in 1745 Jonah Tomlinson had told him about the money making in the Oblong and at the time had showed him a Connecticut twenty shilling bill which had been finished off by Boyce himself. The blacksmith was indicted at the superior court in New Haven in April 1747 for making instruments for counterfeiting and for passing two sixpence quarters to Mrs. Clark, to all of which he pleaded guilty and was sentenced in accordance with law.

Sarah Weed was more fortunate than her husband and most of his accomplices, though she too was arrested toward the end of April 1747 and taken before Justices John Hubbard and Samuel Bassett for examination. She admitted that she knew of Sam's making money, but only after the bills had been struck. In fact, in the beginning she had suspected that Sam was having an affair with the widow Washborn, but when she accused him of this her husband took from his pocketbook about ten Connecticut twenty shilling bills, newly printed but not signed, and explained to her what he was doing. She learned, furthermore, that Boyce had been at their former house for three days, and when she threatened to complain to the authorities unless Boyce departed, Boyce went to Edward Washborn's, where her husband took meat and cheese to the fugitive from justice. When she admitted that all that she had done was not proper, the justices were satisfied and dismissed her.

As the Weed family had foreseen, the estate of Samuel Weed was declared forfeited, as were those of Tucker and Wooster. In May 1747 the Assembly appointed Captain John Fowler and Captain Samuel Bassett as a committee to receive from Sheriff Samuel Mansfield of New Haven County the confiscated estates, which they then were to sell. At the same time Captain Elisha Hall was appointed to start suits for the recovery of the property of Samuel Weed, who had given title to it to other persons in an attempt to protect it from seizure.

It was customary for counterfeiters condemned in Connecticut to imprisonment for life to petition for release, which, as a rule, was granted. Thus, on 12 May 1747, Tucker and Wooster memorialized the Assembly to free them from jail. Wooster set forth that he had never enriched himself by a penny through counterfeiting, that his property had been purchased with the money of his wife, who was very infirm, that they had several children, of whom the youngest was four months old, that his own health was impaired in jail, and that his family must become charges on the town unless he was released to support them. This last was usually a telling point with the legislators. Tucker pleaded that his estate, which in large part consisted of his blacksmith's tools, would no more than pay his just debts. Besides he had a wife and three small children who must, save for the aid of an aged father-in-law with an elderly and infirm wife, become town charges. Both memorialists were set free on condition that each provide a bond of £500 for his good behavior and that each abide within the town limits of Derby. Tucker, after his return to Derby, was, as he put it, of 'a humble and upright behavior,' and in October 1759 he asked the Assembly to restore to him the liberties and privileges which had been lost through his conviction. His petition found favor in the eyes of the legislators, who gave back to him the right to contract, trade, and deal as other inhabitants of the colony might do.

Samuel Weed in May 1747 also besought the Assembly to free him from confinement and permit him to go to Waterbury and reside there permanently, but both houses of the legislature turned down his request. His wife Sarah at the same time petitioned that her son, Samuel, Jr., be allowed to keep the sheep and cattle which belonged to him and bore his mark, all of which was probably a subterfuge to keep some of his father's property from confiscation.

Samuel Weed, denied his freedom by the Assembly, early in October, together with the notorious counterfeiter, Joseph Bill, broke out of the New Haven jail but was captured on 6 November by Nathaniel Gunn and returned to confinement. He managed to escape again, for on 26 December 1748, Justice John Humphrey had him seized in Simsbury, where he was found armed with a pistol and in possession of a milled dollar, forty-two copper pennies, a bed, two goats, a deerskin, a brass skillet, a pair of brass shoe buckles, two chains of silver buttons, a pair of skis, a mare, a saddle, and a bridle. He was committed to jail in Hartford, and the next day the superior court ordered that he be given twenty-five lashes on the naked body as a punishment for breaking jail. Until May 1749 he was kept securely in confinement in Hartford. At that time he besought the legislature for his release, and it was voted that he be put to work under a master in Hartford, with the proviso that, if he should be caught wandering outside of that town, the person who seized him was to be given a reward of £10, while Weed should receive ten stripes on the naked body for so offending. In addition he was required to furnish a bond of £50 for his good behavior. For some reason, probably the failure to obtain a bond, he was kept in jail and in October he sent another memorial in which he stated that he was reduced almost to a skeleton and had but a few rags to cover him. The same measures were voted as before and this time the requisite bond was put up by Joseph Weed of Simsbury and Jonas Weed of Waterbury.

Samuel Weed sent a memorial to the Assembly on 30 April 1752, requesting leave to go from Hartford to Waterbury to see his children and take care of the estate left them by their mother, but the petition was denied. In February 1756 it came to the notice of the Assembly that in various instances Weed had behaved contrary to the tenor of the conditions of his bond and that it was justly suspected that he was confederated with persons who were counterfeiting bills of credit and putting them off to the great disquiet of his majesty's subjects. Thereupon Jabez Hamlin, John Hubbard, and Elisha Sheldon were appointed a committee to examine Samuel Weed, inquire into his doings, and then report back to the Assembly. These gentlemen discovered that Samuel had been at Dover, New York, on what business they could not discover, but they could obtain no conclusive evidence against him. They reported, however, that common fame represented him as a very bad and dangerous man and as one who corresponded with the counterfeiters of bills. As Dover was the headquarters of Owen Sullivan and his 'Money Club,' it seems likely that 'common fame' was correct in this instance. Weed, indeed, made a further attempt at the removal of the regulation which restricted him to the limits of Hartford, for on 4 October 1758 he memorialized the legislators, setting forth that he wished to become a dresser of deer's leather and in that business travel from town to town, a prayer which the Assembly in its wisdom denied.

There were, indeed, other persons who at this period were certainly or probably connected with Weed or the money makers at Dover. Benjamin Barns of Waterbury, arrested in that town by Constable Samuel Scott, Jr., on a charge of passing false bills, very likely obtained them either directly from Dover or perhaps through Weed. Barns was taken to jail in New Haven but nothing more is known of him and he probably made a break as so many others had done. John Dexter was followed by officers from Dutchess County to New Haven, where he was arrested and committed for having made pieces of eight and pistoles, several of which were found on his person. Since his crime had been committed in New York, he was extradited and imprisoned there, but his fate is not recorded, for the minutes of the supreme court for that year are lost. The want of these same minutes also leaves uncertain the lot of Jeremiah Weyman, who, according to a report made to the Connecticut Assembly by Captain John Riggs, was taken up in Waterbury on suspicion of counterfeiting bills and committed to jail in New Haven. In due time he was delivered to an officer to be taken to New York for trial, which indicates that his offense was committed in New York.

Abel Clark of Waterbury was informed against on 3 September 1748 by Hezekiah Kilborn for having that day passed to Nicholas Ayrault of Weathersfield a false twelve shilling Connecticut bill of the emission of 11 October 1744. John Chester, assistant, at once issued a warrant for the arrest of Clark, who was quickly apprehended by Constable Oliver Denning of Weathersfield. At his examination before Justice Chester the prisoner claimed he was not guilty but refused to say where he got the counterfeit bill. Since a number of other false notes were found on his person — two two pound Rhode Island bills and two twelve shilling and one twenty shilling of Connecticut — his bail was set at £2,000 and he was committed to jail in Hartford. Prison fare and conditions in general were so bad that on 17 September 1748 he sent a petition to the Assembly, in which he stated that he, 'a youth,' about the beginning of August had been 'bewitched' and 'seduced' by Samuel Weed to take some £42 in counterfeit bills to pass, with the understanding that he was to retain half the profits. He admitted that he had put off about half of the sum before he was arrested. In his memorial he asked that he be admitted as king's evidence against Weed, a prayer which the Assembly voted to take up for consideration in May.

It so happened, however, that a fellow prisoner with Clark in the Hartford jail was the infamous Joseph Bill. A warrant for Bill's arrest had been issued in New Haven on 19 May 1747 by Justice John Hubbard, on a complaint which stated that Bill had lately engraved a plate for the lower left-hand quarter of a Connecticut two shilling old tenor bill and also a plate for a four shilling Connecticut bill and had also aided in striking and passing counterfeits. When Bill was taken into custody by Stephen Hotchkiss, he pleaded not guilty, but when a four shilling counterfeit bill was found on him, he confessed that he had made it and two pieces of bills which were discovered in his possession. He also had an engraving tool which, along with some small pieces of copper and a crucible, he said he had obtained from Isaac Doolittle in New Haven. He had melted some pieces of copper, fashioned a plate, and then engraved it. Then, when all alone in the woods in Cheshire, he had struck the bills from the plate, though he maintained he had done this only because he had nothing else to do and that he had never signed or passed any bills. He had broken jail in New Haven, together with Sam Weed but, like Weed, was recaptured and imprisoned in Hartford. He now escaped from the Hartford jail in company with young Clark and together they made their way to Boston, where they joined a gang of counterfeiters. By April 1750, however, Clark became desirous of returning to Connecticut and therefore wrote to the Connecticut Assembly, offering to confess all and asking liberty to return home, an only son, to his good parents. His petition met with the negative vote which it probably deserved.

# Chapter 9

## JOSEPH BILL AND HIS MASSACHUSETTS GANG

Toward the end of September 1748 Joseph Bill and Abel Clark escaped from the prison in Hartford and made their way to Boston. Clark was new at the counterfeiting game but Bill was an old hand. His real name was probably Joseph Bill Packer but he was usually called Joseph Bill. He was a Presbyterian, eventually married a New England woman but deserted her when she was pregnant, and later committed bigamy in Virginia by taking to wife a woman in that colony who bore him a son (the New England woman bore him a daughter). Bill was an engraver and, in a speech just before he was executed at Albany in 1773 he stated that he engraved plates in North Carolina, Virginia, Pennsylvania, the Jerseys, and New York for people who made a business of counterfeiting the currency of the provinces. He declared that he never considered it criminal for a mechanic to finish any piece of work that he was employed to execute, whatever mischievous purposes the instrument might be applied to after the artist delivered it out of his hands. In this connection he made the point that he had never passed any bills of credit made from his plates — which, of course, was a barefaced lie.

Now Bill apparently joined forces at once with Isaac Jones in Boston, and in a matter of days, it seems, Jones became embroiled with the law. On Friday, 28 September 1748, Jones was detected in putting off some counterfeits of the seven shilling Connecticut bills of the last emission and was observed to have a large quantity about him. His notes were poorly done, for they were too pale, miserably engraved on both sides, and with the letters and lines very uneven. Some officers of the law followed him to the house in which he dwelt at the bottom of the Boston Common and when they attempted to take him he took a stand at the head of the stairs, armed with two pistols, and threatened the lives of the officers and their assistants. For some two hours he defended his post, while some of his accomplices in the chamber were busy burning the press and bills. Several pieces of the bills and one almost entire flew out of the chimney and were picked up by persons in the crowd below. Finally Jones was rushed by the officers and taken, with one confederate, apparently sooner than they expected, for in the room were found some parts of the press, several quires of paper suitable for making bills, and a quantity of lampblack, oil, and other materials for carrying on the business.

The bills which Jones had counterfeited were of the seven shilling Connecticut variety, and it happened that when the fracas took place at the lower end of the Boston Common Jonathan Trumbull of Connecticut was in that town. When he discovered that the counterfeiter was seized by a person who had thereby exposed himself to great danger, Trumbull thought it fitting for the honor of Connecticut to give the courageous person a gratuity of £8, so he himself made such a gesture, and, no doubt to his relief, the Assembly took the same view of the matter and reimbursed him.

Jones was more than a match for the Boston jail of the

day and in a very short time broke out and went straight to work, with the aid of Bill and others. Their activity came to light through the arrest of some passers of their product in Hebron, Connecticut, where in February 1749 Justice John Bulkley discovered that some individuals in Hebron had been connected with Joseph Bill in counterfeiting paper money. As a result David Wilcox, Jr., and Elias Wilcox were apprehended and examined closely by Bulkley and Joseph Phelps, another justice of the peace. The prisoners, charged with passing Connecticut currency, confessed, implicated others, and said that one Bryant of Boston was the one who had undertaken to put off paper notes manufactured by Joseph Bill. They further explained that the money obtained from Bryant was to be passed 'on shares.'

Since it seemed advisable that someone should go to Boston to alert the authorities there, Justice Bulkley asked John Thompson of Hebron to undertake the business. After a consultation with Jonathan Trumbull and Joseph Fowler, who were of the opinion that the Assembly would reward him, Thompson, accompanied by David Wilcox, Jr., who was to serve as king's evidence, set out for Boston toward the end of February in extremely inclement and rainy weather. Upon his arrival Thompson delivered to the proper authorities letters from Trumbull and Bulkley.

Jonathan Bryant, a shingle maker, was at home and was taken into custody about 8 or 9 March. In his house were found ninety-five three pound bills and nine seven shilling bills of Connecticut and thirty-two ten shilling bills of Massachusetts, all counterfeit. He said that Joseph Bill and Isaac Jones were counterfeiting money in a rented room in a house on Long Island about two miles below the Castle. The officers were extremely gullible, for they permitted

Bryant to seek out the men. He pretended to lead the constables to seize his accomplices but, as might have been expected, he had tipped off the rascals and the birds had flown. All that could be done for the moment was to commit the shingle maker to jail and offer a reward of £50 for the discovery of his associates. Bryant was indicted in April 1750, at a court of assize, for having passed knowingly a false three pound Connecticut bill. He pleaded guilty and prayed the benefit of clergy, which was granted him, and he thereupon was burnt in the hand in open court — surely no way to stop counterfeiting!

The diddled officers were thoroughly aroused and soon picked up the trail of Jones and Bill, who, they found, had removed their plates and utensils to Newton Woods and there set up in business again. This time they were taken red-handed with their implements and a quantity of unsigned bills and committed to the jail in Cambridge. While they were the next day being transferred to Boston, they made a successful break and escaped at Watertown, so that the unhappy officers reached Boston with the plates but no counterfeiters.

It is not known where the rogues went first but some eleven days later, on the last day of March, led by an Indian squaw, the two men arrived at an early hour in the morning at the home of Jedediah Ashcraft in Groton. According to Ashcraft's evidence when he was subsequently examined — and he was probably far from telling the whole truth — the men told him that they came from Rhode Island and had had someone take back their horses. Bill, whom Ashcraft described as a tall, slender, well-dressed man, was going by the name of Doctor Wilson and pretended to be a famous physician. His companion called himself Captain Wright and claimed that he had lost his vessel in the war.

A 'Pine Tree' shilling, obverse (a) and reverse (b), and a shilling (c) of the same type after clipping, as well as a clipped piece (d).

(*Courtesy of the American Numismatic Society*)

A counterfeit twenty shilling North Carolina bill of the emission of 1735, perhaps one of those forged by Thomas Hamilton Scott.

(*In the collection of the American Antiquarian Society*)

A counterfeit ten shilling Connecticut bill of the emission of 1709, forged by Ebenezer Seamore.

*(Collection of Mr. Harley L. Freeman)*

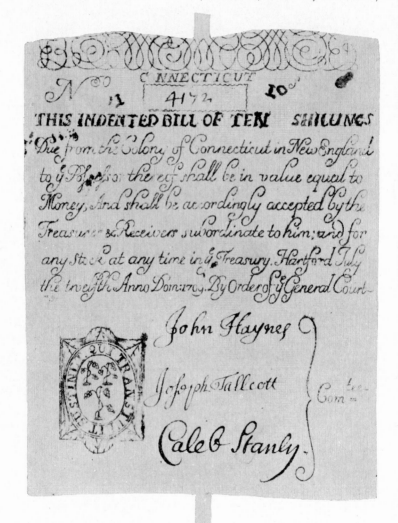

The hanging of Owen Sullivan in New York in 1756, from a woodcut which served as frontispiece to his autobiography printed that same year.
*(Courtesy of the American Antiquarian Society)*

A counterfeit forty shilling Rhode Island bill made by Owen Sullivan and passed by his confederate Joseph Steel.
*(Courtesy of the Connecticut State Library)*

A counterfeit fifteen shilling 'Crown Point' bill of New Hampshire. William Brown of Madbury was indicted for passing it but acquitted by a jury in 1761.

*(Courtesy of the New Hampshire Historical Society)*

The back of a counterfeit New Hampshire eight pound bill, unsigned, made by a mulatto, Caesar Trick, in 1754.

*(Courtesy of the Connecticut State Library)*

The notorious counterfeiter 'Dr.' Seth Hudson in the Boston pillory in 1762. His confederate Joshua Howe on the whipping post. He received seventy-eight lashes and Hudson eighty.

*(From an engraving made by Nathaniel Hurd in 1762 and now in the Boston Public Library)*

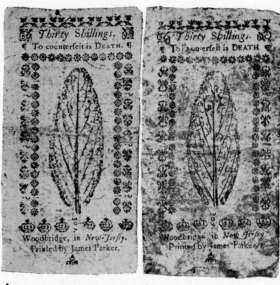

A     B

The back of a genuine thirty shilling New Jersey bill (a) and a counterfeit (b) of the same with part of the stem of the sage leaf wanting.

*(Courtesy of J. N. Spiro)*

The punishment on the pillory of Charlestown in 1768 of one of three coiners. All three had their cropped-off ears sewed on again in a vain attempt to save them.

*(From an engraving by I. Thomas on a broadside in the Historical Society of Pennsylvania)*

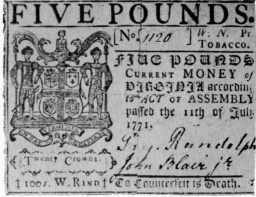

'Tis Death to Counterfeit' on a genuine three pound New York bill.
*(Courtesy of the American Numismatic Society)*

'To Counterfeit is Death' on a counterfeit Virginia bill.
*(Collection of F. C. C. Boyd)*

'Counterfeiters Beware' on a counterfeit twenty shilling North Carolina bill.
*(Collection of Eric P. Newman)*

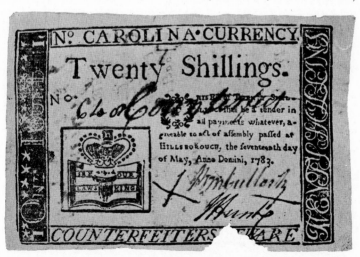

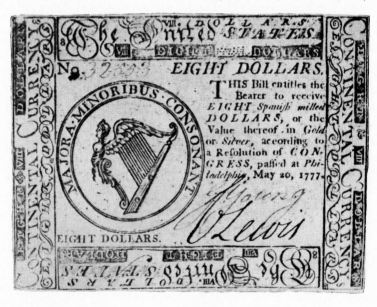

**ADVERTISEMENT.**

Persons, going into the other Colonies, may be supplied with any Number of counterfeited Congress-Notes, for the Price of the Paper *per* Ream. They are so nearly and exactly executed, that there is no Risque in getting them off, it being almost impossible to discover, that they are not genuine. This has been proved by Bills to a very large Amount, which have already been successfully circulated. Enquire for Q. E. D. at the Coffee-House, from 11 P. M. to 4 A. M. during the present Month.

Just opened for Sale.

Advertisement in Hugh Gaine's *New York Gazette* in 1777 of counterfeit Continental currency for sale for the price of the paper per ream.
(*Courtesy of the New York Public Library*)

A British-sponsored counterfeit eight dollar Continental bill.
(*Collection of Eric P. Newman*)

The strangers desired immediate transportation to Sag Harbor on Long Island. Ashcraft took them across in his boat and landed them at their destination, for which service, as he maintained, he received from Dr. Wilson an eight pound Rhode Island bill. Later, however, after merciless questioning and without the benefit of any attorney, he broke down before the examining magistrate and wept, admitting that he had lied and confessing that in reality he had been given a ten pound ten shilling bill, apparently a counterfeit. He added the information that his two passengers went to South Hampton, where they attended meeting and spent the Sabbath at Zeb Howel's tavern.

A warrant for Ashcraft's arrest had been issued at New London on 5 May 1749, and he was apprehended at Groton on 8 May by Daniel Collins, a deputy sheriff of New London County, and examined by Justice Daniel Coit, who questioned the prisoner particularly about a letter addressed to Mr. Willet Larabe living in Norwich Long Society. Collins had found it in Ashcraft's possession, and Ashcraft explained that it had been given to him by 'Wilson.' Justice Coit came to the conclusion that the prisoner had concealed, nourished, and conveyed away counterfeiters and, further, that on Long Island he had passed a false ten pound ten shilling bill to Nathan Fordham. The magistrate therefore bound over Ashcraft to the next superior court to be held in September 1750, and the prisoner was released on bail of £1,000. The case was continued to March 1751, when Ashcraft was charged with aiding in counterfeiting bills. Fortunately for him, the one thing which could be proved against him and to which he had confessed was the passing of the false bill. This offense, however, had been committed on Long Island and so was not actionable in Connecticut. No one appeared to prosecute him and he was freed by proclamation on payment of costs.

The court records do not explain the content of the letter addressed to Willet Larabe and delivered to Ashcraft by Joseph Bill nor do they indicate why Justice Coit questioned his prisoner about the document. It seems, however, safe to assume that there was some message about counterfeiting and that Larabe was one of Bill's gang or at least in the same business, for early in November 1751, Willet Larabe was convicted at the superior court of King's County, Rhode Island, for passing several counterfeit twenty shilling new tenor bills of New Hampshire. He was sentenced to stand in the pillory for half an hour, to have both ears cropped, to be branded with R on each cheek with a hot iron, to be imprisoned for one month, to pay double damages to the persons injured by his counterfeit bills and the costs of prosecution, and to forfeit the remainder of his estate, both real and personal, for the use of the colony. The corporal punishment was executed at South Kingston on 7 November.

For a time Jones and Bill appeared to have dropped out of sight. Then, late in July 1751, Jonathan Woodman of Narragansett was arrested in New York City and committed to jail for putting off counterfeit twenty shilling bills of New York of the emission of 10 December 1737. The counterfeits were done from copperplate instead of printing types, the two X's near the arms were unequal in size, and a point was left between N and YORK, while the word EBORAC in the arms was spelled EBORAO. Woodman admitted that he had passed ten such bills and that he had two accomplices, one of whom was going by the name of Dr. Dustin, whom he believed to be the signer of the bills.

Woodman also had on his person some false four pound bills of New Hampshire which he had obtained from Dustin. The other accomplice he knew only through hearing of him from Dustin.

Within a few days, however, the mysterious second accomplice was captured by Robert Benson and Abraham Mills and turned out to be none other than Joseph Bill, who was confined in jail with Woodman. The three counterfeiters were indicted by a grand jury but did not come to trial. It seems that from the moment of his commitment Woodman apprehended he must die and for some time he was in terror and anguish of mind. Finally, one Friday morning early in September, he was found hanging dead in his garters at the grate of his prison. Bill was jubilant at the death of his accomplice; he boasted that now, since through Woodman's death there was no material evidence against him, he would get clear, as proved to be the case.

Dr. Dustin took a somewhat impetuous course from New York in the direction of Haverhill, Massachusetts, and on his way through Connecticut passed a quantity of counterfeit four pound bills of New Hampshire and twenty shilling bills of New York. He was described as a tall, slim man, wearing red plush breeches and a black wig. He went beyond Haverhill and entered New Hampshire, where he was taken up and in October tried at a superior court of judicature in Portsmouth. He was acquitted by the jury, which was surprising inasmuch as the story of his association with Bill and Woodman and of his flight had appeared in the New York and Boston newspapers and must have been known. His acquittal was attributed to indifference on the part of the people of New Hampshire.

The counterfeiting physician of Haverhill, whose name

appears as Dustin, Dunston, or Dunsten, by no means gave up his wicked ways. Indeed the Connecticut authorities had a reminder of him when in December 1752 they arrested John George of Hampton, New Hampshire, alias George Kimball of Newbury. George had passed three counterfeit twenty shilling New Hampshire bills to Captain John Payson of Woodstock, who, discovering them to be counterfeit, had the passer arrested. George admitted he knew the bills were false and confessed that he had received the money from Dr. Sam 'Dunsten' at Haverhill. Soon after George twice broke out of the jail of Windham County and the second time eluded the pursuit of Sheriff Fitch.

During the winter of 1754–5 Dustin was active in New Hampshire with Owen Sullivan and a large band of New Hampshire counterfeiters, one of whom was Robert Rogers of Rogers' Rangers fame. Early in February 1755 a grand jury in Portsmouth found a true bill against Dustin for having passed twenty false New Hampshire notes of 40s. each to Samuel Gordon at Salem, New Hampshire. The elusive physician, however, was beyond the reach of the New Hampshire authorities, for he had found it expedient to betake himself to Woodstock, Connecticut, where, doubtless with plates cut by Sullivan, he manufactured a considerable quantity of Rhode Island and New Hampshire bills. Somehow Captain Payson discovered what was afoot, complained to Justice Bowen, and had the Haverhill doctor taken into custody. Dustin was indicted, tried, and convicted, but on the night of 10 April 1755, together with an accomplice named David Adams, alias Timothy Green, he broke jail and fled to parts unknown. Eventually he returned to New Hampshire and died at Plaistow in that province on 11 September 1760, leaving behind a widow named Ruth.

Passers of Bill's paper currency were numerous, and, as has been stated above, his activities in co-operation with Jones came to light through the detection of some of the band by Justice John Bulkley in February 1749. Amos and Timothy Fuller of Lebanon, Samuel Ingham, Aaron Wilcox, David Wilcox, Jr., three men of Hebron, and probably Alpheus Wickwire of Norwich belonged to the gang. David Wilcox, Jr., had at his examination made a clean breast of the matter and by turning king's evidence had escaped prosecution. One of his friends, Samuel Ingham, had shared a room with David at the home of Mr. and Mrs. Benjamin Gale. In a chest in her lodgers' room Mrs. Gale discovered a letter, read it, and to her surprise found that its contents indicated that Ingham was passing counterfeit money. Ingham was apprehended and examined at Colchester by Mr. Bulkley, assistant, on 7 March 1749. It became clear that Ingham had received from David Wilcox, Jr., a counterfeit three pound Connecticut bill and passed it off to a Mr. White at Killingworth, and passed a similar note to one Rossiter of the same town, while Mr. Gale had also received false bills from him. Jonathan Factor of Branford secured one of the bills from Gale and sent it to Captain Edmund Ward of Guilford, who turned it over to Samuel Lynde, assistant. If Gale would be willing to swear the bill on Ingham, it seemed that Ingham could be convicted, but Gale, very likely out of friendship for the accused, refused to take this step. As a result, when Ingham was indicted as a passer at the superior court held at Norwich on 28 March 1749, he was tried and acquitted, being released on payment of fees amounting to some £43.

Aaron Wilcox was less fortunate. On 2 March 1749, Asael Phelps and William Sumner complained to Justice Joseph Phelps of Hebron that Aaron Wilcox had uttered counterfeit bills, so the justice issued a warrant for his arrest. Wilcox was taken into custody on 30 March and was examined on the next day and again on 3 April. At first he maintained that he did not know where he had obtained the false three pound bill but later conceded that he had received it from Elias Wilcox in exchange for a deerskin. Finally he confessed that he had passed another of the counterfeit three pound notes to John Alden in Lebanon. When asked if he had ever seen Joseph Collins (apparently known to be a counterfeiter) at his father's house, he denied it, but questioning brought out the fact that he had seen Joseph Bill both at his father's home and in the woods. After these admissions it is not surprising that he was bound over to the superior court to be held in September and was then released on bail of £500, furnished by himself and David Wilcox. At the court he was indicted for having at Hebron in January 1749 passed to Thomas Fuller of Coventry a counterfeit three pound new tenor bill of the Connecticut emission of 8 May 1746. He pleaded not guilty but was convicted and sentenced in accordance with the law of 1724.

From the Hartford jail in October, 1749, Aaron Wilcox sent to the Assembly a petition in which he lamented his idleness in prison and his subjection to 'pinching hunger' and 'chilling cold' and begged for his release. His request was granted on condition that he pay all costs of prosecution and jail charges, secure a bond of £500 for his good behavior for life, and live within the town limits of Hebron and there conduct all lawful business. On 10 May of the next year he again sent a memorial to the legislators, whom he informed that his father had sold his land in Hebron and purchased an estate in Harwinton. He requested leave to move there, and this was granted him on condition that he be restricted to the limits of that town. Four years later, when, doubtless encouraged by his previous success, he besought the Assembly to remove all restrictions laid upon him, his plea was denied.

The two Fullers were indicted by the grand jury at the superior court held at Windham in March 1749, Timothy for having on 23 December 1748 passed a counterfeit ten shilling Massachusetts bill, new tenor, to Samuel Dewey of Lebanon, and Amos for having helped make three three pound new tenor bills of Connecticut of the emission of 1746. Both pleaded not guilty, and Timothy, indeed, was acquitted on payment of some £35 in costs. It was quite a different story with Amos, for he had been passing false New Jersey money in that province under the name of Jeremiah Carpenter and had broken out of the Burlington jail and escaped on 17 September 1747, though the Connecticut authorities do not seem to have known of Amos's escapade in the Jerseys. There was now no doubt of his wrongdoing, for Thomas Hubbard, who was active in Boston in having Bryant arrested and a search made for Jones and Bill, wrote to Colonel Trumbull that Amos had been 'sadly guilty' and that Bryant stated he received the false paper money found in his possession from Fuller and one Clarke — doubtless Abel Clark of Waterbury, who had escaped from the Hartford jail in company with Joseph Bill. This time justice was done, and Amos Fuller was convicted and sentenced according to the severe law of 1724.

It was not often that the sentence of imprisonment for life was actually carried out, so Amos Fuller, like most counterfeiters convicted before him, petitioned the Assembly in October 1749 for his release, stating that he was willing to give valuable evidence against the money makers if he were liberated. The legislators granted his request on condition that he pay all costs and charges, find sureties in the amount of £500 for his good behavior, and remain within the limits of the town of Lebanon. Eight years later he again memorialized the Assembly, requesting that his full rights of freeman be restored to him in order that he might recover by process of law some debts owed him before his conviction, but the legislators turned a deaf ear to his plea.

On 4 April 1749 John Smith, a justice of the peace of Voluntown, issued his warrant for the arrest of Alpheus Wickwire, who was taken up the next day by Constable Joseph Tracy, Jr., and immediately examined in Norwich by Hezekiah Huntington, assistant, on suspicion of being a counterfeiter and passer of the bills of Connecticut and other colonies. The prisoner was evasive in his replies and on point after point he claimed to have forgotten. It became clear that he had ridden from Providence to Voluntown in company with a woman to whom he had spoken freely about counterfeiting and his own part in such activities. He admitted that at the end of December 1748 one 'Carpendor,' obviously Carpenter, had been at his home and that he, Wickwire, had had in his possession a ten pound ten shilling bill. Seemingly the justice of the peace did not know who Carpenter was, but there can be little doubt that it was Amos Fuller, who had been using that name while passing false money in New Jersey. On his first and subsequent examinations it seemed that Wickwire was guilty, so on 8 April he was bound over to appear at the superior court to be held in New London in September and was then released on bail of £1,000, provided by himself, Urian Hosmond, and Ebenezer Barstow. There appears to be no record of his prosecution.

It will be recalled that John Thompson of Hebron, encouraged by Jonathan Trumbull and Joseph Fowler, had gone to Boston in the interests of Connecticut to inform the Massachusetts authorities of the operations of Bill, Jones, and their gang. Unhappily the Assembly was far from open-handed — and as a rule such was the case with other legislatures — so that he was grudgingly and meagerly compensated for his time, trouble, and expense. When the first sum awarded him did not satisfy him, he petitioned for a further amount; in October 1750 he was voted £20 and again, in May 1751, a second £20.

# Chapter 10

## OWEN SULLIVAN AND THE DOVER MONEY CLUB

THROUGH the enterprise of Robert Clarke and the co-operation of the Connecticut authorities the nest of money makers in the Oblong, while not destroyed, had been temporarily restricted in its operations. It was presently to be revived on a vaster scale by the able leadership of Owen Sullivan. This individual is first heard of in Louisbourg, where he was convicted of passing counterfeit dollars. It was indeed in all probability this contretemps which induced him to remove to Boston, either in 1748 or early in 1749, where he carried on the goldsmith's business and attracted attention by being always flush with money, though he lived in an expensive manner and beyond his visible income.

He might have gone on in this way for some time, had he not on one occasion had a difference with his wife, who, having drunk somewhat too freely, called him the forty thousand pound money maker. As the remark was overheard and other evidence was gathered against him, toward the end of August 1749 he and John Tyas of Roxbury were arrested and committed to the jail in Boston. They were suspected of passing false ten shilling Massachusetts bills of the last emission, more than thirty of which were found on them. The bad notes were too black and could be easily distinguished by a comparison with the back of a genuine bill. A search of Sullivan's chest yielded a mold for casting dollars, ink, and other things used for printing from copperplate and pieces of paper on which attempts had been made to imitate the handwriting of the signers of the Massachusetts bills of credit.

While confined in jail in Boston Sullivan used his enforced leisure to cut a plate for counterfeiting forty shilling New Hampshire bills. In some manner he got in touch with John Fairservice of Boston, who, in return for the plate, promised to secure Sullivan's freedom and to find a way to get him exempt from trainband service. The deal was concluded, and, with the plate in question, Fairservice set up his own mint in a barn on Bull Wharf in Boston. The business came to light when Thomas Wilson, master of a sloop, was caught passing some of the bills. Wilson confessed that he had the currency from Fairservice on the understanding that he was to keep half the profits gained from putting it off and told how Fairservice obtained the plate and was keeping it under a sled in the barn on Bull Wharf.

Sullivan obtained sureties for a very large sum, was released on bail, and, along with Tyas, was indicted at a court of assize held in Boston on Friday, 7 September 1750. Tyas was presented by the grand jury for passing, while two indictments were found against Sullivan, one for making bills and the other for concealing some of them with an intent to pass them, on both of which he was tried and convicted. The next day the court sentenced Tyas, who had pleaded guilty, to stand in the pillory one hour and receive fifteen stripes and Sullivan to be pilloried for two hours and to be given twenty lashes. The corporal punishment was inflicted on Thursday, 13 September.

After this unpleasant experience in the pillory Sullivan judged it expedient to move to Providence, Rhode Island, where he set up again in the same nefarious business with a number of accomplices. He did an excellent job of imitating the sixteen pound Rhode Island bills of the latest emission, but in August 1752 suspicion fell upon the gang and all members were arrested. Sullivan, who had acquired considerable experience with courts, juries, and the laws which applied to counterfeiting, strenuously pressed his accomplices to declare that whatever money they had received of him they had considered genuine and passed as such. He assured them that if they followed his directions he would bring them all off clear. One man, Nicholas Stephens, alone, thinking to turn king's evidence, confessed that he had passed the currency he had received from Sullivan in the knowledge that it was counterfeit. Since his evidence did not convict any of the rest, it was taken only against himself and Sullivan, who were tried, convicted, and sentenced each to have his ears cropped, to be branded on each cheek with R, and to be imprisoned.

The corporal punishment was inflicted about the beginning of October but in a quite scandalous fashion. Sullivan, who was described by a contemporary journalist as a man of good address, managed to prejudice the populace in his favor and got his punishment inflicted in such a manner that it did no injury to his person, probably meaning that the brand mark was placed in the hair and just a small piece snipped from each ear. Further, although by his sentence he was to remain a prisoner, he nevertheless obtained liberty to be present when sentence was to be excuted upon his accomplice, saying that he would see it was effectually done as a punishment for the man's folly and perfidy. Accordingly, since he was but slightly guarded, he broke from his keepers, seized a cutlass, went into the ring, and encouraged the executioner to do his duty with rigor. When this was done, Sullivan fought his way through the crowd, escaped, and eluded the pursuit made after him. A few days later, however, he surrendered, boasting that he was doing voluntarily what they could not force him to do, but within a matter of days he broke jail and escaped, sword in hand, and removed to Dutchess County, New York, where he provided himself with a secret retreat. There he gathered a set of accomplices for vending the bills made by him and supplying necessaries, conveniences, and correspondents for putting the business upon a regular footing, that they all might live comfortably from it. As he was an excellent engraver, he counterfeited the currency of almost all the neighboring governments so masterfully that even the best judges could hardly tell his imitations from the true bills. For some time he carried on the business with great success, vending large sums and receiving in return true money, bonds, or other valuable effects. As his exploits were gradually forgotten he ventured to travel about and once even to return to Rhode Island.

The center of the gang, which was known as 'the Dover Money Club,' was in Dover, New York, and there most of the villains had a crop or brand mark upon them, as it was a kind of disgrace for one reputed honest to be seen among them. All the rogues, in all probability, were never revealed, but it is possible to give a partial account of Sullivan's activities and of those of some of his associates. One such confederate was almost certainly Benjamin Force, who in 1741 had been involved in counterfeiting in Rhode Island with Israel Phillips, Henry Bosworth, the Boyces, and others, and who, like the Boyces and Bosworth, had gone to Dutchess County, New York, when things became too hot for him in Rhode Island. In November 1752, not long after Sullivan had taken refuge in Dover, Force, described as a resident of Dover, was arrested in Sharon, Connecticut, on a warrant issued by Justice John Williams of that town, for having passed a false three pound Rhode Island bill to Samuel Elmer. At first Force proclaimed his innocence but soon changed his mind and expressed a desire to be accepted as a witness for the crown against several persons. In May 1753 he testified at Poughkeepsie against some suspected counterfeiters, and on 12 June Justice Williams wrote of this matter to Samuel Pettibone, the king's attorney, and informed him that two of the individuals, Captain Joseph Boyce and Joseph Hicks, had been indicted, while he concluded his letter with the hope that the 'Club' might be broken up.

Sullivan's hand in the production of bogus Rhode Island currency did not escape notice, for on 8 June 1753, on the evidence of Samuel Southworth, a grand jury in New York indicted Benjamin Chase, Jacob Mace, and Sullivan, alias James Shiffel or Benjamin Parlon, for stamping Rhode Island bills and forging the signers' hands. Sullivan, however, was not taken and the other two were not prosecuted. Mace, a blacksmith, in fact slipped over into Connecticut, where about the middle of August he was actively passing off some of Sullivan's four pound Rhode Island counterfeits in Woodstock, with the aid of two accomplices, John Cogswell, a yeoman, and Jacob Wiley, a trader, both of that town. Their doings came to the attention of Henry Bowen, a local justice of the peace, and the rogues were taken up by Constable Daniel Child and Deputy Sheriff John Chamberlain and indicted at the superior court held at Windham in September, when Mace was tried, convicted, and sentenced and the other two bound over to the December term of the court. But Wiley, who was released on bail, forfeited his bond and joined the band of counterfeiters led by David Sanford in Ridgefield.

Cogswell, who was at liberty on bail of £100, ran into immediate difficulty. In June, while in Rhode Island, he had passed to George Gardner seven false sixteen pound Rhode Island bills. As a result a hue and cry after him was proclaimed by the authorities of that colony and he was seized in Connecticut, carried off to Newport, and there tried and convicted. When the superior court met in Windham in December, as he was then safely locked up in the jail in Newport, he naturally did not appear when called, so his bond was declared forfeited. In May 1754, at length released by Rhode Island and back in Connecticut, he petitioned the Assembly in vain for relief from paying his forfeited bond.

The authorities had no occasion to forget about Sullivan, for he was constantly getting others in hot water. By November 1753, three more of his associates, William Shapley, Jedediah Cady, and Jeremiah Lisha, an Indian, all of Killingly, Connecticut, were in the toils of the law. Shapley, on a complaint lodged with Justice William Chandler, had been arrested for being involved in counterfeiting or passing four pound bills of New Hampshire and eight pound bills of Rhode Island, while the same justice had also caused the arrest of Cady. Justice Henry Bowen of Woodstock, who had examined Mace, Wiley, and Cogswell, sent the information to Chandler which brought about Cady's apprehension, so Bowen had doubtless learned about Cady from one of the three when they were questioned. Lisha's behavior caused Constable Hezekiah Cutler to denounce him to Justice Joseph Cady, who had the Indian taken into custody on a charge of aiding Jedediah

Cady in passing false Rhode Island currency of the emission of 1750.

Shapley was apparently completely innocent, for it came out that he had obtained twelve dollars and £150 in paper money from William Carpenter of New Salem, of which he passed two eight pound Rhode Island bills to Widow Joannah Utter of Killingly but in the sincere belief that they were genuine. He was tried at the superior court in Windham on 25 December 1753, acquitted, and released on payment of some £17 in costs.

Jedediah Cady, however, had been recruited into the Dover Money Club by Sullivan, probably because Cady's house was remote from travel and distant from neighbors and therefore convenient for counterfeiting. Cady, in July 1753, had permitted Sullivan, Captain Cogswell, Jacob Wiley, and one Bacon to use the chamber in his home for striking a great number of Rhode Island four pound bills of the emission of 1750. When the printing was finished, Sullivan gave Cady about £400 of the money, which Cady put in a box and then buried in the ground. Later, or so he said, he took the box out and burned all the currency. Lisha, the Indian, on the other hand, related that Cady had given him £128 in counterfeits to pass, with the understanding that he was to keep half the profits. Although he had admitted his guilt upon his examination, Cady nevertheless pleaded not guilty. He was tried, convicted, and sentenced in accordance with law. An order was issued on 2 January 1754 that before the end of that month he was to be cropped, branded with C, sent to the workhouse, and deprived of all his estate. On 7 January Sheriff Fitch carried out the cropping and branding but reported that he could discover no estate. Cady, on 8 May 1754, sent from jail a petition to the Assembly along with a testimonial, signed by a considerable number of fellow townsmen, concerning his good care of his aged father and mother and his fine reputation before he was drawn into the counterfeiting scheme. The legislators decided to release Cady, who was then about thirty years of age, on condition that he pay all costs of prosecution and find surety in the amount of £50 for his good behavior for life and the peaceable surrender of his body to the sheriff if required. Further, he was required to go to Killingly and reside within the limits of the town, where he was free to carry on all lawful business.

Lisha, the Indian, who claimed he had obtained £128 in counterfeits to pass, told how he had uttered it at Smithfield, Narragansett, and elsewhere, giving the names of the persons to whom he had paid the bills. These individuals, however, denied ever having changed any money with Lisha, so it appeared that he had given free rein to his imagination. Apparently the king's attorney was of this opinion, for he decided that there was not sufficient evidence against the prisoner, so that the court ordered the release of the Indian if he would pay costs of £6.5s. Lisha, unhappily, had no money at all, so he offered to go into service to pay the costs. It was then finally agreed that he should work for two years for Eliphalet Dyer, Nathaniel Wales, and Isaac Warner, all of Windham, in return for which they paid his costs.

Another of Sullivan's agents was John Clark, alias Stoddard, a mason of Stratford, Connecticut, who in September 1753 went to Dover, New York, ostensibly to work at his trade. Before long, however, he was back in Stratford with a large quantity of counterfeit eight pound Rhode Island bills which he had obtained from the Money Club in Dover. He quickly secured as a passer Benjamin Beardslee, son of Josiah Beardslee, left eight counterfeit notes with him, and then went off again to Dover to get another parcel of currency. During Clark's absence Beardslee was assailed with qualms and hastened to buy back the four bills he had passed and then to burn all eight. When Clark returned and found that Benjamin would take no more of the money, he promptly found two new accomplices in John Beardslee and Israel Beardslee, 2nd.

Before long Constable Ebenezer Hinman somehow learned what was afoot, complained to Justice Samuel Adams, and brought about the arrest of Clark and Israel and Benjamin Beardslee. In Clark's pocket were found twenty-six counterfeit eight pound bills of the Rhode Island emission of 2 February 1741, and he was indicted for passing at the superior court held in Fairfield. In the light of the evidence against him he decided to plead guilty and was cropped, branded, and returned to jail, from which, however, he soon broke out and escaped. His position was, indeed, difficult for a number of reasons: counterfeiters soon approached him but he both refused to join them and also gave information against them; because of this he was exposed to the hatred and malice of the counterfeiters, while at the same time he was under sentence of imprisonment for life and subject to arrest at any moment; he was tormented with anxiety concerning the future of his wife and two small children. In these circumstances he petitioned the Assembly in October 1754 to give him liberty to go about his lawful business, a request which was warmly seconded by Justice Adams, who pointed out that of late Clark had been co-operative and of good conduct. The legislators lent a receptive ear and granted his request with the proviso that he remain within the limits of Stratford and on the understanding that if he left the bounds of that town his privileges would be forfeited.

Benjamin Beardslee, who was released by Justice Adams as innocent, some three or four weeks later returned to the magistrate and made a clean breast of the business, implicating John Beardslee, who, until then, had not even been suspected. Benjamin was released on bail of £50 and expected, on the basis of encouragement given him by Justice Adams, to be admitted as a witness for the crown, a prospect which evaporated when Clark pleaded guilty and John Beardslee, who had been released on bail of £50, forfeited his bond. Benjamin therefore feared to appear in court, so his bond too was declared forfeit. In May 1755 he appealed in vain to the Assembly to be released from the bond but a year later that body ordered the sum reduced from £50 to £25, if he would pay that amount and all costs to Robert Walker, the king's attorney for Fairfield County.

Israel Beardslee was released on bail of £300 furnished by himself, his father Josiah, and his brother Benjamin. He should have appeared to stand trial but was dissuaded by friend and relatives, including his father-in-law, Samuel French of Stratford, to whom he had passed two of the false bills. The amount of the bond which was forfeited was ruinous to him and his sureties, but in May 1755 he managed to persuade the Assembly to chancer the bond down to £50.

The Money Club in Dover had an extensive chain of passers and agents in both Connecticut and Rhode Island, as well as in Dutchess County, as became more and more apparent to the governments of the three colonies. On 16 January 1754, Thomas Hugford of Greenwich, Connecticut, was arrested by Deputy Sheriff Ephraim Jackson on a writ issued by Justice Platt and charged with helping Sullivan to strike off forty shilling New York counterfeits. The grand jury, however, did not find a true bill against him but the incident again called public attention to Sullivan's activity, as did the arrest and conviction in March of two Connecticut men named Averell and Coggshall, who were charged in Newport with passing Sullivan's forged sixteen pound bills.

But far more irritating to the authorities was the behavior of a band which was apparently a subsidiary of the Dover Money Club and which was led by David Sanford of Salem in the Oblong. This wretch, in the autumn of 1753, kept in his house both Owen Sullivan and Nathaniel Nichols of Woodstock and together they counterfeited the bills of New York and Rhode Island and Spanish dollars. Later Sanford built up his own gang, which included, among others, one of his sons, Joseph Nichols, and Jacob Wiley, who, it will be recalled, had skipped bail rather than stand trial for counterfeiting. Nichols, who was a resident of Ridgefield, had also been taken into custody about the middle of February 1754 on suspicion of counterfeiting. Justice Samuel Olmstead, who examined him, could not find sufficient evidence to bind him over to the superior court and ordered him released on payment of costs, which, however, were considerable. For failure to pay them Nichols was committed to jail in Fairfield but he soon broke out and fled to Sanford and his accomplices.

It chanced that Sanford himself was in Waterbury on 25 January 1754, where he put in a busy day by passing off ten counterfeit New York bills, nine of the twenty shilling and one of the forty shilling denomination. The following day one of his victims, Joseph Hopkins, complained to

Justice Thomas Clark, who issued a warrant and sent out officers in search of the passer. Sanford, who had no idea that trouble was in the making, set out from Waterbury on 25 January for Woodbury and on the way chatted most indiscreetly with two other travelers, Barnabas Merwin of Wallingford and Elisha Hall, Jr., of South Kingston, Rhode Island. Among other things he told them that unless he could change a New York twenty shilling bill he could neither eat nor drink. When they arrived that evening at the tavern of Isaac Brounson, Sanford pretended to be intoxicated and tried to induce the landlady to change the bill, which she refused to do. Another patron, however, James Lewis of Bateman's Patent, finally obliged. Then, as the travelers proceeded on their way, Sanford, who probably had imbibed more flip than was good for him, boasted of being well acquainted with Jacob Mace and of knowing where plates for counterfeiting were to be found. At this Merwin and Hall bluntly informed him that they suspected he was putting off counterfeits but he bade them say nothing and go with him, for he would make them gentlemen and put a thousand pounds in their pockets. Finally, when they approached Hurd's tavern, he told them that he was going to pass more bad money and offered to bear their expenses but threatened to kill them if they exposed him.

On 26 January the officers of the law overtook Sanford and brought him before Justice Clark in Waterbury, to whom he freely admitted his association with Sullivan and Nathaniel Nichols. He was committed to jail, indicted at the superior court held at New Haven on 26 February, tried, convicted, and sentenced, but managed to break out and escape, vowing vengeance on those who had had him imprisoned. About the end of April Sanford and his band incensed the government by further misdeeds. They planned to recover by force some neat cattle which had been attached for debt but the officer in charge of the animals posted a guard of twenty men and the attempt of the desperados came to naught. The same night the villains, enraged at being foiled, set fire to a barn where the cattle were being kept under lock and key but this attempt also failed, as a guard saw them in time and frighted them off by discharging his musket at them. Thereupon they immediately set fire to some fences in a neighboring field, and a high wind fanned the flames. While the people were trying to quench them, Sanford and his followers set new fires on the other side of the field. A week later, at dead of night, the counterfeiters went to the parish of Wilton to the house of Mr. Deforest, who had the attached cattle in his keeping, cut the tongue out of one of the cows and in the vicinity of the house set a brisk fire, which, had it not been discovered in the nick of time, would have consumed the house and barn and probably the people in the house.

But this was not the end of the trouble. One of Sanford's followers, Joseph Nichols, who had been prosecuted for counterfeiting, had been recently convicted of forgery. Now he went to the house which he had acquired through a forged deed and, looking in at the window, saw his daughter Abigail, who was busy weaving, and asked her why she stayed there. When she replied that it was in order to finish the cloth, he told her that she would pay for it if she did, for he, Sanford, and Jacob Wiley would burn or destroy the house that night. He then ordered her to give him all the shot in the house and, when she would not at first comply, he pointed a pistol at her and forced her to do his bidding, warning her, moreover, that he would certainly kill her if she told of his design. The poor girl was terrified but finally ventured to tell a woman in the neighborhood, and she promptly made all known, so that a watch was set. Probably measures were also taken to guard the dwelling of Samuel Olmstead, for Nichols had likewise informed Abigail that he planned to burn the house of Olmstead, the justice of the peace who had prosecuted him. When night arrived, the guards at Nichols's former dwelling saw Sanford's dog and suspected that the criminals were near. In this they were not mistaken, for presently fires broke out at some distance from the house and did considerable damage before they could be extinguished.

Soon after this Sanford showed one man four pistols which he carried and swore that he would be the death of the first man who should venture to lay hands on him. Regardless of this bravado, a number of young men of Ridgefield, with the aid of the constable of Salem, captured Sanford without any bloodshed, and their prisoner was remanded to the New Haven jail. On his way to this prison, from which he had already made one escape, he 'spoke terrible words in defiance of all the goals [sic] in the colony.'

The good citizens of Ridgefield and Norwalk, provoked by these outrages, petitioned the Connecticut Assembly for relief, pointing out that the desperate fellows went about armed in defiance of all law and government. Further, the damage caused by fires set by Sanford's gang was computed to exceed £4,000, while the loss of time and labor of people keeping watch and working to save their property in this time of drought was estimated at £100 a day. The memorialists prayed that Sanford might be kept secure in jail, for if he escaped again he would be more dangerous than before. They likewise besought the legislators to take measures to effect the arrest, which would doubtless be accomplished only with bloodshed, of the rest of the gang, all of whom were distressing people by setting fires and lurking armed about the borders of Ridgefield.

In keeping with a report brought in by a committee of the Assembly appointed to study the situation, the Assembly, in May 1754, ordered the king's attorney to see to it that Nichols and the others in the gang were taken, that the officers of all counties help him, and that he secure as much assistance as was needed. Finally the legislators went on record in commendation of Abigail Nichols for her prudent and good conduct and just attachment to public virtue and the common good 'in Disclosing the wicked Design of certain convicted Desperados and Banditti.' They expressed the realization of the danger she was in of becoming 'a Victim to the merciless Rage of those detestable Miscreants' and recommended her to the special care and protection of the civil authority and the charitable compassion of all true lovers of their country.

In spite of the arrest of some of its agents the Dover Money Club continued to flood Connecticut and Rhode Island with bogus currency manufactured from Sullivan's plates. Connecticut suffered especially and the number of passers detected there must have made the government extremely uneasy. Probably the majority of the scoundrels escaped undiscovered but those apprehended were numerous enough. In August 1754 Jehiel Murray of Merryall was convicted in Litchfield County of passing false Rhode Island bills; David Owen, Jr., of New Milford, a lad of about twenty-one, was found guilty of the same offense and managed to get Samuel Cogswell into trouble by persuading him to cast half and quarter pieces of eight from pewter, a misdeed which was punished with thirty-nine lashes on the bare back; Samuel Little of Litchfield was committed for passing counterfeit Rhode Island money but forfeited his bail bond, and Nathan Knap of Reading did the same when charged with the like offense; in July 1755 Amos Tyler of Sharon was taken up for passing the same bad Rhode Island bills and he too forfeited his bond, though he managed to persuade the Assembly to have it chancered down because he sought day and night to find the 'wicked man' who led him into passing; other passers of the Rhode Island counterfeits were David Ensign of New Hartford, who was convicted, Hugh Gillespy and Eliphalet Stephens, who were taken up at Middletown, tried, and convicted, William Hamilton of Dutchess County, New York, who was arrested at Fairfield but apparently broke jail, William Robinson of Killingly, who was taken and convicted, and George Brown, alias Anderson, who was pursued and captured in a cornfield at Voluntown but was released because he had had the time and foresight to destroy the evidence. In July 1755 Joseph Avery of Norwich, who was a man of considerable means, came home after a trip to Dover, New York, in the company of a certain Cocker and well supplied with counterfeits of Connecticut and probably of Rhode Island as well. Cocker fled to Rhode Island and Avery was released for want of sufficient evidence, though the next April he was again apprehended and this time convicted.

In the fall and winter of 1754 Sullivan spent some months in New Hampshire, where he managed to involve in his iniquitous business Robert Rogers, a blacksmith named Benjamin Winn, James McNeil, and a host of others. Winn printed at least £15,000 from Sullivan's plates, and the others put them into circulation. From the evidence of one of the gang it appears that Sullivan was seldom sober and that he had little use for his New Hampshire partners. On one occasion, while at the home of Ebenezer Martin, he said to some of the band: 'Damn you for a pack of fools. I never was concerned with such a pack of damned fools before.' Again, he complained bitterly that all Martin's callers were 'ministers and ministers' sons, squires and squires' sons.'

Sullivan himself can scarcely have been beloved. He was drunken, quarrelsome, and exacting. He boarded two months at the home of Benjamin Winn, whose wife confided to Ezekiel Greeley of Nottingham West that Sullivan was 'a very difficult man to board. He must have chicken or fresh meat every day.' Indeed, Mrs. Winn told Greeley, she would not board him a year for a thousand pounds or for all Nottingham.

In February, when Sullivan and Dustin were already out of the province, the authorities descended upon the gang and arrested a great number of them. The rogues were terrified, the redoubtable Captain Robert Rogers as much as any. When Undersheriff John Light seized Carty Gillman, that individual had on his person two false bills and a note from Rogers. Carty popped the note into his mouth and began to eat it, but Light retrieved it in time. It is addressed to 'Mr Cartee Gilman att Exeeter' and reads as follows: 'Gilman Sr. for gods sake do the work that you promised that you would do by no means fail or you will destroy me for ever for my Life Lays att your proodence now ons mor I adgure you by your maker to do it for why should such an onest Man be killed. Sr, I am asoured freend, [signed] Robert Rogers.'

The authorities in Rhode Island were fortunate enough to catch and convict at Newport about the end of August 1755 four passers, who admitted that their bills were made

from Sullivan's plates and that they had struck off about
£50,000 of them but had spoiled some £10,000 in the
signing. Peter Bours of Newport now wrote to Lieutenant
Governor De Lancey of New York that the General Assembly of Rhode Island had offered a reward of £400
for the capture of Sullivan, who was at a place called the
Oblong in New York and was apparently using the alias
of John Pierson.

In spite of this letter the government of New York seemingly took no action, and the misdeeds of the gang in Dover
might have continued for a long time, had it not been for
the initiative of Cornet Eliphalet Beacher of New Haven,
who, in the course of his private business, traveling back
and forth through the country, made some discoveries of
the villainous band near the western border of Connecticut.
Beacher laid his information before the Connecticut Assembly in January 1756, and that body voted its conviction that Sullivan — or Johnson, as he was also called —
was living at or near Dover in Dutchess County and there
counterfeiting money of Connecticut, New York, Rhode
Island, and New Hampshire with the aid of Elisha Morehouse, one Hunt, a brother of Ambrose Hunt, and other
individuals. It was further resolved that if Beacher should
undertake to arrest the rogues all reasonable charges
would be borne by Connecticut and he would further receive a reward as provided by law for each counterfeiter
that he should take and have convicted.

Beacher had already secured, on 29 December 1755, a
warrant signed by Chief Justice James De Lancey and two
other justices of the Supreme Court of Judicature of New
York. Armed with this and encouraged by the support of
the General Assembly of Connecticut, he seized Samuel
Griswold, who was living at Dover, and his accomplice,

Jacob Mace, and brought the suspected counterfeiters before Messrs. Haviland and Humphrey, justices of the peace
of Dutchess County. These gentlemen, according to
Beacher, were most unco-operative, for after examining
the prisoners on 10 and 11 February they made him give
recognizance to prosecute and refused to give him a warrant to take the two men to Connecticut. As Beacher at
the moment found it impracticable to bring the necessary
evidences before the justices, the prisoners were released
on bail of £50 each, while Beacher was required to pay all
costs of the examination.

All this was set forth by Beacher in a deposition taken
by Justice Hamlin, and the document was then read in
the Connecticut Assembly. Its members were impressed
by the want of encouragement and assistance on the part
of the civil authority in Dutchess County and therefore
requested the governor of Connecticut to write to Sir
Charles Hardy, the governor of New York, asking him 'to
give all such further & necessary authority & directions to
the said Eliphalet Beacher, or to other proper persons, as
may enable him or them to apprehend such Suspected persons & Secure them in the Government, or send them into
this, for Trial according as the Cases may appear to be
Cognizable by the Courts there or here.' The treasurer of
Connecticut was further instructed to pay Beacher some
£20 for the prosecuting of the suspects.

Beacher now set about his task with grim determination
and a corps of mounted assistants, to whom he promised
pay and a share in the rewards. He himself worked on the
case for ninety-five days, Eliphalet Beacher, Jr., for twenty-
seven, John Thomas for twenty, Howkiah Thompson for
fifteen, Captain Joseph Starr for sixteen, Daniel Starr for
eight, John Beacher for eighteen, Caleb Beacher for six,

Eleazar Berry for six, Gabriel Dickinson for fifteen, John Dickson for eighteen, and Timothy Delivan for twenty-four. The costs, for which he was reimbursed by Connecticut, came to £134.3s.

In the course of 1755 a brisk trade had been carried on with Sullivan's currency, especially among the soldiers, who, not suspecting it, took it instead of or in exchange for true money. Beacher had been active in the discovery of some of the gang and had come to suspect that two tavern keepers, Hunt and Morehouse, belonged to the band. He now went to one of them and, taking occasion to change some money with him, received a counterfeit note as part of the change. He charged the tavern keeper with the fraud, but this individual at first denied that the bill was counterfeit and then denied that he knew it was bad, seeking, however, to give other money to get it back. But Beacher carried him off to a magistrate, who soon extracted from the tavern keeper a confession, by which some of his accomplices and many of the proceedings of the Money Club were revealed. Most important of all the frightened prisoner disclosed the place of Sullivan's retreat.

By now Beacher had seized several suspects and, taking one of them as a guide, he first was led to a swamp in a large, unfrequented wood, where in the side of a small cliff of the hill, made by the stream, his guide removed some brush and the stump of a tree which very artfully concealed the mouth of a cave. Beacher and his company entered the cave and found that it led by a long, narrow passage into a large, handsome room, cased round with planks and provided with many conveniencies for lodging, sitting, and eating, while light was admitted by a window cut from another part of the hill.

Sullivan, however, was not to be found, for, hearing that

some of his accomplices had been taken and expecting that they would betray him, he abandoned his hiding place and fled to the mountains, where he lay concealed from Saturday, 6 March, to Friday, 12 March. Then, compelled by hunger, he ventured to a house where he was acquainted and where he hoped they would be willing to conceal him. In the meantime Mr. Beacher, who was searching every house that he found reason to suspect, arrived just before one o'clock on Saturday morning at the dwelling where Sullivan was hiding. The inmates vehemently denied any knowledge of the fugitive and a careful investigation failed to reveal him. One of Beacher's men, as it chanced, found some dirt which seemed to be newly removed, and this led to a more diligent search. They removed a woman, bed and all, and under the bed discovered a plank which was cut in two and not nailed down. When the plank was taken up, they saw a passage cut in the earth — for there was no cellar to the house — and called on Sullivan to surrender. At this he came forth from a cavity dug under the hearth, a cavity which had its own fireplace whose smoke issued by a vent into the chimney above it.

The prisoner offered Mr. Beacher a large sum if he would let him escape and boasted that he had counterfeited bills to the amount of several hundred thousand pounds, that he could counterfeit any money he had ever seen and that, if he might be spared, he would contrive a plate which it would be impossible to counterfeit. Sullivan, for whom, as one newspaper put it, the gallows had groaned for a long time, was removed to New Haven and then to New York City, where he was arraigned on 24 April on an indictment for counterfeiting the bills of New York, to which he pleaded not guilty. He was tried in the supreme court, presided over by Justices De Lancey, Chambers, and Horsmanden, and the witnesses for the king were Nehemiah Lyon, Jonathan Miller, Edward Hugford, Eliphalet Beacher, and one member of the Money Club, David Sanford, who had turned evidence for the crown. The jury found Sullivan guilty and that he had no lands, tenements, goods, or chattels, except a saddle valued at £5, and on 29 April he was sentenced to be hanged between the hours of ten and twelve in the forenoon of 7 May.

The execution, however, did not take place as scheduled, partly because of the efforts of the condemned man's friends or accomplices. First the hanging was put over from Friday to Saturday for want of a hangman and, as on Friday night the gallows were cut down by persons unknown and as Jack Ketch was still wanting, the ceremony was postponed to Monday. On that day Sullivan made a speech, which was printed and put on sale at Henry Deforrest's, in which he confessed that his sentence was just and expressed the wish that his accomplices would destroy the plates and quit the money-making business. His associates, whom he would not betray, for, as he put it, he would not be guilty of shedding their blood, were twenty-nine in number. He revealed that some years past he had struck off nearly £12,000 of Rhode Island money and passed more than £1,600 of it in a single day, while he had also made £10,000 or £12,000 of New Hampshire currency, £3,000 of Connecticut, and large sums of four different emissions of New York. In his work he had four sets of accomplices, who from his plates had printed and passed other large amounts at times unknown to him. He approached death with the greatest resolution imaginable and just before he was hanged he took a large cud of tobacco and, turning round to the people, said: 'I cannot help smiling, as 'tis the nature of the beast.' When asked, for the benefit of the public, to reveal the denomination of the New York bills which he had forged, he answered, 'You must find that out by your learning.' And so he died obstinate.

Although the maker of the plates was hanged, the plates were still in the hands of his twenty-nine accomplices, so that the New York Assembly, on 9 July 1756, passed a law making it an offense punishable by death to conceal Sullivan's plates or to aid in counterfeiting the currency of the province. Eliphalet Beacher, who had proved to be the nemesis of Sullivan, proceeded to hound the remainder of the gang. He prosecuted in Connecticut Elijah Keeler of Ridgefield and Elisha Hunt, a tavern keeper of the Oblong. Keeler forefeited his bail bond but Morehouse was convicted and punished. Ambrose Hunt, who lived east of Sheffield in Hampshire County, Massachusetts, was taken up as a passer but, like Keeler, chose to have his bond declared forfeit rather than stand trial. Daniel Cornall of Croton River, New York, when seized by Beacher, was taken to Fairfield for trial and was acquitted.

So far the score was not impressive, for only Sullivan and Morehouse had been punished. Yet Beacher, far from being discouraged, soon laid hands on some of the most dangerous of the gang, Joseph Boyce, Sr., Joseph Boyce, Jr., Joseph Steel, Benjamin Pierce, Amos Fuller, William Hamilton, all of Dutchess County, and Jacob Pattengill. The authorities in Connecticut, following the surest way to obtain convictions, accepted Hamilton as king's evidence and released him on bail of £50 to appear in court and testify against some of his associates, all six of whom were in the Litchfield County jail awaiting trial. Unhappily the government, which should have known better, failed to keep a proper guard, and the Boyces, who were old hands at breaking prison, slipped out with Fuller, Pierce, and Pattengill on the night of 13 June and eluded all pursuit. Steel, whom they left behind, was tried and acquitted, doubtless because Mrs. Gaylord, the woman to whom he had passed the bad bill mentioned in his indictment, had died and therefore could not be used as evidence against him.

Two others who were associated with the Money Club, Daniel Galusha of Dover and young Ebenezer Lothrop of Norwich, were arrested but Lothrop broke away from the grasp of the officer who was leading him to prison and fled to distant parts, while Galusha, after sitting some five months in the Norwich jail, was released for want of sufficient evidence.

The Dover Money Club was thus broken up but it should be noted that this had been achieved through the initiative of a private person, a situation which was frequently repeated in colonial times. The whole affair demonstrated how difficult it was to obtain convictions, how readily, in Connecticut at least, a counterfeiter could escape punishment by forfeiting his bond, and how frequently and easily counterfeiters escaped from the flimsy and poorly guarded jails. Many of the gang remained at large and surely contributed to the enormous growth of counterfeiting, which posed a constant threat to the trade, commerce, and credit of the various provinces.

# Chapter 11

## SILVERSMITHS AS COUNTERFEITERS

Engraving of plates or making false coins required considerable technical skill of a nature which was possessed by silversmiths par excellence. Coining *might* be somewhat risky, for in England it was punished as high treason and such was the case in some of the colonies, so the would-be coiner should have realized that he should select with caution the place for committing his crime. Thus in 1703 in New York the silversmith Onclebag got off with a small fine for coining, while in Philadelphia in 1720 Edward Hunt, who was in the same profession, was hanged for the like offense; in Rhode Island in 1742 the goldsmith, Obadiah Mors, suffered an hour in the Newport pillory, had his ears cropped, and was sold into service to pay his fine and costs, but fourteen years later Owen Sullivan died on the gallows.

Virginia was a bad spot for coiners, for that colony treated such wrongdoing as treason. Though this must have been well known, in 1750 Low Jackson, a silversmith of Nansemond County, with the aid of his two brothers, John, a watchmaker, and James, a blacksmith, and Edward Rumney, who had kept a tavern in Annapolis, Maryland, made some Spanish double doubloons and was soon detected. All the gang fled, but Low, with a reward of £50 on his head, was presently taken up in Charleston, South Carolina, and extradited to Virginia. This slender young man, some five feet nine or ten inches in height, with a face full of red carbuncles, was tried on 15 April 1751 in Williamsburg and convicted. Justice Blair pronounced sentence of death on 6 May but execution was put off pending the results of an appeal for royal pardon, so poor Jackson was confined in jail until March 1753, when word arrived from London that the king had refused mercy. On 13 April the condemned man was drawn on a sledge from the prison to the gallows, where he addressed himself to the spectators in a moving and pathetic speech on the fatal consequences of an early habit of vice, which had brought him to his shameful and untimely end. He died in a very penitent manner, and his body, placed in a coffin which bore the inscription 'Mercy! triumph over Justice,' was delivered to his friends for burial in Nansemond County.

While Low Jackson was in prison under sentence of death another silversmith, Gideon Casey of Exeter, Rhode Island, at that time about twenty-eight years of age, was in Philadelphia, where he took occasion to pass off some false doubloons, probably samples of his own workmanship. On Saturday, 1 August 1752, he was arrested and committed to jail. During the third week of October he was tried in the mayor's court, convicted, and let off with a fine of £50. This he apparently paid, for on 1 June of the following year he purchased from his brother Samuel a half interest in his property and the brothers continued as partners in the silversmith's business until May 1763, when Gideon sold back his interest to Samuel and moved to Warwick. Both men, unfortunately, did not confine themselves to their legitimate trade, at which they were masters, but preferred quicker ways of getting rich, as will presently be related.

New York had become as perilous for coiners as Virginia, since a law of New York, passed on 29 November 1745, fixed the penalty of death for counterfeiting or knowingly passing counterfeit Spanish, French, or Portuguese gold or silver money. In spite of this Charles Hamilton, the first known silversmith in Poughkeepsie, became associated with Samuel Cogsdale, who had belonged to the Dover Money Club, and started making base Spanish cobs, which he coated with quicksilver. One April evening in 1761 at a tavern he foolishly displayed some cobs to a shoemaker named Lewis Bennett of Stratford (who was later found to be one of a gang of counterfeiters in contact with Gideon Casey) and boasted that he had made them, while soon afterward he sold nine of his dollars for one good dollar to Gersham Hubble, Jr., of Fairfield, Connecticut. Word of the matter came to the ears of the authorities, and Hamilton was taken up and examined in Poughkeepsie by Justices Bartholomew Noxon, Lawrence Van Kleek, and Anthony Yelverton, who committed him to the keeping of Charles Everit, sheriff of Dutchess County.

Attorney General Kempe of New York was determined to bring Hamilton — and Cogsdale, if he could be taken — to justice, so on 1 May he wrote to the sheriff: 'I know not in what condition your Gaol is in, but trust that you will keep them secure. . . I should be very sorry should you be liable to be punished so severely as the Law directs for the Escape of a Felon. . .' After such a warning, resort was probably had to heavy irons on the prisoner and an armed guard. Hamilton, seeing that his case was hopeless, saved the government trouble and expense by making fast his handkerchief to a spike that was driven into the wall of the jail and then hanging himself.

The *Connecticut Gazette,* published in New Haven, of

7 January 1764 briefly noted that a person in Killingworth had been taken up on suspicion of altering Connecticut bills and had been admitted to bail. This person, it
developed, was Abel Buell, whose father was dead and
who had just completed his apprenticeship to Ebenezer
Chittenden, a silversmith of Guilford. Abel had just married and, being desirous of setting up in business for himself, had induced his guardian, John Spencer, to purchase
for him a house and nine rods of land 'conveniently situ-
ated for a silversmith' along the post road. Spencer likewise
advanced the money for finishing the house, erecting a
shop, and providing for the support of Abel's wife and
workmen, with the understanding that when Abel came
of age he would execute a deed for enough of his estate
to repay his guardian.

With the expenses he had to meet Abel apparently felt
the need of more ready cash and so, in December 1763, he
tried his hand at altering four bills of 2/6 to 30s. each,
which he then passed off. A local constable, Niel Buell,
discovered the fraud, complained to Justice Benjamin
Gale, and the young silversmith was arrested and bound
over to appear at the next superior court to be held at
New London in March. Bail of £400 was furnished by
Abel, Spencer, and Abel's former master, Ebenezer Chittenden. His trial took place as scheduled and after his
conviction he was sentenced in accordance with the harsh
law of 1724. It is recorded, however, that the executioner,
taking pity on Abel's youth, inflicted the cropping and
branding in such a way that these marks of shame would
be concealed by the hair of his head. The young man's
estate was sold by Matthew Griswold, acting on orders of
the General Assembly, and the proceeds were used to pay
the costs of prosecution and reimburse the holders of the

bills which Abel had altered, while the residue went into the public treasury.

According to the law Abel was to be imprisoned for life but as a rule a convict might obtain his release by appealing to the Assembly. In May 1764, Abel, then confined in New London, sent a memorial to the legislators in which he set forth that he had no means of support, was in ill health, and in danger of perishing. The Assembly thereupon passed a resolution permitting his release on condition that he secure a bond of £100 for his good behavior and that he not depart from the limits of Killingworth without special license of the Assembly. By 21 July Abel had secured the bond and was set free. Encouraged by the success of his plea, in October 1765 he again besought the legislators to lift the restriction which confined him to the limits of his town, pointing out that he was under many disadvantages because of it and that he might be a more useful member of society if free to trade and deal in Connecticut. This time his prayer was denied by both houses.

The young silversmith was a talented inventor, as he showed throughout his life, and his ability now won him the freedom which he desired. In October 1766 he memorialized the Assembly, setting forth that in the course of his business he had discovered a method of grinding and polishing crystals and other stones of great value which were found in Connecticut, by which discovery great saving and advantage would accrue to the colony. Arguments which involved possible profit readily impressed the legislators, who now released him from the punishments enjoined by the law and restored him to the liberties and privileges which he had forfeited. The sole condition required was that he furnish a bond in the amount of

£200, with good sureties, for his good and peaceable behavior and that he never again offend in like manner
against the laws of the colony. Buell's invention was, of
course, a lapidary's wheel, and the stones to which he referred were doubtless tourmalines from the vicinity of
Haddam and other semi-precious stones, such as garnets.

Before long this ingenious mechanic distinguished himself by learning the art of type-founding and by designing
and casting types. About 1770 he turned to copperplate
engraving, in which field in 1784 he produced the first
map of the territory of the United States to be made by
one of its citizens. The following year he invented a
machine for striking copper coins and for a few years was
again a money maker, this time, however, with the sanction and supervision of the state. His many ventures, which
included the construction of a cotton mill at New Haven,
brought him no lasting financial rewards, and he died in
an alms house in New Haven at the age of eighty-one.

In February 1763 another New England silversmith,
Joseph Billings, about fifty-three years of age, six feet five
inches in height, long-necked and raw-boned, was in jail
in Reading, Pennsylvania, for having counterfeited New
Jersey three pound bills of the emission of 8 April 1762.
His counterfeits did not do credit to his skill as an engraver, for the strokes in the arms were too black and
clumsy, the letters irregular, the type not good, the red
ink too dirty, and the sage leaf on the back too small; in
the first line of the face of the counterfeit the o in POUNDS
was shorter and thicker than the other letters and in the
third line the last E in JERSEY was more like a written
than a printed E.

Billings, who often styled himself 'Doctor,' had been
convicted of counterfeiting in other provinces, had been

obliged to leave New England because of coining, had been whipped out of a regiment at Pittsburgh for the like offense, and had once escaped from a Maryland prison. Early in 1762 he took up his abode in the house of Frederick Weiser under pretense of getting a living by engraving and printing. His three pound bills, however, soon attracted notice and he was arrested and brought before a magistrate, to whom he complained that he thought it hard a poor man should suffer for a crime in which rich men were equally concerned with him. There is no evidence as to whether he was justified in thus casting aspersion on Weiser, but he did have one accomplice, though this was not proved at the time. This accomplice, a certain Herman Rosencrantz, a native of Esopus in the Province of New York, was arrested in March 1763 by Constables John Kelley and William Dungan of Bucks County on the charge of having passed bogus thirty shilling New Jersey bills. The accused maintained that he had received the currency from Billings in exchange for a horse and managed to get his case postponed for a year on the plea that a vital witness was missing. When he was finally tried, in March 1764, he persuaded the jury that he had accepted and passed the money in the belief that it was good and he therefore was acquitted, though in the light of what is now known of him there can be no doubt of his guilt.

Rosencrantz was not long out of jail before he associated himself with an Irishman named John Hannah at Squan in Monmouth County, New Jersey, in making and procuring a quantity of false twenty shilling Pennsylvania bills of the emission of 1 May 1760. Hannah was about six feet one inch tall, much pock-marked, long of visage, and lacking a left ear lately cropped on a conviction for putting off bad money. He and his partner set about passing their false bills, but on 17 August came to grief. On that day, in Woodbridge, New Jersey, they bought three horses from Samuel Jacques, Jr., paying him with their spurious twenty shilling notes, and also passed some of the bills in Perth Amboy, where Hannah, at least, is known to have put off four of the bills to Anne Brooks, wife of James Brooks. The deceit against Jacques was detected and the following day the men were arrested and committed to jail in Elizabethtown. They pleaded guilty and were sentenced each to stand one hour, between five and seven in the afternoon, in the pillory of Elizabethtown and to be imprisoned in that town until the last day of October. In addition, Hannah had his remaining ear cropped, while Rosencrantz was fined £50.

The prisoners still had to answer for their offense in Perth Amboy, so in May Sheriff Moses Ogden took them to the supreme court in that town, where they were indicted in September, pleaded guilty, and were sentenced to stand an hour in the pillory of that place, between ten and twelve in the forenoon, and then be returned to Elizabethtown to serve out their sentences. Probably both were detained beyond the end of October for non-payment of costs. In any event, about the beginning of November 1764, Hannah escaped from the jail and a reward was offered for his capture by the sheriff.

No sooner was Rosencrantz released than he returned to his old business of counterfeiting, this time with fatal results. About the middle of December 1769 a rather corpulent man of about sixty, some five feet ten inches tall, at dusk entered the shop of Robert Taggart on Market Street in Philadelphia and purchased some goods, tendering in payment a three pound New Jersey bill of the emission of 16 April 1764. The shopkeeper, suspecting that the note was counterfeit, went out, professing that he must get change, and showed the bill to several gentlemen, all of whom doubted that it was genuine. When, however, he returned to the shop, the customer had departed, leaving the goods behind him. Taggart immediately went after him from tavern to tavern, until he finally found him in a tavern in Strawberry Alley. The stranger was arrested and turned out to be Herman Rosencrantz, who, when searched, was found to have sixty-eight three pound Pennsylvania bills in his breeches. He was indicted at a court of oyer and terminer held in Philadelphia in April 1770, pleaded guilty, and died on the gallows that same month.

Billings, however, was still at large and about his nefarious work, for on 15 January 1770 Lieutenant Governor John Penn of Pennsylvania offered a reward of £50 for the capture of the silversmith, who was charged with counterfeiting the bills of the province. In March, news reached Philadelphia by way of Carlisle that Billings and an accomplice, after a long and obstinate resistance, had been overpowered at Winchester and committed to jail in that place. There is no further record of them, so it is not improbable, in view of the sorry state of the prisons of the time, that both escaped.

Another silversmith, like Billings a New Englander and a counterfeiter, was Gilbert Belcher, from a branch of the distinguished family of that name. He got what was then a common education, which meant that he learned to read and write, and then he served an apprenticeship to a silversmith. He was, as he once said of himself, 'of an unsocial, refractory disposition,' extremely inquisitive about the affairs of his neighbors, but careful that nothing should transpire relating to his own. In 1761 he married in Hebron, Connecticut, a worthy woman by whom he had nine children. Being, as he admitted himself, far from industrious, and dissatisfied with the profits from his legitimate business, he made some Mexican cobs, of which he passed away six in Killingly on 15 July 1764. The deceit was discovered, and he was arrested by Hezekiah Smith and then examined by Justice Jonathan Trumbull in Hebron. The magistrate bound him over to the superior court held in Windham in September, at which he was indicted, tried, convicted, and sentenced to pay a fine of £50 and costs of some £29 more.

Soon after his conviction and doubtless as a result of it, Belcher removed to the neighborhood of Great Barrington, Massachusetts, where he met with people as perversely inclined as himself. 'No gain,' he stated, 'afforded me so much pleasure as that which I acquired by illicit means. Coining and counterfeiting engrossed my attention, and those who first advised me to transgress, persuaded me to continue my iniquitous practices.' His iniquitous practices and those of his associates by 1772 had attained such alarming proportions that on 3 October Sir William Johnson advised Governor Tryon of New York that of late various New Englanders in their traffic with the Indians had passed so many counterfeit Spanish dollars that, if some means were not quickly devised to prevent this imposition, he feared the savages would retaliate by carrying off the horses and cattle of the whites.

Tryon, who had no stomach for troubles with the Indians, encouraged the justices of the peace to bestir themselves, with the result that by the first week in November nine counterfeiters were behind bars in Albany, despite widespread sympathy for the criminals. On 24 November Justice John Munro of Fowlis in Albany County wrote to the governor that he had just spent ten days examining counter-

feiters and their associates, 'of which the country abounds.'
Two constables had released coiners whom he had ordered
jailed, while the same night some of the miscreants' associates had broken and destroyed his potash works. By
the confession of the felons he had learned that there
was a 'line of money makers' from New Jersey to Cohass
back of New Hampshire. Munro was convinced that even
his constables were concerned in the mischief and that
the whole country was combined against the magistrates,
so he tendered his resignation.

Other justices, however, notably Matthew Adgate, William Whiting, James Savage, and Nathaniel Culver, were
less timid or vulnerable, and by their vigilance twelve
counterfeiters were committed to the jail in Albany.
Colonel Elijah Williams, sheriff of Berkshire County,
Massachusetts, obtained a warrant from the justices mentioned above and laid hands on the notorious Joseph Bill
(or Joseph Bill Packer, as he sometimes called himself)
at White Plains. Further, provided with a writ from a
justice in Albany County, the sheriff also set out to arrest
some suspected counterfeiters in a part of Berkshire County
which was also claimed by New York. For this purpose
he also obtained a warrant from an obliging justice of
Massachusetts, Joshua Ashley of Sheffield, authorizing him
to seize his quarry and then haul the suspects off to Albany.
This is just what Williams did, taking into custody, among
others, Gilbert Belcher. At this there was a furor in the
Massachusetts legislature, since persons residing in that
province had been dragged off to New York for trial and
since their offense was punishable by death in New York
but was no more than a trespass in Massachusetts. The
screams of rage became louder when it was learned that
smallpox was rampant in the Albany jail and that some

of the counterfeiters had become infected and had died. The remainder were tried by a special court of oyer and terminer.

On the night of 14 December 1772 the counterfeiters nearly escaped from the jail by breaking out near the chimney but they were heard by the guard which had been posted ever since their confinement and thereafter were kept more closely confined. Five of the rogues were convicted and sentenced to die on the gallows: William Hulbert, Joseph Bill, John Wall Lovely, Gilbert Belcher, and John Smith, though Hulbert was pardoned because his early confession appeared to have been a consequence of the justices' promise to recommend mercy. There is no record of Smith's hanging, so very likely he fell a victim to the smallpox.

Bill, Lovely, and Belcher, who were to be 'turned off' on 2 April 1773, gave Albany a thrill long to be remembered, for the day before they were to be hanged, they got off their bolts in the night and escaped from prison, though they were soon retaken and fastened in new irons. The next morning, however, they had their fetters off again, barred the room in which they were confined and bade defiance to the sheriff and his party, threatening to kill anyone who should try to take them out. At this the militia of the whole city was got under arms, but the counterfeiters kept the forces of law and order at bay. Thereupon the rascals set fire to the jail, expecting to die in the conflagration, but the citizens soon brought up the fire engines and extinguished the flames. Next John Wall Lovely contrived to get from some mischievous fellows about two pounds of powder, which he put into a bottle, and a match to put to it if the sheriff or anyone else should venture in. Thus for some time the city was kept in an uproar, until at length a party burst in upon the villains. Lovely promptly fixed a match to the bottle of powder, which he was holding in his hand, but by the mercy of Providence the powder did not take fire and the rascals were carried off to the gallows, singing psalms on the way.

Their fate was what inspired Colonel Schuyler to propose to the New York Assembly that a device be added to the bills representing 'an eye in a cloud . . . a cart and coffins . . . three felons on a gallows . . . a weeping father and mother, with several small children . . . a burning pit . . . human figures forced into it by fiends, and a label with these words, *"Let the name of a Money Maker rot"*; and such other additions as they [the commissioners] may think proper.'

Justice Munro's report to Governor Tryon that there was a line of counterfeiters from New Jersey to Cohass was no exaggeration, and one newspaper estimated the clan at about 500 from New England to North Carolina. The money making of the two brothers Casey, 'Silver Sam' and Gideon, sheds some light on the extensive network of criminals who plagued the colonies with bogus currency and base coins. As the Caseys seem to have become involved in the business through Joshua Howe, it will be instructive to relate what is known of him and two of his associates, 'Dr.' Seth Hudson and Glazier Wheeler.

Howe and Hudson were commited to jail in Boston in October 1761 for having made and passed off some £800 in forged treasurer's notes, all of which were very like the genuine ones. The printed part was a most accurate imitation but the written part was contrived by placing a true note over a counterfeit, tracing the writing with a sharp instrument, and then filling up with ink the impression on the false note.

Howe, who lived in Westmoreland, New Hampshire, had other charges against him, namely, that he had procured and kept in his possession tools for counterfeiting dollars and had solicited and tempted various persons to be concerned with him in such business. For these offenses he was tried at a court of assize held in Charlestown the last week in January 1762, and was sentenced to stand in the pillory one hour, to be whipped twenty stripes, and to pay a fine of £20, while upon another indictment for making dollars (for which he had been convicted some years before), he was sentenced to twenty years at hard labor in the House of Correction. After receiving the corporal punishment in Charlestown on Tuesday, 2 February, he was returned to jail in Boston, where his accomplice, Hudson, was imprisoned. Hudson, doubtless uneasy at the prospect of suffering what his confederate had just experienced, attempted to break jail on Thursday night but was discovered just in time and prevented.

The two malefactors were to be tried at the superior court in Boston on 1 March but when the time came the concourse of people was the largest ever known at any trial in that city, so that, as the courthouse was too small, the court was adjourned to one of the largest meeting houses in town. The fact was proved so plainly against the accused by the testimony of witnesses that the jury, without leaving the courtroom, brought them both in guilty. Hudson was sentenced on each of four indictments to stand one hour in the pillory, to be whipped twenty stripes, to be imprisoned for one year, and to pay a fine of £100; Howe was sentenced on each of two indictments to stand an hour in the pillory, to receive thirty-nine lashes, to be imprisoned for a year, and to pay a fine of £100. Nathaniel Hurd, a noted silversmith and engraver, who had a shop near the Exchange, made a humorous print of the pair and sold copies to the curious spectators.

Hudson did not serve his two years in prison, for on 8 July 1762 he shipped on board the man of war *Launceston;* he had probably persuaded the legislature that it would be more advantageous to have him in the navy than as a public charge in prison. By December of the following year he had been released, for a Boston newspaper warned its readers that Dr. Seth Hudson had arrived in town as a passenger on a vessel from Halifax. He eventually went to Albany, New York, where he died of the smallpox early in September 1767, after having given the disease to one of his old comrades who came to visit him there.

Howe and Hudson had obtained their tools for making dollars from Glazier Wheeler, the head of a gang of coiners with headquarters at Cohass, New Hampshire, on the Connecticut River. In 1763 this Wheeler was arrested and jailed in Worcester, Massachusetts, tried and sentenced to imprisonment for twenty years, but soon broke jail and escaped. Wheeler remained at large and at work counterfeiting until the night of 21 January 1774, when Major Simpson, high sheriff of Grafton County, New Hampshire, acting on a warrant issued by Colonel John Fenton, a justice of the peace of that county, seized Wheeler and an accomplice named Peter Hobart. The high sheriff, with the assistance of Colonel Hurd, made a diligent search of Hobart's house at midnight and was rewarded by the discovery of fifteen counterfeit dollars. Both prisoners were examined by three justices of the peace — Colonel Fenton, Major Sewall, and Colonel Porter — all through the cold night and the greater part of the next day. Hobart broke down under the questioning, made a full confession, and turned king's evidence against Wheeler, who was presumably given his deserts at last.

Howe, after a year or two, was set free but was presently arrested and jailed in Springfield, where he became indebted to Isaac Colton, keeper of the prison, for numerous charges. He offered to settle his account by deeding to Colton a tract of land in Westmoreland, New Hampshire, a proposal which the jailer readily accepted, only to find out later that the land in question belonged to a brother of Howe. When the fraud was detected, Howe gave Colton his promissory note for £40 and then broke out of jail and fled to New Hampshire. He is probably the counterfeiter who, according to the newspapers, was one of a group of prisoners who undermined the Springfield jail and then escaped by the tunnel on the night of 15 November 1766.

In 1767 and the early part of 1768 it became very generally suspected that there were large numbers of persons in New York, New Hampshire, Massachusetts, Rhode Island, and Connecticut who were combined in gangs for counterfeiting and passing many different foreign coins. As these evils seemed to increase to an alarming degree they became the objects of public notice and attention. The governors of several provinces, of which Massachusetts was one, fixed upon Isaac Colton of Springfield to run down the federated gangs, and to this purpose he was provided with proper credentials and warrants. He set about his task at the beginning of January 1768, and devoted himself to it for a year, during which, at great peril to his life, he brought several offenders to justice and broke up and dispersed a number of clans of money makers.

Apparently his first move was against a group in Killingly, Connecticut, not far from the Rhode Island border.

The counterfeiters carried on their coining in a subterranean habitation, constructed for that purpose, in the woods near Killingly. Fifteen individuals were taken into custody, including the person immediately concerned in making the money, who said he had been hired by the Killingly gang and that he came from Cohass, where he had left another nest of coiners. As soon as news came of the raid on the counterfeiters, Gideon Casey, who was residing in Warwick, fled from Rhode Island, with his two sons and Daniel Wilcox, in a schooner commanded by Tibbet Hopkins. They put in at Fairfield, Connecticut, where they spent some six weeks and at once made contact with a counterfeiting band consisting, among others, of William Imus, Nathaniel Bunnell, Samuel Sturges, 3rd, Archibald Phippeny, Elnathan Hubbell, Jr., John Mallet, Seth Porter, and Lewis Bennett. The Rhode Islanders, after passing some counterfeit New York bills, eventually departed for New York City.

As luck would have it, the Connecticut gang was discovered and many were apprehended. Some of them must have implicated Casey, for a gentleman in Fairfield sent off a letter posthaste to the Honorable William Smith, Jr., in New York. Smith notified the mayor, who sent officers on board the schooner, which was then on the point of sailing, ostensibly up the North River but really to North Carolina. On board the officers found a small bag containing all the instruments for coining and milling dollars of the years 1763 and 1764, two plates for North Carolina currency, molds and stamps for making pistareens, receipts for smelting and varnishing metals, and several counterfeit forty shilling bills of New York of the emission of 21 April 1760. At first the five men, who were placed under arrest, denied all guilt, but upon further

examination Gideon Casey admitted that some of the bad
bills had been passed in New York. He also explained the
presence of the coining instruments by stating that three
years previously Joshua Howe, the noted money maker,
had left them all in his custody. The *New-York Journal or
General Advertiser,* in noting the arrest of Casey and of the
gang in Connecticut, remarked: 'It is said they have established a regular Chain of Communication throughout
the whole Extent of the British Dominions in America,
and that there are above an Hundred of them concerned
in the different Provinces.' Despite Casey's admissions and
the objects found on the schooner, he and his four associates were all acquitted in April 1768 'for want of
sufficient evidence.' Thereupon Gideon disappeared permanently from the scene, unless, as is not at all improbable,
he operated elsewhere under an alias.

On 27 February 1768 Isaac Colton made one deposition
and two sworn declarations before Thomas Hutchinson,
chief justice of Massachusetts, in which he told of several
trips to Westmoreland, New Hampshire, where Howe
lived with his wife and two children, in a vain attempt to
obtain payment of the promissory note. There he saw in
Howe's possession forged Spanish cobs, stamps for making
pistareens, and a bar of base metal for coining. On one
occasion Benjamin Leonard and Joel Ely of Springfield
accompanied Colton and procured from Howe some bars
of the base metal. One may guess at the contents of such
bars, for Howe informed Colton that with an alloy of one
quarter silver he could make dollars that would never be
discovered and that for such operations he had a press at
a small distance from his house.

While at Howe's Colton made the acquaintance of Lieutenant John Snow of Chesterfield, who told him that he

had been at great expense to have Howe obtain for him counterfeiting tools and that he had just purchased an instrument with which to draw bars to just the right thickness of a dollar. In July 1767 at Chesterfield, Colton had discovered further details about the source of counterfeiting instruments, for there he met a certain Brown from Dover, New York, who was so indiscreet as to inform his new acquaintance that he had paid Glazier Wheeler of Cohass sixty dollars for tools and stamps. Indeed, Wheeler soon came to Chesterfield in order to get steel with which to finish the job but decided against doing the work in Chesterfield because he feared 'it would make a noise.' Somewhat later, as Lieutenant Snow told Colton, Brown returned to Dover, accompanied by one Sawyer who was to help him in money making and taking along the completest set of tools and press that Snow had ever seen. At the same time Snow showed Colton a dollar, containing not more than one quarter silver, which had been fashioned by Glazier Wheeler and which, to Colton at least, looked like a good coin.

On one of Colton's trips to New Hampshire he learned from Howe that sometime earlier Howe had gone, together with a German from Philadelphia, to Esquire Casey's at Little Rest in Rhode Island and had received from Samuel and Gideon Casey 500 dollars for instructing them in making money. Further, Howe complained that Thomas Colton, having stolen from him a set of counterfeiting tools and stamps, had taken them to Samuel Casey, who was carrying on some counterfeiting at Mohawk River, whither Casey sent the German from Philadelphia and Thomas Colton.

The sworn statements made by Isaac Colton were sent on to the government of New Hampshire, where the authorities made a raid on the gang at Cohass; there they took into custody Joshua Howe and Lieutenant John Snow. Unfortunately Glazier Wheeler, who made the molds and tools, escaped. 'It is said,' reported a Boston newspaper, 'a great Number are concerned, and sent into every Province on the Continent to pass away their Counterfeits.' Howe stoutly denied being concerned in manufacturing money but he readily acknowledged that he let out certain tools at ten dollars a day. He and Snow went on trial at the superior court held in Portsmouth, New Hampshire. Public opinion, in the other provinces at least, was aroused, and at least three important newspapers printed an article in which it was charged that a band of at least 500 counterfeiters were corresponding throughout the colonies. The jurymen in Portsmouth, however, were difficult to convince, for they acquitted Howe because the evidence was not thought sufficient, while Snow, who was convicted, got off by paying a fine of £30 and furnishing a bond for his future good behavior.

The Rhode Island government must have kept an eye on Samuel Casey from early in 1768 but it was slow to take any action. 'Silver Sam' as a silversmith was an excellent craftsman, and it has been thought that he was led into evil ways because of a disaster which befell him on Tuesday morning, 25 September 1764, while he was living in Exeter with his wife, Martha, and his children, Mary, Samuel Jr., William, and Willet. The day before he had kept in his goldsmith's forge a fire which was so intense that a post at the back part of the chimney caught fire, and his house was reduced to ashes. Most of his books and a small part of his furniture were saved but one newspaper account estimated his loss in furniture, European goods, drugs, and medicines as nearly £2,000 sterling. The mention of these items would indicate that Samuel kept a store, as did many another silversmith of the day, to supplement his earnings as a craftsman. This very considerable loss would be a plausible partial explanation for Samuel's turning to crime in order to recoup his fortunes but, if the confession of one of his accomplices can be trusted, Samuel had been in the counterfeiting business long before, for he boasted that by the work of his hands he had aided Benjamin Barber of Hopkinton and Samuel Stewart of Voluntown to get their estates and that they had never been found out.

After the fire, at any rate, Samuel removed to Little Rest, where he secured as his new home Helme House, built ten years before by James Helme. In it he conducted, to all appearances, his legitimate trade, but in reality he was the leader of a gang of coiners, of whom two, Noah Colton of Coventry, the brother of James Colton, and William Reynolds of Richmond, and possibly a certain Harvey, were also silversmiths. Joshua Howe, as Casey admitted, spent a night at his home and Daniel Wilcox was hidden there for a week since he wanted 'to be secreted from the officers.' Through these men or perhaps others Samuel Casey, on the basis of his own confession or the testimony of others, was acquainted with a number of makers of counterfeiting tools and dies — Azariah Philips of Smithfield, Amasa Jones of Colchester, Samuel Hoxie of Dutchess County, who lived for some time at Casey's in 1764, and Daniel Tonkray. Philips sold Casey for some ten or twelve dollars a die for making moidores; Jones brought him two dies for striking half joes; Hoxie, under Casey's supervision and in Casey's house, made a set of dies for dollars; Tonkray, who had served his apprenticeship with Harvey, fashioned dies for dollars and, according to an accomplice of Casey's, 'one of the neatest screws in the government.' Through Noah Colton, Casey also obtained three sets of dies for making half joes and a milling instrument, all manufactured by Glazier Wheeler at Cohass.

Experience had shown that one of the gravest dangers to any gang of counterfeiters was betrayal by a member, so each member of the band assembled by 'Silver Sam' was required to take a solemn oath not to reveal 'the secrets of any other man, woman or child without the consent of company or companions' and to swear: 'If I am not true to you and do not keep all your Councell & your Secrets I pray God to shut me out of Heaven and to make all my Prayers to become Sin.'

The actual counterfeiting was chiefly carried on in Samuel Casey's garret or in the garret of 'Dr.' Samuel Wilson, who lived at Tower Hill, and to some extent at the home of William Reynolds. Casey and Wilson had great screws with which they stamped out false moidores, half joes, and dollars, using gold or silver mixed with base metal. They varied the proportion, sometimes to suit the wishes of their customers, who would bring or send them good coins and broken pieces of coin or metal for melting down and mixing. Sometimes the blanks would be made by confederates and then taken to Casey and Wilson to be stamped. On occasion a number of persons were present and helped in the stamping, namely, Noah Colton, William Reynolds, Samuel Hoxie, William Pollock, Samuel Wilson, Jr., Gideon Casey, Jr., Samuel Casey, Jr., and William Coon of Hopkinton. Others who were receivers or passers of the bad coins were Joseph Babcock, Elisha

Reynolds, Robert Campbell (an innkeeper of North Kingston), Nathan and Benjamin Barber, William Corning, Thomas Clark, Jr., Caleb Bates of Coventry, Immanuel Case (a trader of South Kingston), Palmer Sheldon, a deputy sheriff of Kings County, and William Hiams, an innkeeper. 'Silver Sam' was proud of his work and boasted to his nephew, Samuel, that the dollars of his making were so good and so well done that 'they would pass through the world.'

The flood of false coin put into circulation could scarcely escape notice, and ever since February 1768 the Massachusetts authorities had been informed of Samuel Casey's connection with Joshua Howe. At length the officers struck, beginning with the arrest of the innkeeper Hiams on 10 July 1770. Hiams, when examined, admitted receiving bad coin from Thomas Clark, who told him that the pieces were made 'by the ole Man upon the Hill,' meaning Casey. Clark was then taken up and a search was made of Casey's home, where a press was found. In a neighboring cornfield the officers came upon three stamps for half joes and two for dollars, while in Casey's 'Neserary House' a deputy sheriff discovered the proper tools for milling the edges of dollars and half joes.

Shortly before the raid Casey was somehow tipped off and he in turn attempted to get hold of Wilson, to whom he sent the following letter, addressed to 'Doctor Samuel Willson, Tiptop Tower Hill': 'friend Willson I Desire you to Cum here this without fail as your Cumming will be of Great Service to me and you therefore I Beg you for the Love of God to Cum a way upon Sight of this Letter for Colten and all the Boys are gone to Meeting and I am all allone and want you to Cum I tell you if you Dont Cum Directly you will be Sorry but once therefore you

now have a friend Be Good Enough to keep him or I
tell you you will be Sorry for it Cum and Bring ▢▢ with
you your Compliance will oblige Both you and me y^r
Sincer friend to Serve ⫟
P S I pray Dont Loose on Hower of time but Cum Directly
I say ⫟ .'

This message may have been intercepted or, if delivered,
at least it was not destroyed, for it fell into the hands of
the magistrates who examined Casey. He admitted that
the handwriting was his but when they asked him the
meaning of the two squares his only reply was: 'What is
written is written.' Four days later, however, upon further
examination he confessed that the two squares indicated
dies.

Of the numerous suspected counterfeiters taken into
custody, five — Samuel Casey, Elisha and William Reynolds, Thomas Clark, and Samuel Wilson — were indicted
at the October session of the superior court of Kings County
and put on trial. The attorneys for the king were James
Honeyman and Henry Merchant and those for the prisoners were Matthew Robinson, William B. Simson, and
James N. Varnum. When Casey was tried, the jury brought
in a verdict of not guilty, but the court found their verdict
so contrary to law and evidence that it could not be accepted and the jury was sent out again. The second time the
jurors found the prisoner at the bar guilty if his confession might be considered lawful evidence, otherwise not
guilty. The court promptly ruled that Casey's confession
was lawful evidence, whereupon the attorneys for the
defense moved that the verdict be set aside as a mistrial
on the basis that three of the jurors, William and James
Congdon and Edward Perry, had prejudiced the subject
matter of Casey's indictment and condemned him un-

heard and also on the basis that evidence had been produced by William Congdon after the jury had retired and that the grand jurors did not belong to the court where the alleged fact had been committed. The same day, however, the motion of the defense was retracted and the court sentenced the silversmith to be hanged until dead between the hours of nine in the morning and two in the afternoon on a day left blank in the records.

Wilson's trial lasted ten hours but the jury convicted him in ten minutes, and he was sentenced to stand an hour in the pillory on Little Rest Hill in South Kingston on 26 October, to be branded with a hot iron with the letter R on both cheeks, to have his ears cropped, and to pay a fine of £600 and costs. Clark, also convicted, received the same sentence as Wilson, save that his fine was £100. William Reynolds refused to contend on one indictment, threw himself upon the mercy of the court, and received the same sentence as Wilson except that in his case the fine was £300. The *Connecticut Courant* pointed out that 'a more horrid and extensive combination to defraud the public' had never been heard of in New England and assured the public that it extended much further. Interest in the affair was so keen that a concourse of more than 3,000 persons gathered on Tower Hill on Friday, 26 October, and witnessed the infliction of the corporal punishment on Wilson, Clark, and William Reynolds. Elisha Reynolds does not seem to have been tried, and it may be suspected that he was received as king's evidence.

Casey sent a memorial to the General Assembly in the hope of escaping death, and his petition was referred to the next session of that body. His fate, however, was decided in another way, for on Saturday night, 3 November, a considerable number of persons, with their faces black-

ened, riotously assembled in Kings County and proceeded
to the jail. Then, with iron bars and pickaxes, they broke
open the outer door, smashed all the locks, and liberated
all the money makers except Wilson, who could not flee
because he was ill. Governor Wanton offered a reward of
£50 for the capture of Casey and a like amount for the
discovery of one or more of the men who broke open
the jail. Numerous arrests were presently made, and at
the April session of the superior court eleven rioters were
indicted. Several of them who were young and were supposed to have been inadvisedly drawn into the affair were
admitted as king's evidence, but John James, Nathan Barber of Hopkinton, and Timothy Peckham, a blacksmith
of South Kingston, were all punished, Barber with a fine
of £300 and the other two with a fine of £100 each. At the
same session of the court William Carlisle, described by the
*Providence Gazette* as one of the gang's emissaries 'employed as a post to the most distant connections of the
numerous gangs of money makers throughout the colonies,'
was convicted of passing and sentenced to stand an hour
in the pillory, to be branded with R on both cheeks, to
have both ears cropped, and to pay a fine of £30 and costs.

Samuel Casey was never recaptured, and it is possible
that he was one of a group of silversmiths, of whom Noah
Colton was one, who went from New England to New
Jersey and there engaged in counterfeiting. In September
1779 the General Assembly of Rhode Island granted a
petition made by Martha, Sam's wife, 'fully, freely and
absolutely to pardon and restore' the silversmith, but there
is no evidence to show that he availed himself of the pardon
to return to his native state. Indeed, it is reported by a
Canadian descendant that Sam was a loyalist and fell fight-
ing for the king during the revolution.

# Chapter 12

## THE PITTSYLVANIA AND MORRISTOWN
## GANGS

THE operations of the Dover Money Club, the flourishing business of Wheeler, Howe and Hudson, the coiners at Little Rest, the trials in Albany, all pointed to counterfeiting on a wide scale and as a highly organized business. Two major gangs were busy in 1773, one in Pittsylvania County, Virginia, and the other in Morristown, New Jersey.

The Virginia emisisons of 1769 and 1771, early in 1773, were found to be counterfeited, and the treasurer of the colony, Robert Carter Nicholas, held a conference in Williamsburg with the leading merchants of Virginia. On 1 February Thomas Adams wrote from that town to Messrs. Perkins, Buchanan, and Brown: 'The Counterfeit Bills which have appeared at this meeting have put a stop to all business.' Five days later James Hill, Washington's new steward on the Custis plantations, who also attended the gathering in Williamsburg, wrote to Washington that he would accept no cash for the corn he had sold because 'there was so much bad money' that he could not receive it with safety.

Under such circumstances Governor Dunmore, acting with the advice of the council, adopted a device which in the past had often proved efficacious and offered a reward of £500 for the discovery of the principal offender and of £100 for the apprehension of any of the passers. The proclamation of the rewards brought immediate results, for John Short, a former constable and accomplice, came to the governor and informed him that a gang of sixteen persons was busy in Pittsylvania County turning out bad bills and coin. Dunmore at once sent out Captain Joseph Lightfoot, who at about two o'clock one afternoon descended upon Benjamin, Joseph, and James Cooke, Benjamin Woodward, and Peter Medley at work in their shop. The men were arrested, and Lightfoot also laid hands on all their tools for engraving, frames for making paper, a rolling press, dies for dollars and half pistoles, a large quantity of false five pound bills, and a plate for making forty shilling notes. Further, at about the same time, suspected money makers were arrested in other counties, one of whom, John Ford, Jr., promptly escaped from the jail of Amelia County in spite of the fact that eight men had been set to guard him.

A number of the prisoners were taken to Williamsburg, then sent to York for examination, and finally tried in Williamsburg, a change of venue which greatly exasperated the members of the Assembly against the methods of the governor. At the trial the testimony of John Short, the main witness against the counterfeiters, was invalidated by various witnesses, who proved him 'a most atrocious Villain.' This he probably was, but at the same time there was no doubt about the guilt of the prisoners, who had been taken red-handed. The accused, however, because of some defect in the act of Assembly on which they were tried, were all acquitted and, as the *Virginia Gazette* commented, 'again let loose as beasts of prey, and suffered to roam at large on their fellow creatures.'

In the meantime a new flood of forged bills, Pennsylvania currency of the denominations of three pounds and
of thirty shillings, both dated 1 March 1769, were discovered circulating in July 1773. They were done with
printing types and were so like the true bills that, unless
they were examined very attentively, many persons might
be deceived by them. The authorities were justifiably
alarmed, and, on 19 July 1773, Lieutenant Governor Richard Penn issued a proclamation in which he adverted to
the circulation of counterfeits of these two denominations
and offered the extraordinary reward of £500 to any person,
other than an accomplice, or of £250 to an accomplice,
who should denounce the criminals and bring about their
conviction.

At the time that this proclamation appeared the New
Jersey authorities already had information as to the identity
of the counterfeiters of these Pennsylvania bills. The last
week in June two silversmiths, John Swan and Stephen
Waterman, were arrested in Middlesex County, New
Jersey, on suspicion of coining dollars and half joes. One
of them finally made an ample confession by which several
persons in different places appeared to be concerned with
them. This confession and those of other coiners in Middlesex and Monmouth counties led, as Governor Franklin
stated, to the discovery of another gang of villains in Morris
and Sussex counties 'who had for several years past been
employed in counterfeiting and passing the Paper Currency of this and the neighbouring Colonies.'

The information secured by the government of New
Jersey was imparted to the grand jury of the court of
quarter sessions of Morris County then sitting in Morristown, and Samuel Ogden, a justice of the peace of Morris
County, together with another justice, Samuel Tuthill,

apparently in consultation with Attorney General Cortland Skinner, displayed great energy in attempting to discover the counterfeiters, and their efforts were crowned with success. Indeed, the Provincial Council subsequently praised the conduct of Justice Ogden as that of 'a vigilant and upright Magistrate' and expressed the opinion that it was 'in a great measure owing to his Activity and Zeal for the Publick Good, that a Gang of Villains, very mischevious to this and the neighboring Provinces, have been detected and some of them brought to Justice.'

The leader of this gang was Samuel Ford, one of the most resolute and skillful counterfeiters of the entire colonial period, whom a contemporary designated as 'the most accomplished villain that this country ever produced.' Samuel Ford was the son of Samuel Ford, Sr., and Sarah Baldwin, and the grandson of John Ford, who in 1721 settled in Monroe, two miles east of Morristown, on a tract of land given to him by John Budd, who desired to have the region settled. Samuel Ford, Jr., married Grace Kitchell, the daughter of Joseph Kitchell of Hanover and the sister of Squire Aaron Kitchell, who was a United States Senator from 1807 to 1811. By Grace Kitchell, Ford had four children — Betsy, Phebe, William, and Samuel.

Not long before 1765 Ford was engaged in the iron industry at Hibernia in company with Lord Stirling and Benjamin Cooper, a son of Daniel Cooper (one of the early judges of Morris County). The Hibernia industry, perhaps in 1764 or 1765, became involved in financial difficulties, and it would seem that Benjamin Cooper suggested to Ford that he counterfeit money to help them out of their financial problems. At least, in 1773, Ford wrote to Cooper: 'You describe me as being the chiefest promoter and first introducer of the money making affair. Did you

not in the time of our depressed circumstances at the
furnace first move such a scheme to me?'

It is not known whether Ford at that time acted on his
partner's advice. In any event, in 1765 Ford sold out his
share in the Hibernia furnace and his property there to
Cooper and to James Anderson, each of whom paid him
£265. With the proceeds he made a trip to Ireland, where
he proceeded to marry an Irish girl of some means, and
with her he returned to America in 1766. The young lady,
of course, then discovered that Ford already had a wife
and children, so she promptly left him and is said to have
married an Irishman and to have resided at Whippany,
New Jersey. It is probable that Ford returned early in
June 1766, and that he imported with him counterfeit
New Jersey bills made in Ireland, for on 28 June the
Governor of New Jersey issued a warrant for the treasury
to pay the Honorable John Stevens to send an express to
warn the inhabitants of the province that a large sum of
false Jersey bills had just arrived in a vessel from England.

Benjamin Cooper, under examination on 24 September
1773, before Justices Ogden and Tuthill, gave a detailed
and probably fairly accurate account of Ford's activities.
His story was that sometime in 1767 Ford went from
Hibernia to a money maker named Coon at Stony Hill.
Coon had some false New York forty shilling bills and
New Jersey six shilling bills with plates for striking them,
and it was agreed that Coon should send the money and
plates to Ford by John Cooper, Benjamin's brother. John
brought about £40 of this bogus currency to the home
of Thomas Kinney, Esquire, no less a personage than the
high sheriff of Morris County! At the sheriff's house Ford
and his associates viewed the bills, decided they were very
poorly done, and sent them all back to the maker except

for a few six shilling notes which Ford kept. Early in 1768 Ford removed to New York City, where he secured counterfeiting materials and studied the technique of making paper money. He remained there at the lodging house of a Mrs. Blaw until he finally procured a house in the back part of the town, after which he lived part of the time in this dwelling and part of the time at Mrs. Blaw's.

He was busily engaged in fabricating three shilling and six shilling New Jersey bills when, late in 1768 or early in 1769, the New York authorities arrested him and clapped him in jail on suspicion of making money. On the way to prison he somehow arranged with his brother-in-law Kitchell to have his money and tools put away in a safe spot. Ford was admitted to bail, and on 18 April 1769 he appeared before the supreme court of judicature in New York City to answer to the charges against him. His case was put over to the 21st, then the 22nd, the 24th, the 27th, the 28th, and finally the 29th, when, after proclamation was made three times and no person appeared to prosecute, it was ordered on a motion of the king's attorney that he be discharged. Thus, doubtless for want of sufficient evidence, a most accomplished criminal managed to slip through the fingers of the authorities.

Even while out on bail Ford set about preparing materials to renew his nefarious business. The day before his arrest he told Dr. Barnaby Budd, commonly called 'Bern,' that during his residence in New York he had learned to carve from a woodcarver and had obtained types from a journeyman printer, a drunken fellow, who lived with Hugh Gaine, publisher of the *New-York Gazette: and the Weekly Mercury* and printer of the New York bills of the emissions of 5 January 1770, and of 16 February 1771. Ford boasted to Budd that he had counterfeited thirty and sixty shilling bills of Pennsylvania, numerous notes of New Jersey, and the three pound bills of New York, but gave up making the New York money because the paper was so thin that he could not do a good job of imitation.

Immediately after his difficulty with the law in New York Ford removed to Hanover, Morris County, New Jersey, where he resided on his farm of some 130 acres which went by the name of the 'Hammock.' He traveled often to Philadelphia, where he formed a connection with a certain Captain Joseph Richardson, from whom he got a supply of types. After the Pennsylvania emission of 1769 came out, these two miscreants made a trip to Ireland and thence to London and the manufacturing towns. While abroad Ford applied himself to learn the business of an engraver and type maker, and from his previous knowledge of the art of carving and an uncommon natural genius he became so skillful that he later made all the types for his own press. Now that the purpose of their mission was accomplished, the two rogues returned in 1772 by way of Halifax and Boston, and in August Ford settled down again at the Hammock.

From this time on he gave himself over to counterfeiting large sums of paper money, especially of New Jersey and Pennsylvania. His press and all his implements were about a mile from his house in an almost impenetrable swamp, in which the water, for the greater part of the year, was half a leg deep, so that no person could track him and so that he had to crawl on his belly for some rods before he could reach it. No person, except Joseph Richardson and one John King, knew where he did his work or had ever seen the place, and these, as all others concerned with him as passers, were sworn to secrecy. He used to go to his work at daybreak, in the morning, with his gun, so that no person would suspect him. He struck off bills from types he had made in so masterly a manner and his imitations of three pound and thirty shilling Jersey and Pennsylvania bills were so exact that the difference from the genuine could not be discovered without the strictest examination by a person well acquainted with the true bills. His notes, indeed, stood the test of several treasurers' examinations and had their sanction, to secure which he made it an invariable rule before he passed any of his new emissions. He signed his own money and his admiring associates called him the 'treasurer for the three provinces.'

The gang of counterfeiters who put off Ford's bills had quite a few members. Prominent among them were his most trusted cronies, King and Richardson. John King, who had been an undersheriff of Morris County, was a square, well-set fellow, about five feet eight or nine inches tall, with short, brown straight hair, a full face, and a rather dark complexion; he had been frequently in Philadelphia and at Fort Augusta, while in 1770 and 1771 he was at Wyoming and served under the government of Pennsylvania against the New England people.

Richardson was described in a proclamation issued by Governor Dunmore of Virginia and published in Rind's *Virginia Gazette* of 9 September 1773 as about forty-three years of age, above six feet in height, very stout, active and resolute, of a fair complexion, with very light brown hair, well dressed, and smooth of speech.

Another of the band was Squire Ayres, a justice of the peace of Sussex County, who worked for a time in collaboration with Ford but eventually broke away from his criminal associates and lived so exemplary a life that the congregation to which he belonged promoted him to the rank of deacon. The remaining accomplices whose names have been recorded were residents of Morris County — Samuel Haynes of Morristown, Benjamin Cooper, Esquire, David Reynolds, and the physician Barnaby Budd. These persons were remarkably handsome men, three of them about thirty years of age, the other forty, all married and all fathers. They were descended from the first families of the province and all had parents living.

It is known that Reynolds was a farmer. In an evil hour he chanced to make the acquaintance of the notorious Herman Rosencrantz and by him was led into the scheme of making and passing counterfeit money. Shortly after the death of Rosencrantz on the scaffold, Reynolds struck up a friendship with another counterfeiter, Captain Richardson, who in time introduced him to Ford, Haynes, Cooper, Budd, King, and the rest of the Morristown gang.

The plundering of the public by this group went on without interruption until Friday, 16 July 1773, when the authorities, under orders from Justices Ogden and Tuthill, arrested Ford and locked him up in the county jail in Morristown. On Saturday night, however, aided by his confederate John King, Ford broke out and fled. The high sheriff, Thomas Kinney, allegedly 'at his wit's end' because of the unfortunate incident, offered a reward of £25 for the capture of King and of £50 for the taking of Ford, whom he described as follows: 'He is a well built Fellow, about thirty Years of Age, five Feet ten Inches high; had on when he went away, a Nankeen Waistcoat and Breeches, a brown Coat, plain brown Thread Stockings, a good pair of Shoes, and silver twisted Buckles: It is supposed he has taken with him a suit of pale sky blue Clothes, with a large silver Twist gay Button, he has short brown curled Hair, very red Cheeks, and a remarkable Dimple in his Chin. He is an artful Fellow — with the Serious and Grave, can put on the Face of Seriousness, Religion, and Gravity, and with the Gay, can behave with as much Levity as any one.'

It seems, however, that the high sheriff himself had been largely to blame for Ford's escape. John King, after his flight, wrote to Governor Franklin of New Jersey, laying charges against Sheriff Kinney in respect to Ford's breaking jail. The high sheriff was afforded an opportunity to reply thereto but the Provincial Council, after a careful study of all the evidence, reached the conclusion that Kinney was 'blameable for negligence in his Office respecting the Escape of Samuel Ford.' The grand jury of Morris County also indicted Kinney 'for Misbehaviour respecting the said Escape.' The sheriff's later conduct in the pursuit of the fugitives added further to the suspicions about him.

After the flight of Ford and King every effort was made to discover the identities of their accomplices. One person who had been seized for helping the two fugitives in their escape and who lay under the censure of three convictions, one of which was for his aid to the jail breakers and the others for high misdemeanors, on being hard pushed and in order to mitigate his punishment for his crimes, began to make a confession. This in turn so alarmed another accomplice that he then freely and fully revealed the details of the counterfeiting, whereupon Reynolds, Cooper, Dr. Budd, and Haynes were apprehended and tried before a special court of oyer and terminer. All pleaded guilty to their indictments and on 19 August were sentenced to be executed on 17 September.

Their numerous friends and relatives poured into the town of Perth Amboy, and an eyewitness wrote that among a thousand people there was scarce a dry eye and that the spectators were particularly moved to sympathy for the unhappy criminals since they appeared to have been led to wrongdoing through the art, cunning, and persuasion of the villain Ford. A correspondent wrote in a letter from Perth Amboy on 15 September that the wives and relations of most of the unhappy money makers, then under sentence of death, were there with the governor in order to solicit him for a reprieve and that so many unhappy people wandering about the streets made an affecting sight.

The pressure brought to bear on the chief executive had its effect, for Budd and Haynes were respited by the governor until 17 October, but Cooper and Reynolds were ordered to prepare for execution at the time appointed. A few minutes before sentence was to be carried out Cooper suddenly confessed himself privy to the robbery of the provincial treasury at Amboy and he stated that he had received £300 of the loot. Thereupon he too was respited until he should make further discoveries, and Reynolds alone was hanged.

Cooper's last-moment confession seemed to clear up a sensational robbery which had been perpetrated in 1769. According to Cooper, the theft was planned by Ford and carried out by him together with three soldiers who were then quartered at Perth Amboy. The scheme was first to attempt to carry off the iron chest that contained a large sum in bills and, if that failed, next to take the key from the bedroom of Mr. Skinner, the treasurer, and to kill him or any person who should discover them, and that, if afterward any of them should be suspected and convicted, they were to turn king's evidence and accuse Mr. Skinner as being the only accomplice with them. When some of the scoundrels were shocked at this proposal since thereby an innocent person might lose his life, Ford met their objections by replying, 'No, damn him. He will only be condemned; he has friends enough to save him from the gallows.'

Cooper related how, after breaking into the treasurer's office adjoining his bedroom, the burglars first attempted to carry off the money chest but found that too difficult and set it down again. They then broke open a desk in hopes of finding money but instead came upon an old, rusty key to the chest which had been discarded as unfit for use. With it, however, they unlocked the iron chest, and through this the lives that would have been exposed by their search for the other key were probably preserved. Treasurer Skinner had political enemies, and James Kinsey, an attorney and member of the House, examined the evidence adduced against Ford in connection with the robbery of the East Jersey Treasury, declared it unreliable, and persuaded the majority of the House that such was the case. The whole issue became one of partisan politics, a fact which has beclouded the entire affair.

By his confession, whether true or false, Cooper saved his neck, for in December Governor Franklin granted a pardon to him as well as to Dr. Budd and to Haynes. As for Squire Ayres, his fate is not recorded. When he was first arrested, his parson was so fully convinced of his innocence that on the Sunday after the commitment of Ayres he prayed in church for the squire's protection from 'false accusers,' and when on the following Sunday a report prevailed that Ayres was released, the parson returned thanks for it. To the preacher's chagrin, however, before the third Sunday reliable accounts were received that the squire had admitted his guilt. In all probability Ayres was accepted as king's evidence in order to secure the conviction of Reynolds, Budd, Haynes, and Cooper and thereby escaped prosecution for his crime of passing counterfeits.

The view of the press of the day was that these persons had through Ford been 'brought into the most shocking and desperate circumstances.' The governments concerned, because their bills had been so artfully imitated, published offers of rewards for the capture of Ford and some of his associates until by December the sums offered amounted to £750 for Ford, £600 for Richardson, and £75 for King. Reports concerning the whereabouts of these men appeared in issue after issue of most of the newspapers of the colonies. Rivington's *New-York Gazetteer* on 9 September stated that a little earlier Ford had been on the west branch of the Susquehanna, with a posse in hot pursuit. A week later the same newspaper reported that in a swamp had been located Ford's press, a set of plates for making the currencies of Maryland, Pennsylvania, New Jersey, and New York, and a quantity of types and other utensils. The counterfeiter himself, in the course of his flight, had put off some Jersey bills of his own manufacture among the Indians, who, when apprised that the notes were false, had very willingly joined in the pursuit. Information had reached the paper that Ford and King had been at Fort Augusta and on 5 September were at a village called Annquauga. Ford had been seen asleep under a tree, guarded by King and another well-armed man, and they were said to take their rest alternately in this manner. Ford, it was claimed, was reduced by a fever, 'joined to a complication of the most loathsome distempers,' so that he could travel no more than five miles a day, and it was expected that the chasseurs would soon take him either dead or alive.

Despite all these detailed rumors concerning his flight, Ford was the whole time at Smultz's cabin in the mountains near the Hibernia furnace, the scene of his former partnership in the iron industry. News of the villain's presence at the cabin seems to have finally forced Sheriff Kinney to act, for on a Sunday morning in mid-September he went with a posse to Rockaway, where he picked up Abraham Kitchell, Ford's brother-in-law, as a guide, and he then proceeded in a leisurely fashion toward Smultz's cabin. Young James Kitchell, Abraham's son, told a certain Joseph Herriman what was afoot, and Herriman, throwing off his coat, ran off along a short cut to the cabin and warned Ford, so that when the sheriff arrived it was too late, Ford had decamped. It was rumored that Sheriff Kinney himself had been involved with Ford and had purposely tarried and that Abraham Kitchell had that Sunday remarked to the high sheriff: 'You dare not, for your own sake, arrest him.'

Speculation was now rife about the fugitives from justice. Some said that Ford, King, and a certain Thomas Budd had embarked at Barnagat for St. Kitts and thence intended to go to St. Eustatia. Greater credence, however, was given to the report that the men had headed toward the Ohio with the intention of going to the Mississippi and then to New Orleans, where they had promised Samuel Haynes that they would wait for him until after Christmas. Governor Franklin proposed that trusty persons be sent to the governor of West Florida and New Orleans to seize Ford and his friends on their arrival. The posse that had been pursuing abandoned the quest but sent one man ahead to go down the Ohio and then to proceed to New Orleans. Colonel Guy Johnson, hearing of the flight of Ford and his companions, likewise dispatched one of the best runners of the Mohawk Indian nation with exact descriptions and proper instructions to follow them down the Ohio. All these efforts, however, were in vain, for apparently Thomas Budd, Ford, and King were never taken. Governor Franklin had reason on his side when in an address to the General Assembly on 12 December he said: 'In all Probability, if Government had been empowered to hire a Number of active Men to have gone off immediately in different Parties, in Pursuit of these Delinquents, they would ere now have received the Punishment due to their Crimes.'

It turned out that Ford had left many creditors behind him, and the Morris County inferior court of common pleas, on or before 30 October, appointed Samuel Tuthill and Jonathan Styles of Morristown and Thomas Millidge of Hanover to adjust and settle the demands of his creditors. Sheriff Kinney sold off Ford's farm and all his property, 'even to a tin cup containing milk for the babe.' Sheriff Robertson, who purchased Ford's house, in making some repairs, apparently at a much later date, found counterfeiter's tools hidden in the walls.

Ford himself went to Green Brier County, Virginia, now West Virginia, where he assumed his mother's name of Baldwin and, together with a partner, engaged in the business of silversmith. During a severe illness, from which he did not expect to recover, he told his partner's wife his real name and his evil past. He was, however, restored to health, and when his partner later died, the partner's wife married Ford, although she knew full well that he already had a wife in New Jersey, who, indeed, died in 1818 at the age of seventy-seven. At first Grace Ford had been intensely loyal to her rascally husband and had refused to believe ill of him. When at length news somehow drifted back to Morristown that he was still alive, she made no attempt to join him. Their eldest son, William, however, accompanied by a friend named Stephen Halsey, later paid a visit to Ford in Virginia, where they found him living with a new wife and the children she had borne him. To his son and Halsey, Ford vehemently denied any guilt in connection with the robbery of the treasury but expressed repentance for his general bad conduct. William and Halsey reported that they found him 'a most melancholy man.'

Although nothing further is known of Thomas Budd and John King, word of Captain Joseph Richardson reached New York and then Boston through a gentleman who came from Philadelphia. This person stated that it was currently reported in that city that Richardson was taken in Virginia, where he had been pursued by three men. It was said he had killed two of them and made a pass with a sword at the third, who, with his hand, parried the blow and took away the weapon.

This yarn, it turned out, was made up out of whole cloth, but an item which was dated Baltimore, 13 November, and was printed in a Boston newspaper, may have been based on fact. It quoted a letter from someone in Lancaster County, Pennsylvania, to a gentleman in Baltimore. The correspondent wrote that Richardson 'after taking leave of his wife and family, who lived in the Great Valley, lodged, the night before he took flight towards the Ohio, at Mr. M . . . . . . s; during his stay there, which was about nine hours, he discovered symptoms of a mind rather warily than fearfully agitated, and seemed resolvedly fixed to defend the most desperate attack on his person. He was well armed, as was also a man that attended him, who, as soon as day dawned, took his station before the house, watching narrowly every person who passed, until they departed. On Richardson's going off, being asked if he was not afraid of being taken, he replied, "No; damn me! A man whose pockets are lined with money, and his heart with courage, has nothing to fear but God; and before I am heard of again in Pennsylvania, I shall be out of the reach of pursuit." '

For all his bravado, Richardson was eventually captured and confined in the jail of Lancaster County. On 19 June 1777, he was allowed to secure bail if he could and in the spring of 1780 he was discharged from confinement on condition that he leave Pennsylvania and never return without special permission. He could probably thank the Revolution, with its confusion and change of authorities, for the fact that he escaped death on the gallows.

# Chapter 13

## JOHN BULL TURNS COUNTERFEITER

THE outbreak of the Revolution found counterfeiting for profit flourishing in all the provinces, and the emissions of new currency to finance the war, both by the Continental Congress and by individual colonies, increased the amount of paper in circulation and afforded unscrupulous money makers a golden opportunity. In addition, for the first time in history, counterfeiting was resorted to by a government to undermine confidence in the currency, and thereby the credit, of the enemy.

The British government soon conceived the idea of forging the Continental currency, perhaps at the suggestion of Dr. Benjamin Church and his brother-in-law, a printer named John Fleming. Church, a distinguished physician and able writer supporting Whig policies, had been discovered in secret communication with General Gage and other British leaders only a few months earlier.

In any event, as early as the first week in January 1776, if not before, a printing press on board H.M.S. *Phoenix,* a ship of forty-four guns lying in New York harbor, was turning out counterfeits of the thirty dollar bill of the emission of 10 May 1775. When General Howe took New York City in 1776, that city became and remained the chief source of counterfeits made by the British or with British sanction. So open was the whole business that New York newspapers of 14 April 1777 carried the following advertisement, unique in history:

> Persons going into other Colonies may be supplied with any Number of counterfeit Congress-Notes, for the Price of the Paper per Ream. They are so neatly and exactly executed that there is no Risque in getting them off, it being almost impossible to discover, that they are not genuine. This has been proved by Bills to a very large Amount, which have already been successfully circulated.
>
> Enquire for Q.E.D. at the Coffee-House, from 11 p.m. to 4 a.m. during the present month.

The American intelligence service of course sought to detect the persons immediately concerned but without success. One agent early in September 1779 advised General Washington of 'a new emission of bills of sixty dollars lately done in New York' and informed him that 'a great quantity of this kind is put into the country by way of Kingsbridge and Bergen.' Then, some two months later, a confidential correspondent in New York wrote to the general of the indefatigable endeavors of the enemy to increase the depreciation of the Continental currency by putting off counterfeits and told him that for that purpose reams of the paper made for the last emissions struck by Congress had been secured by the British from Philadelphia.

Responsibility for the wholesale imitation of the American money could be fixed upon the highest British officials when an American privateer intercepted a ship carrying a letter written on 30 January 1780 in Savannah by Sir Henry Clinton to Lord George Germain, British secretary of state. In it Clinton referred to the 'futility of calculations' founded on the failure of the American currency. 'No experiments,' he wrote, 'suggested by your Lordship; no assistance that could be drawn from the power of gold, or the arts of counterfeiting, have been left unattempted . . . I shall . . . continue while I have the honor to command in America, assiduous in the application of those means entrusted to my care; if they cannot work its [the American currency's] destruction, yet they embarrass Government.'

Further proof of counterfeiting by the enemy was obtained when in April 1780 Captain Marriner captured two British ships off Sandy Hook, the *Blacksnake* and the *Morning Star,* with a large amount of counterfeit Continental currency on board them and brought them as prizes into Egg Harbor, New Jersey. Previously a raid on a dwelling a mile and a half from the Sandy Hook lighthouse carried out by Captain Rudolph of Major Lee's Rangers, a sergeant, a corporal, and eight privates, had netted eight prisoners and some 45,000 counterfeit Continental dollars.

One device used by the British for putting off false bills was a Trojan Horse, filled not with men but with counterfeit money, in the form of a wagon train of clothing and supplies for British prisoners in Lancaster. It was sent out from Philadelphia by General Howe under a flag of truce in January 1778, but was halted by the Americans at the Spread Eagle public house, and two British officers who were present in excess of the number permitted were sent back to Howe. During the delay a heavy rain soaked some of the shipment, including two bags which were opened and discovered to be filled with Continental bills of credit, while four of the wagon drivers, when the party reached Lancaster, were found to be well supplied with counterfeit bills.

One of the craftsmen engaged in counterfeiting the money was probably James Smither, a well-known Philadelphia engraver, who before the Revolution had made cuts for some issues of the Pennsylvania currency. Thomas Paine, in a letter to the President of the Continental Congress dated 11 April 1788, named the engraver as being a participant in forging Continental currency for the British. When the British abandoned Philadelphia and returned to New York, Smither accompanied them, and on 15 June 1778 the Supreme Executive Council of Pennsylvania issued a proclamation ordering him to answer to charges of treason.

The most effective scheme for getting the bad money into circulation was the use of Tory passers. Such persons were animated by motives of loyalty to the crown and doubtless found double pleasure in making profits at the same time that they injured the credit of the patriots' currency. In the main such persons had been, before the outbreak of hostilities, law-abiding individuals of standing in the community. A good example of Tory passers was Colonel Stephen Holland of Londonderry, New Hampshire. He was born in Ireland, served during the Seven Years' War as a lieutenant and adjutant in Goreham's Rangers, retired from the army in 1762, and settled in Londonderry, where he busied himself as merchant and tavern keeper and by 1775 owned real estate in excess of 10,000 acres. This good-looking, ruddy-faced, pockmarked Irishman, fleshy and five feet eight in height, was affable, popular, and a leader in the community and province. He was a justice of the peace, clerk of the court of common pleas, and clerk of the peace for Hillsborough County. He held a commission as colonel in the militia, while in Londonderry he served as selectman, and from 1771 to 1775 represented the town in the General Court. He was a warm friend of Governor John Wentworth and was secretly devoted to the interests of the crown.

In April 1775 Governor Wentworth persuaded Holland to remain in New Hampshire and use all his arts 'to circumvent and disappoint' the views of the patriots. The Londonderry Tory, among other acts of devotion to the British cause, organized an elaborate chain of friends and acquaintances as passers of counterfeits. Some of them went, ostensibly on business, to the southward, secured quantities of British-made counterfeit bills, and brought them back to loyalists and their wives to be passed off.

One of the gang, John Moore of Peterborough, while in Connecticut on the pretense of buying flax, came down with the smallpox in Wallingford and died there. A boy at the house where Moore had stayed, while looking for eggs in the barn, found a stone in the hay and under it a packet of letters from Governor Wentworth and other New Hampshire Tories in New York, some of which were addressed to Stephen Ash of Londonderry, which turned out to be a covering name for Stephen Holland. As a result of the discovery, Holland and others were detected.

One accomplice was William Stark of Dunbarton, a former captain in Rogers' Rangers and the brother of Colonel, later General, John Stark. William was also a brother-in-law of Holland, for they had married sisters, Mary and Jane Stinson. Stark was indicted for counterfeiting but when released on bail he chose to forfeit his bond and fled to the British in New York, where he obtained a colonel's commission. Like Stark, Thomas Cum-

mings, a prominent lawyer of Hollis, after being indicted
for counterfeiting also fled, while free on bail, to the British
and joined Governor Wentworth's Volunteers, with whom
he served until 1782 and then removed to Nova Scotia.

Among the members of the gang were two physicians,
Dr. Silas Hedges of Dunbarton and Dr. Jonathan Gove
of New Boston. Others were Benjamin Whiting, deputy
surveyor of his majesty's woods in America and sheriff of
Hillsborough County, his brother, Captain Leonard
Whiting, John Stinson of Dunbarton, a prominent attorney of Amherst, Joshua Atherton, who after the Revolution was attorney general of New Hampshire and a member
of the United States Senate in 1792, Major James Richardson of Dover, John Holland, who escaped to the British
and after the war became sheriff of the County of St. John
in New Brunswick, John McLaughlin, James Ryan, and
many others.

Two of the band, David Farnsworth of Hollis and John
Blair of Holderness, had the misfortune of being arrested
in Danbury, Connecticut, and being brought to the headquarters of General Enoch Poor. There it was discovered
that they had brought from New York City more than
10,000 dollars in counterfeits, and upon examination Blair
asserted that another of the gang, Moses Gerrish of Lancaster, had passed some 40,000 or 50,000 dollars in bad
bills. Farnsworth admitted that he had gone to New York
'to get Counterfeit Money' and that what he brought with
him was to be delivered to Samuel Abbott in Hollis. His
confession also implicated the wives of William Stark,
Stephen Holland, the two Whitings, and two Cummings as
passers, while he stated that Oliver Parker of Stoddard,
Richard Peck of Marlow, and Captain Samuel Tarbell of
Mason were engaged in the counterfeiting. Their confes-

sions did not win leniency for Farnsworth and Blair, for after conviction by a court-martial they were executed in Hartford.

Three of Holland's friends in Londonderry, John Clark, John Moore, and William Cox, were suspected, probably with good reason, of being in on the scheme, while it was reliably reported that Moore had stated that Dennis Haley, an active carrier of false bills from New York, 'had Neer the Bignes of A Bible of Counterfit Money and . . . would give Any of his Comrads a Thirty Dolar Bill for a Gill of Rum.' To the list of Holland's associates may be added the names of Simon Baxter of Alstead and his three sons, William, Benjamin, and Simon, Jr., as well as Annanias and Ziba Hall of Keene.

Holland, the organizer of the band, was twice imprisoned in Exeter and twice escaped, the second time while under sentence of death. He reached the safety of the British lines and was given a well-earned commission in the intelligence service. It is small wonder that John Langdon, later governor of New Hampshire, said with reference to Holland: 'Damn him . . . I hope to see him hanged. He has done more damage than ten thousand men could have done.'

Langdon's feelings about the damage done by Holland are probably warranted, when one considers the disastrous effect of British counterfeiting on the American paper money. Benjamin Franklin, in an essay composed in his eightieth year, wrote as follows on the subject:

Paper money was in those times our universal currency. But, it being the instrument with which we combated our enemies, they resolved to deprive us of its use by depreciating it; and the most effectual means they could contrive was to counterfeit it. The

artists they employed performed so well, that immense
quantities of these counterfeits, which issued from the
British government in New York, were circulated
among the inhabitants of all the States, before the
fraud was detected. This operated considerably in depreciating the whole mass, first, by the vast additional
quantity, and next by the uncertainty in distinguish-
ing the true from the false; and the depreciation was
a loss to all and the ruin of many.

Unhappily Holland and other Tories like him were not
the sole offenders. Men on the other side were not backward
in forging their own currency for gain, for, as Isaac Ketcham
of Long Island testified in 1776, three of his accomplices,
Henry Dawkins and Israel and Isaac Young, had said that
Tories would counterfeit money, so that they might as well
do it too. Dawkins had been born in England, where he had
been apprenticed to an engraver, but he seems to have
come to America some time after 1750. There he worked
for a time in New York City but in 1757 removed to Philadelphia, where he soon set up on his own account as an engraver and in 1764 was elected junior warden of his masonic
lodge. In 1775 or 1776 he was jailed in New York, probably
for debt, and the Young brothers of Cold Spring on Long
Island, who had a mind to do some counterfeiting, sought
him out, secured his release, and gave him money with
which to pay the rent on his shop. Upon his being let out
of prison, he went, with his small son, to live with the
Youngs. They first secured for him a bookbinder's press,
but as this would not serve the purpose, Dawkins rubbed
off a few counterfeits of the forty shilling Connecticut bills
with a burnisher, and one of the Youngs signed them.

The false bills were soon detected, and to Dawkins' de-
light, Hugh Gaine, publisher of the *New-York Gazette: and
the Weekly Mercury,* printed a detailed description of the

counterfeit, pointing out how it differed from true money. From the newspaper item Dawkins made suitable changes in his plate, especially causing the two small crosses after the asterisk and before the obelisk to join together. With the corrected plate and a suitable rolling press, which the Youngs had brought from New York, Dawkins was prepared for mass production. His only difficulty was proper paper, for first Levi Lott and then Isaac Ketcham had gone afield in vain attempts to secure just what was wanted.

Rumors of what was going on at Cold Spring reached Charles Friend of Westbury in Queens County, and he went before the Provincial Congress and gave information which caused the legislators to take prompt action. On the evening of 11 May 1776 Captain Jeremiah Wool crossed the East River to Long Island and proceeded to Huntington, where he was joined by Thomas Weeks. With a party of minutemen they arrived at two o'clock on Sunday morning at the house of Isaac Young, whom they found at home. A search revealed a secret door and stairway leading to a garret, in which were discovered a printing press, an imperfect copy of a twenty shilling Connecticut bill, and several unfinished counterfeits. Everything was seized as evidence, put in a wagon, and taken to Williams' Tavern, whence men were sent out and brought in Dawkins and John Henderson.

After being imprisoned in New York City, the Youngs were jailed in Litchfield, Connecticut, and Dawkins in White Plains, where conditions were so bad that on 9 October he petitioned the Provincial Congress to have the death penalty inflicted upon him. By 1778 he had been released and was so far restored to favor that he was then engaged in making the first engravings for the New York State coat of arms and had been employed by the Continental Congress to engrave and alter the border and back pieces for striking the bills of credit.

Continental soldiers joined in the epidemic of counterfeiting: Michael Lynch and Thomas Hickey were confined in New York City in 1776 for passing and then sent to General Washington for trial by court-martial; David Gamble in 1780 deserted from the Continental army and, when caught and found to have counterfeits in his possession, was executed. Even officers did not hesitate to take a hand in the game. In North Carolina David Craig, a second lieutenant in William Temple Cole's company, apparently passed bad bills and was concerned in fashioning and engraving a plate for striking five dollar notes of his state.

Wholesale counterfeiting and the profligate emission of currency brought about such a tremendous depreciation in the value of the paper money that George Washington wrote to John Jay, 'A wagon-load of money will scarcely purchase a wagon-load of provisions.' So worthless, indeed, did American currency become, that in May 1781 an angry mob in Philadelphia paraded the streets with paper money in their hats as cockades and with a dog tarred and plastered with the paper dollars of the Congress. 'Not worth a Continental' became and has remained a household word in our language.

Counterfeiting in the colonial period both by individuals and increasingly by organized and co-operating gangs posed a constant threat to the credit and commerce of the provinces. Frequently the colonies were put to the trouble and expense of recalling whole emissions. Sometimes trade was greatly hampered or, as in Virginia in 1773, came to a complete standstill.

A great number of persons seem to have been on the verge of destitution and ready to cheat their neighbors by forging coin or bills, while often many well-to-do and respected individuals had no compunctions about seeking greater wealth through illicit means. To be sure the risk of punishment was not too great. Considerable sections of the population, including upon occasion constables, sheriffs, or even magistrates, were sympathetic to the counterfeiters or indifferent about their being brought to justice. Lack of funds at the disposal of the government gravely hampered the prompt pursuit of criminals or the guarding of jails in which they were imprisoned if taken. The ease and frequency of jailbreaks, the extreme difficulty of securing the conviction of counterfeiters, defects in the laws against imitating bills or coin, antagonism between the officials of the colonies coupled with lack of interest in each other's problems, the great disparity of the punishments imposed for the same offense between province and province — all these items conspired to make counterfeiting not too great a risk.

In the course of time, however, the death penalty was set by law as the reward of convicted counterfeiters and passers in most of the provinces, though New England was more lax in this respect. On the other hand, even in New England, flogging, the pillory, branding, cropping, imprisonment, heavy fines, or, as in Connecticut, confinement in the horrible underground shafts of the copper mines at Newgate were not punishments to be taken lightly. Despite all this, the offense grew more and more common, while during the Revolution official British counterfeiting and aid and comfort to counterfeiters and passers afforded this type of wrongdoing a stimulus never before known in history. It is little wonder that the new country was plagued by a complaint which had become chronic and which in our own time requires the constant vigilance of the Secret Service.

# BIBLIOGRAPHY

MOST of the material for this volume consists of unpublished
court records, items in colonial newspapers, official provincial papers, correspondence of governors, and occasional refer-
ences in diaries and letters. *Law Enforcement in Colonial
New York* by Julius Goebel, Jr., and T. Raymond Naughton
(New York: Commonwealth Foundation, 1946), though not
directly concerned with counterfeiting, deals with many cases
in New York. Mr. Eric P. Newman has generously made available manuscripts of two articles dealing with counterfeiting
during the Revolution. Published books and articles on colonial counterfeiting are the following:

Bowen, Richard LeBaron, *Rhode Island Colonial Money and
its Counterfeiting* 1647–1726 (Providence: Society of Colo-
nial Wars, 1942).
*Early Rehoboth, Massachusetts, Documented Historical
Studies of Families and Events in This Plymouth Colony
Township*, privately printed, 1945–1950.
Broome, John, 'The Counterfeiting Adventure of Henry Daw-
kins,' *American Notes & Queries* (March, 1950), 179–84.
Gillingham, Harrold E., *Counterfeiting in Colonial Pennsyl-
vania* (New York: The American Numismatic Society, 1939).
Lee, Francis Bazley, 'Paper Money and Counterfeiting in the
Colony of New Jersey,' *Proceedings of the American Numis-
matic Society* (1894), 103–10.
Scott, Kenneth, 'New Hampshire Tory Counterfeiters Operat-
ing from New York City,' *The New-York Historical Society
Quarterly* (vol. 34, 1950), 31–57.

'The Counterfeiting Venture of Abel and Samuel Chapin,' *Rhode Island History* (vol. 2, 1952), 93–5.

'The Middlesex Counterfeiters,' *Proceedings of the New Jersey Historical Society* (vol. 70, 1952), 246–9.

'Counterfeiting in Colonial Virginia,' *The Virginia Magazine of History and Biography* (vol. 61, 1953), 3–33.

*Counterfeiting in Colonial New York* (New York: The American Numismatic Society, 1953).

'Gideon Casey, Rhode Island Silversmith,' *Rhode Island History* (vol. 12, 1953), 50–54.

'Two Counterfeit Connecticut Bills of Credit,' *The American Numismatic Society Museum Notes* (vol. 6, 1954), 215–17.

'Samuel Casey, platero y falsario,' *Numisma* (vol. 4, 1954), 35–40.

'A letter and a porringer by Silver Sam,' *Antiques* (vol. 68, 1955), 462.

'Colonial silversmiths as counterfeiters,' *Antiques* (vol. 67, 1955), 54–5.

'A British Counterfeiting Press in New York Harbor,' *The New-York Historical Society Quarterly* (vol. 39, 1955), 117–20.

*Counterfeiting in Colonial Pennsylvania* (New York: The American Numismatic Society, 1955).

'Punishment of Coiners in the Colony of Connecticut,' *Numisma* (vol. 5, 1955), 73–9.

'Caesar Trick: Colonial Counterfeiter,' *The Connecticut Antiquarian* (vol. 7, 1955), 14–17.

'Some Counterfeiters of Provincial Currency,' *The South Carolina Historical Magazine* (vol. 57, 1956), 14–22.

'Counterfeiting in Colonial Maryland,' *Maryland Historical Magazine* (vol. 61, 1956), 81–100.

Spiro, Jacob Newman, 'A Provincial Note Raiser,' *American Journal of Numismatics* (vol. 21, 1886), 10.

' 'Tis Death to Counterfeit,' *Numismatic Review* (vol. 1, 1943), 30.

# INDEX